GERIATRIC PSYCHOTHERAPY

GERIATRIC PSYCHOTHERAPY

T. L. Brink, Ph.D.

College of Notre Dame,
Belmont, California

HUMAN SCIENCES PRESS
72 Fifth Avenue   3 Henrietta Street
NEW YORK, NY 10011 ● LONDON, WC2E 8LU

Copyright © 1979 by Human Sciences Press
72 Fifth Avenue, New York, New York 10011

Printed in the United States of America
123456789   98765432

Library of Congress Cataloging in Publication Data

Brink, Terry L
    Geriatric psychotherapy.

    Bibliography: p.
    Includes index.
    1. Geriatric psychiatry.   2. Psychotherapy.
I. Title.
RC451.4.A5B74   618.9'76'8914   LC78-26232
ISBN 0-87705-344-8
ISBN 0-87705-346-4 pbk.

CONTENTS

Introduction   7

1. Bio-Psycho-Social Crises   15
2. Psychopathology   35
3. Theoretical Perspectives   60
4. Prophylaxis   80
5. Psychopharmacology and Related Topics   98
6. Behavioral Modification   116
7. Perspectives on Geriatric Psychotherapy   132
8. Basic Strategy   151
9. Specific Techniques   174
10. Dream Therapy   194
11. Group Therapy   211
12. Family Therapy   233

13. Institutionalization   258

14. Milieu Therapy   271

References   288

Index   309

INTRODUCTION

This book is written for those people who are involved, or who would like to become involved, in counseling or providing mental health care for the elderly. It is meant to serve as an introductory text for psychologists, psychiatrists, physicians, social workers, clergy, psychiatric nurses, and other mental health professionals who have some expertise in psychotherapy, and who seek some specific information about how they might apply their skills to a new area: aging. In this capacity, the book is designed to acquaint mental health professionals with psychological gerontology and also to point out the most fruitful strategies and techniques of treatment. However, great caution has been taken to make this book sufficiently elementary, not only for those who are new to the field of aging, but also for those presently involved in geriatric treatment (facility administrators, activity directors, physical therapists, nurses, and community workers) who have had no formal training in psychotherapy but would like to apply some of the book's insights and tactics to their own contact with the aged.

A few definitions are in order.

Aging. The dictionary definition of the verb "to age" is to become older or to show the characteristics peculiar to advanced age. When scientists study this process, they are greatly influenced by the parameters of their specific disciplines. In other words, biologists and medically trained researchers tend to define age in terms of bodily functions, psychologists study aging in terms of mental processes, while social psychologists and sociologists are most concerned with changes in attitudes, interpersonal relations, roles, and institutions. All of these perspectives can yield fruitful information for those directly concerned with the care of the elderly. Because this book is written for practitioners of psychotherapy, the perspective will be multidisciplinary, with the focus on practical application. Theoretical and methodological issues will be explored insofar as they are relevant to practice. If the reader wishes more depth on these issues, he should consult the bibliography listed below. Text references will not be thorough on matters that are usually of only tangential interest to practitioners, but will be comprehensive on those points directly bearing on the practice of psychotherapy with the aged.

Elder. This book prefers this term to denote an aged individual. I am indebted to a colleague, Fritz Schmerl, M.D., who has advocated the use of this term as being less connotative of negative images of aging.

Cohort. A group of individuals born during the same time period (for example, 1890–1900) is a cohort. At any subsequent point in time, the members of this cohort will be at the same age level. For example, in 1917 this cohort was between 17 and 27. Cohort analysis is important to the study of aging because the members of a given cohort have many common experiences different from those outside the cohort. The 1890–1900 cohort was the one most likely to participate in World War I, while those who were born a decade earlier or later were either too young or too old. Different cohorts are influenced by different historical events, and the same historical event has different effects on different cohorts because it finds them in different phases of the life cycle.

Gerontology. The suffix *ology* refers to the study of something. The prefix *ger* refers to aging. Therefore gerontology is the study of aging. This broad field has many subdivisions, of which biological, psychological, and sociological are the most basic. Each of these has more minute subdivisions. For example, some social gerontologists study elders at work (industrial gerontology) while others study their family life, or their attitudes, or society's attitudes about them, or recreational patterns, or religious habits.

Gerontologists study aging by doing research involving experiments, surveys, or in-depth case studies. These can be *cross-sectional* studies, which gather data by comparing different cohorts, or *longitudinal,* which compare the data gathered from the same cohort at different points in time. The former method has the danger of mistakenly assuming that the differences noted represent age-determined changes, and not mere differences between cohorts which would have existed had both groups been examined at the same age. Longitudinal studies, which must reassemble the original group of subjects some years later for a retest, are rarer because they are more difficult to plan, finance, and follow up. There is also the danger of mistakenly assuming that the results indicate a generalized pattern of development, rather than a specific trend found in the particular cohort studied.

Geriatrics. Here we have a word with the same prefix, but with a suffix indicating doctor or treatment. Therefore geriatrics concerns the treatment of disorders of later life. Because this is a book on geriatrics and not gerontology per se, it necessarily focuses on disease, disorder, disturbance, and the crises that provoke them, for these are the conditions which the geriatric practitioner must be prepared to confront. In the field of gerontology there is a solid trend to present aging in a positive light by considering successful aging as a reality with most elders, and something realizable for all elders. This is a noble and necessary endeavor, but one in which this book will not participate. The focus on geriatrics is necessarily a focus on the unhealthy minority, the abnormal who need professional help.

Psychology. In its broadest sense, this is the study of thought, emotion, and behavior in humans and animals. Like gerontology, research is accomplished via experiment, survey, and/or case study, and there are many subspecialties within the field. One of these is abnormal psychology, or psychopathology, which is concerned with the disturbances of thought, emotion, and behavior (mental illness).

Psychiatry. Here again we find the suffix indicating treatment. A psychiatrist is a medical doctor specializing in the diagnosis, treatment, or prevention of psychopathological disorders. A clinical psychologist also specializes in these disorders, but differs from the psychiatrist in two important ways. First, he is not medically trained. Second, he cannot prescribe medication. Otherwise, they may use the same methods of diagnosis and treatment, and frequently work together on a case.

Psychotherapy. This term comprises a broad range of treatment for mental/emotional disorders. The common factor in all psychotherapy is that treatment takes place as a result of communication between a patient (or client) and a therapist, who may be a psychiatrist, psychologist, social worker, member of the clergy, nonprofessional, or even a peer.

Why and how psychotherapy works will be discussed in a later chapter. Theoretically, psychotherapy differs from counseling in that the latter is intended to focus on problems that fall short of being a psychopathological illness. The counselor seeks to assist the client in making personal decisions; the psychotherapist seeks to bring about a return to normal (or healthier) levels of functioning. In practice, especially with geriatrics, there is no clearcut distinction between counseling and psychotherapy. The key question for anyone working with the aged is to identify his own expertise, to do as much as he can with it, and to make a referral to another competent professional when the requirements of the case exceed his expertise.

Psychoanalysis. This term is not synonymous with psychotherapy, but refers to a specific type developed by Freud and the Vienna school. Many psychotherapists are influenced by psychoanalytic theories and have utilized modified psychoanalytic techniques, but full-fledged psychoanalysts are psychiatrists who have taken advanced training from a psychoanalytic institute, and have been psychoanalyzed themselves for many years. The inappropriateness of psychoanalysis for geriatrics is discussed in a later chapter.

Now that the basic terms have been defined, and the parameters of this book have been specified, I shall present a brief annotated bibliography on the best books related to the field of aging. Probably the best single comprehensive introduction to gerontology and geriatrics for the layperson would be Butler (1975). The layperson interested in the aging body should read Knopf (1975) or Taylor (1973). Those seeking a medical text on geriatric physiology should consult Caird and Judge (1974) or Hodkinson (1975). For general psychology of aging, Botwinick (1973) and Neugarten (1968) are two of the best. For the social psychology of aging, Neugarten (1968) is the standard

work, but Gubrium (1976) is more recent, and quite profound on a theoretical and methodological level. Riley and
Foner (1968) remains the most complete storehouse of
indexed data on physiological, psychological, social, and
economic aspects of aging. For psychopathology and psychiatric treatment of elders, Busse and Pfeiffer (1973) is
unsurpassed, but quite difficult reading for the nonpsychia-
trist. On widowhood, Lopata (1973) is the standard work.
On death and dying, Kübler-Ross (1969) is the big name on
the lecture circuit, but Kastenbaum and Aisenberg (1972)
and Weisman (1972) are superior technically and have
more applicability to death and dying in geriatric patients.
For sexuality in elders, look to Burnside (1975) or Butler
(1976). Regarding nursing homes and their alternatives,
Butler (1975) is adequate, but Hoffman (1970) can give one
the information and flexibility to rethink many of the issues
involved in the status quo.

The most recent and some of the best information on
aging will not be found in books, but in specialized periodicals. Rarely do newspapers or weekly periodicals or magazines have any profound or new information on aging.
Some tabloids go in the other direction and present research or case studies which are unconfirmed or taken out
of context. Several magazines directed to elders are *Aging*
(Department of Health, Education, and Welfare), *Retirement
Living* (formerly *Harvest Years*), *Dynamic Maturity, Modern
Maturity,* and *National Retired Teachers Association Journal.*
Much of their writing concerns nostalgia, but some practi-
cal self-help articles also appear.

The scholarly journals in psychology, medical care,
pastoral care, and social work sometimes have useful articles, but by and large, this is infrequent. *Postgraduate Medicine* and *Geriatrics* provide practical information for the
primary care physician. A more technical medical journal is
the *Journal of the American Geriatrics Society.* It usually has an
article or two on psychopathology or psychiatric treatment

in each issue. *Journal of Gerontology, Experimental Aging Research,* and *Experimental Gerontology* report research on aging in humans and animals. Most of it is physiological, but usually each issue has something of interest for the psychologically oriented reader. The *International Journal of Aging and Human Development* is one of the foremost journals in social gerontology. Its editor also puts out *Omega, the Journal of Death and Dying.* The *Journal of Geriatric Psychiatry* occasionally has good articles, but in the main it suffers from a psychoanalytic approach. *Gerontologist* is a broad-based journal and considers treatment, social services, and many other concerns of practitioners, in addition to research.

Geriatric counselors and psychotherapists should also keep up with the new concepts and techniques being introduced in psychotherapy and counseling journals. *American Journal of Psychotherapy, Psychotherapy: Theory, Research, Practice, Journal of Contemporary Psychotherapy, American Journal of Orthopsychiatry, Counseling Psychologist, Journal of Counseling Psychology,* and *Journal of Consulting and Clinical Psychology* should be useful. Some of the psychiatric journals may also have relevant articles on psychotherapy: *Psychiatry, American Journal of Psychiatry, Psychiatric Opinion, Journal of Nervous and Mental Disease,* and *Psychiatric Quarterly* should be noted. For group work, the *International Journal of Group Psychotherapy* is the foremost. The *International Journal of Social Psychiatry* is occasionally a valuable source. One way to keep abreast of recent publications in the field is to look in the back of the *Journal of Gerontology,* where Nathan Shock indexes all the published literature on aging.

In addition to books and journals, much valuable information on aging and social services for elders can be obtained from government agencies. Congressional and legislative hearings provide an excellent examination of public policy directed toward the elders in America. The problems with nursing homes and the public response to those problems are better documented in these hearings than in any book. Publications of federal, state, and local agencies are usually free, including newsletters and periodicals. These are usually excellent sources of what is new in the way of social services.

I strongly recommend that the prospective geriatric psychotherapist become thoroughly acquainted with the literature on aging and available services for elders. Just as no physician can practice medicine without a knowledge of disease and treatment, so no geriatric psychotherapist can practice without a knowledge of aging. This book is an introduction to the literature relevant to geriatric psychotherapy. It must never be considered the last word on the subject.

Chapter 1

BIO-PSYCHO-SOCIAL CRISES

Essentially, the later years involve a progressive loss of many of the things that make life most meaningful: health, beauty, careers, financial security, status, and a stable self-image. The fear of loss of life itself may be another factor. Most individuals endure these losses and creatively adapt to unavoidable changes. Where the losses are light or the individual's total resources for coping are high, mental health can be preserved or even enhanced in the later years. However, many times these losses become crises necessitating the intervention of mental health professionals.

PHYSICAL DISABILITIES

The life expectancy for the American male is now about 72 years. White females can expect to live about six more, whereas Black males have a life expectancy of five less.

(Black women are somewhere in between.) The life expectancy has gone up steadily during the century. As a result, so have both the number of elders in the U.S. and their percentage of the total population. In 1900, persons over 65 accounted for only 4% of the total population. This was due to a high birth rate in addition to the lower life expectancy. (Most of the developing countries today have populations comprised chiefly of younger individuals, with elders usually not exceeding 3%.) By 1950 the percentage of elders in the American population had risen to 8%. By 1975 one out of 10 Americans was over 65. Because of the continuing increase in the number of years of life, and also the declining birth rate, elders will constitute between 12 and 20% of the total population of this country by the year 2000.

Most of this increase in life expectancy has come from public health measures that have wiped out childhood diseases and mass epidemics of cholera, smallpox, and plague. The increase in life expectancy does not reflect improvements in controlling the diseases that disable and kill the elders. As a result, the life expectancy of a person who has already reached 65 is about 12 additional years, and has not changed significantly over the past two decades. Despite centuries of medical progress, the conditions that kill, cripple, and incapacitate elders are still with us. It is an open debate whether the improvements in medicine have made aging healthier, or whether they have merely permitted the more frail elders to live longer, and thus to prolong their misery.

Older people are less likely to be afflicted by acute physical conditions, such as infections, and more likely to suffer from chronic conditions. This has been true for centuries. Hippocrates, who lived several centuries before Christ, noted, "Old people, on the whole, have fewer complaints than the young, but those chronic diseases which do befall them generally never leave them." A U.S. national health survey in 1959 found that the number of chronic conditions rose with age. Three-quarters of all men over 65 had one or more chronic conditions, of varying degrees of severity. The female rate was even higher at 81%. Even more serious was the rate of multiple impairment: 28% of the men and 34% of the women had three or more chronic conditions. These rates were about three times higher than those for younger age groups.

Old age itself is not a disease. It is just that certain types of diseases and impairments occur with greater frequency among elders. Loss of hearing and visual acuity are the most prevalent function impairments. Severe hearing loss affects one out of eight elders under age 74, and one in four of those over 75. The lens of the eye progressively loses its elasticity. Blindness occurs in less than 3% of those aged 65 to 74, but it climbs to over 8% after age 75. Accidents, primarily falls, increase with age, and so do the chronic disabilities in their wake. Wound healing usually take about five times longer in old age compared to childhood. Before age 55, only about one-fifth of all Americans lose their teeth. The rate goes up with age. Two-thirds of elders over 75 are edentulous. Arthritis and rheumatism affect over a quarter of elders. Cardiovascular disease is found in varying degrees among one-fifth of all elders.

Paralleling the rapid increase in chronic conditions, there is an augmentation in the number of days of restricted activity and/or confinement to bed. The National Center for Health Statistics reported that elders aged 65 to 74 average 32 restricted-activity days a year, and 11 days in bed. For those over 75, the numbers go up to 36 and 15 respectively. Heart conditions and arthritis are the largest causes of activity limitation, while impairments of visual or auditory senses merely reduce the quality of the activity. The number of physician visits and acute hospital admissions increases after age 65. So does the average length of stay in the hospital. While elders constitute only 10% of the

population, they account for one-fourth of the drug prescriptions, and over one-third of the nation's total health
bill.

In addition to physical changes that necessitate health
care or impair activity, some physical changes do neither of
these, but nevertheless pose a threat to mental health. The
prime factor here would be changes in beauty and body
image. The hair becomes thin and grey. The skin is perhaps
the most accurate indication of the years. The soft, smooth
skin of the infant gradually becomes hard and wrinkled like
parchment. Overly pigmented spots appear. The posture
becomes more bent and stooped, and the gait may become
a hobble. These changes in the body, while not a direct
threat to health, may disturb the elder's body image and
affect his mental health indirectly. Menopause, on the other
hand, appears to be weathered quite well by most women,
who regard it more as a relief than a threat to femininity.

Sexuality is a related factor. There is a marked decline
in sexual activity among the aged. While most couples who
are 60 to 74 are sexually active, only one-quarter of those
over 75 report marital coitus. Some masturbation takes
place, particularly among the widowed. The changes in
rates of activity reflect both psychosocial factors and definite physiological changes. Beyond age 60, the male slows
in the development of a full penile erection, the time required for ejaculation, and the quantity of semen ejacu-
lated. Although this may reduce the frequency and
pleasure of sex, it does not preclude sexual activity. Although impotence is widely feared by aging males, it is
usually temporary and treatable (Masters & Johnson, 1966;
Butler, 1976; Burnside, 1975).

In women there may be some changes in the urogenital tract after menopause. The vagina shrinks and the quantity of natural lubricants diminishes. While this does not
prevent orgasm, it may delay it or produce concomitant
pain. This condition, known as dyspareunia, is medically

treatable (Burnside, 1975; Masters & Johnson, 1966). Vaginitis, an infection accompanied by a painful discharge, is another gynecological problem in elderly women that may affect sexual activity. Altered body image due to heart condition, diabetes, mastectomy, or colostomy may also impair sexual function. The mental health professional must keep in mind that any loss of sexual capacity, role, or activity may contribute to a general sense of loss in certain elders.

One unfortunate fact that tends to compound the physiological limitations of elders is the tendency of all parties to postpone treatment. Elders, their families, and even health professionals frequently overlook the symptoms of the slow advance of impairment, writing them off as the high and inevitable toll of the years. For example, one centagenerian complained that his left knee was stiff. His physician responded that, after a hundred years of use, he should expect some problems from his knee. But this elder would not accept a brush-off, and retorted, "But my other knee is a hundred years old and it feels fine." Elders and their caretakers must assume a different attitude toward treatment. It is true that the quantity and duration of impairments increase, but this should not lead us to a passive acceptance of the limitations. Rather, it should make us even more vigilant in spotting those conditions and assertively seeking treatment for them. Delay only permits the condition to worsen and become more resistant to treatment.

One last psychosocial point must be made about the physical health status of elders. Mental health depends not only on one's physical status, but also on one's perception of that status. In other words, a physically disabled individual who did not regard himself as disadvantaged would be less likely to deteriorate mentally than an individual of the same physical status with a more negative self-evaluation. Likewise, elders with relatively minor physical impairment, but who believe that their impairment is significant, are more likely to have emotional disturbances.

RETIREMENT

At the turn of the century, only one-fourth of the men over 65 were retired. Now the rate is up to 70%. Most American workers expect to retire sometime during their seventh decade. The vast majority of them maintain favorable attitudes toward retirement, and almost half would prefer to retire sooner if they could. However, as people approach retirement, their attitudes may change and become more negative. Until recently there was very little interest in preparing workers for retirement, and insufficient financial and psychological preparation was given. Therefore many elders who have retired with high expectations are disillusioned after a few months of retirement. Many times the decision to retire is forced by declining health, or the job simply becoming too much for the elder. Cases of truly compulsory retirement, against the expressed will of the elder, probably constitute less than one-third of the total.

The majority of retired elders would not give up retirement and accept a full-time job if the opportunity arose. There is no clear-cut evidence that retirement has any health benefits or hazards, or that it lengthens or shortens life expectancy. Retired elders tend to be in poorer health, and to die sooner, but this may simply reflect the fact that people in poorer health are the most likely to retire sooner.

A major factor in adjustment to retirement is the elder's level of income, education, and occupation. Those at the higher levels have a definite advantage. Elders in the professions and those who are self-employed can avoid mandated retirement. In addition, many of them can taper off their work load rather than accept the abrupt curtailment that the factory worker experiences. For example, a

70-year-old lawyer could decide which cases to work on, choosing only the ones most interesting and/or least taxing, leaving the remainder for the firm's younger partners. College teachers can reduce the number of courses to those that are the most convenient and interesting. Writers can write about what pleases them, for however long it pleases them, and where it pleases them. Some workers, like teachers, are used to long vacations, and this makes retirement less of a readjustment crisis.

Elders in the professional occupations also find that their status often persists after retirement. Membership in professional societies, degrees, honors, and titles endure. The physician is still "Dr. X" and the professor may be granted the title "emeritus." Professionals may still keep up on the scholarly literature in their fields, and may be consulted by younger colleagues on specific matters. All of this is excellent for preserving a feeling of importance and achievement. Finally, professionals have been used to working with their minds rather than with their hands. Hopefully, they have acquired a wide range of interests and interpersonal skills that can be pursued after retirement.

The blue collar factory worker has one of the highest incidences of poor adjustment to retirement. This is true even when those workers are very eager to leave the humdrum of factory routine for what they presume will be a life of uncomplicated leisure. For these workers the change is necessarily an abrupt one. There is a loss of occupational status. The retired elder is no longer the shop steward or the man with the top seniority. If his primary social life during his working years was a beer after work with his coworkers, he is really lost after severing that tie. Workers at any level who have failed to develop interests beyond their occupation and transferable social skills may find retirement a psychosocial crisis. This crisis will not be confined to the retired elder, but may also affect his family, particularly his wife. Her stable routine is disrupted by having a husband underfoot all day. The problem is compounded when living quarters are cramped and the husband's mood is essentially negative.

FINANCIAL CONCERNS

As a result of their lower participation in the labor force, the earnings of most elderly couples are substantially less than those of younger adults in the prime of life. Some couples have investments, but most rely on small savings and personal pensions or social security. The Bureau of Labor Statistics attempts to gauge the adequacy of family budgets by estimating what it would cost a retired couple to live at a comfortable level (high budget), modest level (intermediate budget), and the bare minimum above poverty (low budget). These budgets are somewhat higher in urban areas, and somewhat lower in the southern states. For 1975 the absolute essentials (the sum of food and medical care costs) took 44% of the low budget, 38% of the intermediate, and 31% of the higher. Housing and transportation were viewed as luxuries, with the higher budget families spending not only more on these items, but also a higher percentage. Housing and transportation took 40, 43, and 47% of the three model budgets. In none of the budgets was there very much room for personal care, clothing, and recreation. The really disappointing statistic is that only 56% of the nation's five million older couples are in the upper two brackets. It is even more shocking to realize that 22% are below the low budget! Although Social Security and other pensions have been raised in the 1970s, the trends in income adequacy have persisted for about a decade because of double-digit inflation. They are likely to continue.

The relation between poverty and psychosocial crises in elders must be examined. The actual material deprivation is rarely the major factor (although six million aged Americans lack telephones). The average American on welfare probably has a material standard of living surpassing that of 70% of the earth's population. But material deprivation can be the major factor if it causes the elder to skimp on food so much that he or she brings about a vitamin deficiency, which would then directly threaten mental health. However, the greatest threat to mental health resulting from the financial problems of elders is due to relative rather than absolute standards (Williams, 1960). Here we are not talking about the level of material deprivation, but the feeling of being deprived. In the land of the billionaires, the millionaire would feel inferior and insignificant. American elders live in a land of the affluent. In addition, adjustment to retirement income requires them to lower their previous standards of living, which is more difficult for them than for someone who is accustomed to doing without.

Perhaps the most deleterious effect of inadequate income is that elders may skimp on transportation and housing. They must then live in the poorer areas of the city, where rents are cheap, and become stranded there. Taxis are too expensive and private automobiles too costly to maintain. Public transportation is cheap, but it may appear too confusing and dangerous.

CRIME

The prime fear expressed by the urban elderly is crime. Therefore the real problem of poverty is that elders are subjected to the environment of the American poor—one that is drab, dirty, and dangerous. Crime is higher in these areas, and the elders become its chief targets. They rank extraordinarily high in statistical tabulations of crime victims. This is especially true in the poor areas, where muggings and purse snatchings go up right after the Social Security checks come out. The evasive response taken by many elders is to stay indoors, all locked up, and not to let anyone in. While this is a wise move to defend against several types of street cime and burglary, it does have its toll on their mental health. This unfortunate situation is likely to continue as long as there are poor elders who must lock themselves in because American society has not locked its criminals up.

In addition to the crime of the slums, elders are often victimized by more sophisticated criminals. The elders are the chief targets of con artists. One of the simplest tricks, and one of the oldest, is still reported in the news now and then. The "pigeon drop" takes place when a team of confederates arranges for one of them to be with an elder (the victim) when a large amount of money is found. One con man offers to share the money with the elder, but only on the condition that he withdraw a substantial sum from his savings account to prove his "good faith." The swindlers make off with this money, plus the original money that was "found," and usually leave their victim holding a bag of paper.

Other frauds on the elders usually involve an alleged service to meet some real need of theirs. For example, numerous dancing lessons clubs, lonely hearts clubs, and so on spring up, and many misrepresent themselves in order to take in desperate victims. The most profitable types of fraud involve medical quackery or investments. Each year elders spend about 20 times as much on arthritis "remedies" as this nation spends on arthritis research. Many tabloids carry ads for antiaging remedies or medications designed to restore failing beauty or sexual prowess. The fact that new ads keep appearing means that this venture must be successful, at least from the advertiser's point of view. A more recent problem has been phony investments, especially out-of-state land deals. These hucksters

618.9768914 B771g
C.1

prey on the well-to-do elders and can make off with a good portion of their life savings.

DEATH

Most elders do think about death, but they are hardly obsessed with it. Usually, it is realistically considered and prepared for (Roberts, Kimsey, Logan & Shaw, 1970; Kastenbaum & Aisenberg, 1972). Most of their views on death involve positive recognition that it is frequently an end to suffering. This attitude is found even in the dying aged (Kastenbaum, 1966). Looking forward to death is most frequent in those of poor health or in institutions. Fears of death may be due to other anxieties: the unknown, loneliness, loss of identity, loss of significant others, loss of body, loss of control, regression (Pattison, 1967). Fear of death rarely occurs as a separate attitude; it is a manifestation of an underlying neurosis (Lepp, 1968; Rhudick & Dibner, 1961). Specifically, those who have been a failure at living fear death, whereas those who are having a fulfilling life do not (Erikson, 1950, 1959). In the aged, fear of death correlates with living alone (Shrut, 1958; Swenson, 1958) and with a low level of education (Swenson, 1958). While fear of death is not a major worry for most elders, they do worry about the possible death of their spouse, the effect of their own deaths on the spouse, and the problem of living beyond usefulness and becoming a burden on one's family.

WIDOWHOOD

Far more serious than one's own impending death is the effect of an elder's death on the spouse. The worry over the possibility of widowhood is a major concern of American women from middle age on. There are almost 10 million widowed women in the U.S. and only one-fourth as many widowed men. The gap has increased steadily over the past 50 years, when the ratio was only two to one. The differential is due to a combination of longer life expectancy for women and the social custom of men marrying women several years younger than themselves. The average American woman, who marries a man three years her senior, can predict about eight to 10 years of widowhood.

Widowhood causes a severe psychosocial and perhaps also an economic loss. All widowed elders lose the psychosocial role of being a spouse, and also the consortium of the deceased. This is obviously a great loss for those whose marriage joined them in a long and deep relationship with a confidant, friend, and lover. But the sense of loss can also be profound in loveless, stormy unions, as a result of the deprivation of a stimulating opponent. Sometimes these widows develop guilt complexes because they wonder if their evil hopes for the partner were the material cause for his death, or because they did not do more good things for him while he was alive (Brink, 1976b).

Sometimes the widowed spouse may unconsciously interpret the death of the spouse as a rejection by the deceased, almost as if he had died on purpose (Wahl, 1970). This feeling of rejection can lead to a hostility toward the deceased, which can also be displaced onto other close relations or friends (Stern & Williams, 1951). It could also explain the extreme irritability of some recently widowed persons (Wahl, 1970). In most cases, however, widows do not recognize any psychological problems that are directly traceable to the death of the spouse. A more common course is that the widow experiences numerous physical complaints, especially during the first six months of widowhood (Stern & Williams, 1951; Gramlich, 1968; Sturges, 1970; Wahl, 1970; DeVaul & Zisook, 1976). The rates of mortality, physician visits, hospitalization, and institutionalization are higher for the widowed than the married. The rates of mental disorder and suicide show similar trends, but they are not as high as the rates for divorced or separated persons of the same age. (These statistics may reflect the superior mental health of the married, compared with the widowed, or they may simply indicate that the married are more likely to avoid ends such as institutionalization because they have someone who is willing to take care of them at home.)

Many things can ease the pain of widowhood. Time is probably the most effective. The more time between the present and the death of the spouse, the lower the degree of deleterious effects on the widowed person. Time helps in another way also. The older the widow or widower at the time of the death of the spouse, the less this particular loss seems to affect the person. The timing of the death of the spouse in relation to other events is also significant. Widowhood, when coupled with loss of a career for a man, or failing health, or financial insecurity, can yield a crisis which is more severe than if both had occurred separately. Another aspect of timing is preparation. The widows who had to care for the terminally ill spouse for a long time report more of a feeling of relief than of loss.

Another aid in coping with widowhood is the bereavement ritual. Even when the individual disavows belief in such ceremonies, they tend to case the grief. Perhaps this is because they legitimize the feelings experienced by the widow. Furthermore, the rituals channel bereavement into nonpathological outlets. Finally, they prescribe a period of mourning, after which the bereaved is supposed to be capable of normal functioning within the social order. Thus bereavement customs serve as guidelines for psychosocially hygienic grief experiences.

One final comment on widowhood is in order. All losses are relative to the sum total of all the pluses. Widowhood is always a loss, but it will affect some individuals more than others. Especially vulnerable is the woman with a poor education, who never had a career, who devoted her entire life to her husband and family. With her children grown, her role as spouse is the main pillar of her identity. When that is removed, she has very little to fall back on, except living in the past. If she also depended on her husband to fix things around the house and to handle the finances, she will be totally lost.

FRIENDSHIP

Friendship is important throughout life, and the later years are no exception. Many of the other problems of aging also reduce old friendships, and make the formation of new ones more difficult. For example, the reduced use of transportation discussed above makes one immobile and less able to get out and see friends or attend social functions. Diminished sight, hearing, and speech also impede interpersonal communication. Nothing is more frustrating than trying to talk to a deaf person who cannot read lips or communicate in any other way. Finally, old friends die or move away to live in nursing homes or with their children.

One of the keys to avoiding psychopathology, particularly depression, in later life is the maintenance of a confidant relationship (Lowenthal & Haven, 1968). These relationships are most likely to be found in the better educated female elders who are in a high socioeconomic bracket and are practiced in the social graces. They are less likely to be found among those elders who do not have these qualities, particularly those who are poorly educated, and single men. Eldest daughters sometimes complain that they must serve in the confidant role for both parents, spending long hours daily debriefing the parent on the activities, frustrations, and fears that have recently transpired. This role is sometimes burdensome, and causes the daughter to face guilt feelings if she rejects or neglects her parents, while she ends up sacrificing some other part of her life if she tries to accommodate them.

INTERGENERATIONAL RELATIONSHIPS

The quality of intergenerational communication deteriorates with modernization, industrialization, technology, and mass education. The bonds of the extended family are weakened by social and geographic mobility. Social welfare programs relieve the young of the responsibility of caring for dependent elders in their families. In stable, traditional, nontechnological agrarian societies, multigenerational households are the norm. Elders feel useful by performing household chores and caring for the children while the adults work away from the house. When elders are in stages of advanced physical deterioration, older children care for them, and in such societies, the ratio of children to elders is very high. This contact between old and young stimulates communication within prescribed guidelines: the old teach the young, and the young respect the old. The old entertain and edify the young with folklore, customs, religious catechesis, and the technology appropriate to the functions of a society built upon animal-powered agriculture or hunting.

In a technological society such as the U.S. today, the rapid pace of change in knowledge and customs makes the elders appear ignorant and foolish instead of wise. Edification and entertainment are provided by public education and the mass media. Literacy has replaced oral tradition. One of the most profound moments of intergenerational communication was the death bed farewell, combined with advice and a patriarchal or matriarchal blessing. This has been replaced by evacuation of the dying to an acute-care hospital. These losses of intergenerational communication may be particularly hard for those elders who recall good relations with their own grandparents and wonder why they do not have them with their grandchildren.

STEREOTYPES AND PREJUDICE

The word *agism* has been coined by socially concerned gerontologists. Agism is like racism or sexism in that it is a pervasive set of stereotypes and prejudices that underlines generalized differences between the majority of Americans (in this case, the young) and a specific minority group which is in somewhat of a disadvantaged position. Agism emphasizes the negative images of growing old. The elders are viewed as feeble, frail, conservative, narrow-minded, and crotchety. Unlike the negative images involved in racism and sexism, those of aging are learned when the person is young; they do not affect him directly, but become transformed into negative self-images as the person himself ages. The discriminating majority group slowly becomes the minority group that is discriminated against.

The next chapter will demonstrate to what extent some of the stereotypes of aging are true and to what extent they are harmful. However, I would now like to make one generalization about elders, and that is that they tend to be resistant to incorporating socially held images of old age into their own individual self-concepts. Consequently, agism is rarely a precipitating cause of psychopathology (Hall, 1976). Elders who identify their problems as "old age" or who attribute their limitations and diminished achievement to old age in general (rather than to specific causes) are rare, and they are looking for reasons to justify and excuse their own failures.

The real negative effect of agism on mental health in later life is that many individuals are slowly conditioned to accept lower levels of activity, achievement, importance, and interaction as inevitable. This is true, not only of the elders themselves, but of their caretakers as well. It is agism that causes acceptance of physiological deterioration without treatment because doctor and patient alike are convinced that such decline is normal. Agist views have also guided the architects of the sociopolitical establishment and encouraged such policies as compulsory retirement and funding of nursing homes.

DISENGAGEMENT

Galen, the most famous medical man in ancient Rome, remarked that "employment is nature's best physician and essential to human happiness." Throughout the centuries the philosophers of the West have believed that activity is best for a healthy organism, and that the mental cobwebs of an idle mind slowly become shackles. One French philosopher went so far as to say that "growing old is no more than a bad habit which a busy man has no time to form." The first great American geriatric psychotherapist, Lillien Martin, accepted the activity theory wholeheartedly.

> The really happy old are too concentrated on their life work to be aware of what makes them happy. They are going from level to level of achievement in that which gives them joy, mastering life with enthusiasm, and so life seems good and zestful to them until the end. (Martin & DeGruchy, 1930)

The long-standing activity theory was finally challenged around 1960 when some of the results of the Kansas City longitudinal study of aging were published (Cumming & Henry, 1961). Using various measures of life satisfaction and social activity, the research team concluded that there was an inevitable mutual disengagement between the elder and his society. Interaction in the form of various roles was progressively diminished. Such disengagement could take place either by reducing the number of interactions within each specified role, or by reducing the number of roles, or both. Almost all adult social behavior can be described in terms of ten roles: parent, spouse, child of aging parents, homemaker, worker, user of leisure time, club member, church member, friend, citizen (Havighurst, 1957). The process of disengagement is initiated both by the society and by intrapsychic factors within the elder himself. The next chapter will explain more fully this process of intro-version, but now I would like to focus on the Cumming and Henry thesis. Disengagement is not only an empirical real-ity, but also a norm for successful aging, inasmuch as they seemed to uncover a positive correlation between disen-gagement and life satisfaction. The rationale behind this relationship is that freedom from the burdens of social roles and from the old commitments they entailed goes hand-in-hand with the diminished physical and financial resources of later life.

In the last 17 years disengagement has been one of the hottest and most enduring topics in social gerontology. The issues of whether elders disengage, and whether they should disengage, have been attacked, defended, and reformulated many times over (Neugarten, 1968; Gu-brium, 1976). The position I would like to take is that the social gerontologists' debate about whether elders do in fact disengage is largely irrelevant to the geriatric practi-tioner. The practitioner's concern is not with averages in large populations, but with the type and extent of disen-gagement in individual patients. Likewise, the question of the effect of disengagement in general should be applied most cautiously to individualized treatment. The real ques-tion confronting the geriatric psychotherapist is "What is the effect of my patient's life-style (to what ever extent he is engaged) on his mental health, and what can be done to improve it?"

Nevertheless, I will put my two-cents-worth of insight into the disengagement debate. Voluntary disengagement from a specific role, initiated by the elder or done with his consent, seems to be better tolerated than other role losses that are thrust upon the elder by forces beyond his control. Yet another helpful perspective on role loss is gained by considering it not only as freedom from activity and responsibility, but also as freedom to develop new activities and responsibilities. Therefore we must speak of the process of disengagement and also of a process of re-engagement.

One idea common among geriatric counselors is that their clients should be placed into hobbies as a means of re-engagement. In general, this is a good approach. However, several guidelines are necessary. Stonecypher (1974) has offered six. First, the individual must be interested in it. Maybe the elder in question considers knitting or arts and crafts boring. Respect his decision. You may expose him to the hobby, invite him to participate, and provide sufficient opportunity and encouragement, but more than this is contraindicated. Second, it should not take more time than he is willing to give. He may not be willing to become re-engaged with something that requires too much responsibility. Those elders who are willing to take on an activity requiring much time should be given the opportunity, but those who are not should not be imposed on. Third, it should offer a financial reward. This is good not only because it eases the financial situation of the elder, but also because his sense of dignity may be inextricably tied to financial compensation which somehow validates the quality of his work. Fourth, it should require skills and problem-solving ability. Fifth, it should bring him into contact with other people. Sixth, it should develop new resources, especially social skills or personality resources.

CONCLUSION

The most significant threats to mental health in later life are not any vague or pervasive fears about death or negative self-image due to agism. Specific losses, particularly those of health, spouse, or career, seem to pose the most serious crises. When these losses occur simultaneously, they mount a formidable assault on mental health. When the elder lacks financial reserves, access to community services, and a confidant relationship, his resources for meeting crises are likely to be inadequate. Although the concrete losses of elders, coupled with poor resources, do not always produce poor mental health, these factors are the most significant and the ones with which geriatric psychotherapists must concern themselves.

Chapter 2

PSYCHOPATHOLOGY

The purpose of this chapter is to examine the rates, origins, dynamics, and consequences of the mental disorders that are common to or more prevalent in later life. Statistically, old age is the time when the risk of mental disorder is greatest. The World Health Organization in 1959 reported that the mental hospital admission rates for elders were about three times that of the general population. These data are particularly revealing because during the 1960s there was a move to get elder patients out of the mental hospitals and into less expensive nursing homes, whether the patients were senile or long-term schizophrenics. Mental hospitals then refused many geriatric admissions. Therefore the more recent mental hospital admission rates for elders are artificially low and do not reflect the real incidences of mental disease in that age group.

The chief cause of these high rates must be found in the preponderance of life crises that occur in old age, which were discussed in the previous chapter. Bellin and Hardt

(1958) found that among women over age 75, only 10% of those who were married, in good physical condition, and financially secure were certified for New York State mental hospitals. Certifiability was over 41% for women of the same age group who were widowed, in poor health, and financially insecure. Although the events of later life comprise a main factor in geriatric mental health, it is not the only one. Personalities, life styles, and coping patterns are fashioned in early life and are fairly resistant to major change. One 40-year longitudinal study concluded that old age merely perpetuates the patterns launched in early life (Haas & Kuypers, 1975). Most of those elders who adjust poorly to later life had a history of personality problems (Livson & Peterson, 1962). Nevertheless, the degree to which poor coping patterns become translated into geriatric psychopathology is a direct function of the quantity and severity of the crises in later life.

One factor which cannot be neglected is the great delay in treating many of the mental disorders of later life. Here we find a disquieting parallel with the physical deterioration experienced by elders. Everyone accepts the development of these symptoms as an unfortunate but inevitable part of the aging process. The ones who should be most concerned, the elders themselves, tend to have nineteenth century views on mental health. A greater proportion of the aged than of any other age group views mental illness as something inherited and irremediable, the wages of sin, or the result of the patient's not trying hard enough to get well. Likewise, elders are more likely to be unsympathetic toward those who receive psychiatric treatment, putting them in the same category as criminals. Finally, elders are very suspicious of psychologists and psychiatrists. Those elders who are most in need of mental health care are the very ones who are the most suspicious and the least likely to avail themselves for treatment (Brink, 1976b).

The remainder of this chapter is devoted to examining specific conditions.

IQ DECLINE

On cross-sectional tests of intelligence, those in their late teens and early twenties outperform all other age groups. The scores then decline in direct proportion to the age of the older groups. We must always keep in mind that intelligence is what intelligence tests measure. Cohort differences may account for this score differential. For example, the cohort now in its twenties probably had the best educational opportunity, and certainly had more experience taking tests than any other cohort. Other possible explanations could be that the test items are not appropriate to adult life. The declining sensory capacity and increasing reaction time would also serve to depress scores. There might be some way that the scores are affected by poor health, social isolation, or limited motivation.

Longitudinal tests of intelligence show a different pattern over the life cycle. There is no rapid decline of scores. Relative stability is maintained into the later years. Crystallized intelligence (total knowledge) is most resistant to decline and continues to rise the longest for most individuals. Fluid intelligence—the ability to learn new things—is more subject to decline, but nothing like that seen in cross-sectional tests. Tests of divergent intelligence—creative problem solving ability in situations in which there is no one "correct" answer—are the most subject to decline. Longitudinal studies should not necessarily be considered a better measure of intelligence than cross-sectional tests. The factor that biases longitudinal studies is that the sample recovered for the second test is generally the most intelligent and motivated. Their survival rates are better and they are more easily located, and thus the second sample is biased.

Ford and Roth (1977) provide a good introduction to where intelligence testing of the elders stands in 1977.

RIGIDITY

Rigid personality traits cover a variety of specifics associated with elders: political conservatism, religious fundamentalism, dogmatism in all attitudes, less flexibility in attitudes, less susceptibility to attitudinal change, greater control over impulsiveness, greater caution in high-risk/high-reward situations, and resistance to creative new approaches in problem solving. The aforementioned traits are somewhat stereotyped, and it would be grossly inaccurate to imply that all or even most elders demonstrate some of these traits. However, cross-sectional and longitudinal tests give a similar result: There are significant differences on any measure of rigidity, showing that, as a group, elders are more rigid. These differences hold even when such factors as IQ, socioeconomic status, education, and health are controlled.

However, a few things must be kept in mind about rigidity. First, it is not a unitary concept. There are many different aspects of rigidity and it is possible to be rigid in one form and not in another (Botwinick, 1973). For example, rigidity does not become a defensiveness which unrealistically denies one's shortcomings. Elders are more willing than any other age group to admit to errors and deficiencies in their personalities.

There are several possible explanations for the generally higher rigidity levels found in elders. The least convincing is that it is an inherent developmental process (Botwinick, 1973). Other possible explanations are that elders unconsciously assume the cultural stereotypes of rigidity, or that rigidity and cautiousness are aids to survival. The latter rationale is that impulsive individuals live shorter lives, and fewer of them make it to old age. The most likely explanation is that rigidity is a defensive posture assumed in the face of a hostile environment. Elders tend to view the world as more complex and dangerous, while younger groups tend to see it as rewarding boldness and risk taking (Neugarten, 1968). Rigidity may grow out of the elder's increasing awareness of his diminishing sensory and cognitive ability to understand his world and the simultaneous diminution of his coping resources. Under these anxiety-producing conditions, individuals tend to stick tenaciously with well-known strategies, even when they initially meet with failure. Therefore rigidity in elders can be seen as a sign of poor adjustment (Havighurst, 1957). In this way, there is a correlation between rigidity and psychopathology.

Many contemporary counselors tend to jump to the conclusion that the correlation between rigidity and psychopathology is that the former causes or exacerbates the latter. Therefore, they reason, the purpose of therapy should be to attack the underlying rigidity and thereby liberate the patient's natural, creative coping abilities. I hold a different view: Even if geriatric rigidity is defined as a neurosis, it represents the patient's imperfect attempts to cope with physiological and social changes that have approached crisis proportions.

This view of neurosis was suggested by some of the later writings of both Freud and Adler. Jelliffee, a member of Freud's inner circle, successfully applied orthodox analysis to geriatric cases. However, he carefully screened his patients and deemed most of them unsuitable for analysis. His rationale was that in these cases the "disorder" was actually a better solution than what could be offered by a psychoanalytic assault on the neurosis. In this respect, Jelliffee (1925) was most reluctant to attack rigidity—one means that the patient has for coping—unless he knew that he could offer a better means. Another pioneer geriatric psychotherapist, Kaufman (1940), viewed rigidity as an ego defense.

I have numerous acquaintances, elders not in need of psychiatric treatment, who are extremely rigid. I see that in many cases their personality patterns have played a positive role in mental health and have enabled them to cope with several crises. Rigidity can reflect a strong will which prevents the external environment or intrapsychic forces from getting out of hand. As such, it is an ego defense, a learned technique for coping with loss which may be extremely effective when resources are limited. It can channel one's thoughts and prevent the brooding that works itself into depression or anxiety. Therefore the psychotherapist should be very careful not to confuse rigidity with psychopathology. He should attack specific blocks to effective coping, such as obsessional thinking and phobias, but not rigidity in general.

INTROVERSION

Jung (1966) thought that there was a shift from extraversion to introversion as one entered the second half of life. This view has been confirmed by various measures, such as the Rorschach and Thematic Apperception Test, and by the amount of time spent in fantasy behavior, which is higher for elders than for any other age group. Some authors have offered the explanation that ego energy diminishes with age (Neugarten, 1968). Such ego energy is defined as the ability to integrate stimuli; the readiness to perceive and deal with challenging situations; the tendency to perceive vigorous and assertive activity in the self and others. A more likely explanation of this introversion and increased fantasy is that, like rigidity, it is a defensive response to a sense of bleakness and impotence which the elder gets when confronting harsh reality. Such fantasy or introversion is not in itself pathological, but it can reinforce the pathological behavior and thinking that is frequently found in the second half of life. Wherever such introversion interferes with effective reality testing, the counselor must attempt to counteract it.

INFERIORITY

Most of the bio-psycho-social crises of aging produce a loss of activity or significance and a reduction in self-esteem. In addition to the crises enumerated in the last chapter, elders may develop feelings of inferiority because we live in a youth-oriented culture that emphasizes sexual attractiveness and physical recreation. Elders may be incapable (or consider themselves incapable) of performing the modern dances or sports like surfing, skiing, sky diving, snowmobiling, dirt biking, mountain climbing, or shooting the rapids in a canoe. For some time it has been recognized by geriatric psychopathologists that inferiority feelings constitute the intrapsychic dynamics of most problem aging (Cowdry, 1939; Gilbert, 1952; Busse et al., 1954). Inferiority feeling leads to a sense of hopelessness and despair.

PARANOIA

There are several common themes found in most episodes of paranoid thinking: (1) projective thinking; (2) suspiciousness; (3) hostility; (4) centrality; (5) delusions; (6) fear of loss of autonomy; and (7) grandiosity (Swanson, Bohnert & Smith, 1970). In its most extreme manifestation, schizophrenic paranoia, the individual concludes that outside forces are controlling his feelings, thoughts, or actions.

Adler (1956, 1964) speculated that paranoia was an out-growth of inferiority feeling, for which the paranoid attempted to compensate by seeing himself as the target of a grandiose conspiracy.

However, the paranoid thinking of elders does not correspond to this pattern. Their paranoia does not involve the delusion that they are totally under the control of outside forces, nor does it usually involve fantasies of complex or grandiose plots. The fearful fantasies of persecution are usually quite simple. "My postman takes out all the good mail." "The man at the garage took out my new battery and tires and put on some old ones when I brought my car in for servicing." Perhaps the worst one is, "The doctors and nurses give me medication to make me crazy so they can send me to a nursing home." Such ideas are usually short of full-fledged delusions. The patient is usually able to maintain good reality testing and social relations in the other areas of life. Therefore such paranoid thinking, if it can be called such, is primarily due to misunderstanding, particularly misunderstanding of the intentions of the other persons in their immediate environment. The previous chapter detailed the diminishing sensory capacity of elders. Hearing part of a conversation enables one to fill in the gaps with fantasies spun from one's innermost fears, producing suspicion. When suspicions go uncorrected, they become the foundation for further selectively based perceptions. The best way to cure such paranoid thinking in elders is to explain one's actions and intentions in detail beforehand.

CRIME AND PERVERSION

Crime rates are highest for teenagers and young adults. It is exceedingly rare for elders to commit crimes requiring great strength, speed, or agility. Consequently, few crimes committed by elders are crimes involving violence or destruction of property. The few crimes committed by elders usually fall into the categories of petty theft (usually shoplifting for necessities or simply as a result of forgetting to pay) or various offenses such as gambling, drunkenness, exposure, and vagrancy. Popular belief has it that elders become attracted to sexual perversions, especially with children. The usual explanation given is that old "flashers" are fearful of the loss of sexual potency, and therefore relieve their castration anxieties by exposing themselves and interpreting the strong reaction of the victim as proof of the absense of castration. Actually, much of the exposure among the very old is due to confusion, especially in the desire to find a place to urinate. Much of the alleged fondling of children represents feeble attempts to establish contactual relations. These attempts are misinterpreted and labeled as perversion (Weinberg, 1969). However, the hospitalized male patient who intentionally fondles the female members of the staff, or uses suggestive or obscene language, is looking for verification of his masculinity. He may also become combative or try other strategies to be regarded as a "male" even though he is in a dependent position.

GRIEF

Grief is the normal psychological reaction to loss of any important aspect of life, for example, terminal illness, amputation, or widowhood. The most comprehensive work on grief is by Schoenberg, Carr, Peretz, and Kutscher (1974). The severity of the loss is an important factor in determining the severity of the grief, but not necessarily the degree to which the grief becomes pathological and precludes effective coping. For example, Ullman (1962) listed the factors predisposing the victims of CVA's (cerebral vascular accident, or stroke) to psychiatric problems: (1) brain damage sufficient to cause cognitive defect; (2) the resultant physiological disability; (3) previous personality; and (4) a life situation to which the patient returns.

Perhaps the foremost grief-producing event for elder women is widowhood. In many cases there is a relative paucity of overt grief or conscious feelings of guilt (Stern & Williams, 1951). The following symptoms are more common: self-isolation, extreme identification with the deceased, and pronounced hostility, usually directed toward some living person (Stern & Williams, 1951). Occasionally, widows develop the irrational belief that the decedent died on purpose as a rejection of their love (Wahl, 1970). This can lead to feelings of guilt, protracted apathy, irritability, hostility, or frantic hyperactivity (Wahl, 1970; Sturges, 1970). Perhaps the greatest pathology of widowhood is psychosomatic. Rates of visiting the physician and hospitalization for widows go up dramatically in the six months following the death of the spouse. Psychosomatic imitation of the deceased's symptoms is a particular problem (Sturges, 1970; Wahl, 1970; Gramlich, 1968). Many times the patients are totally unaware of the connection between their physical symptoms and the grief. It comes as a great relief to them when they hear that future resolution of the grief will bring about a termination of the symptoms (Gramlich, 1968).

The most advanced theory linking grief to psychopathology was proposed by DeVaul and Zisook (1976). They suggest that there are three stages to grieving, and that if a patient fails to resolve that particular stage, a specific clinical symptom results. The first stage is shock, and the clinical symptom that can develop in this stage is psychotic denial. The second stage, acute mourning, has three substages: an intense feeling state, social withdrawal, and identity with the deceased. The first substage carries the danger of an agitated depression. Social withdrawal may lead to hypochondriasis. Identity with the deceased poses the danger that the widow will psychosomatically produce the persistent physiological symptoms of the deceased. The final stage is resolution. Widows who fail to complete this stage fall victim to chronic mourning.

DEPRESSION

The symptoms of depression include withdrawal from activity and social contact, diminished self-esteem, lack of concern about how one appears to others, and a pervasive pessimism that produces a gloomy evaluation of one's own future. Physiological concomitants include disturbances in bodily cycles, such as sleep (insomnia at night and frequent napping in the day), appetite (anorexia or gorging), elimination (constipation or diarrhea), and diurnal mood shifts (usually bad in the morning, and occasionally incorporating a manic phase). Depression constitutes the major type of psychiatric problem in elders, and most likely constitutes a majority of the clinical cases (Clow & Allen, 1949; Straker, 1963; Busse & Pfeiffer, 1973). The increasing proportion of cases of depression among the aged is a general trend. No other age group has such a high percentage of cases (Swab, Holzer & Warheit, 1973; Scott & Gaitz, 1975; Levitt & Lubin, 1975).

Most individuals report a greater incidence of unhappiness as they grow into advanced age, but only a minority of these cases become clinically significant depression. These geriatric depressions are usually reactive in nature (Stern & Metzger, 1946). Most likely, they are due to major life events which represent exits from the social field in the previous six months (Paykel et al., 1969). Geriatric depression is more common among the physically ill, the widowed, and the retired than in the physically healthy, married, and employed. The chief intrapsychic dynamic of these depressions is not guilt, but inferiority feelings (Busse et al., 1954).

SUICIDE

The suicide rates for elders are higher than for any other age group, including adolescents. Although elders constitute only 10% of the population, they account for a quarter of all suicides. The rates for elder females are four times the national average. The rates for elder males are twice the national average (Resnick & Cantor, 1970). There are over a dozen possible psychodynamics involved in attempted suicide (Hammer, 1972). Geriatric suicide usually comes in the wake of depression, grief, or painful physical illness (Kiφrbe, 1951; Batchelor & Napier, 1953; Gardner, Bahn & Mack, 1964). Suicide is only rarely provoked by institutionalization, marital conflicts, poverty, or loneliness (Kiφrbe, 1951). Motives such as vengeance and feelings of guilt rarely lead to suicide in elders (Batchelor & Napier, 1953). Elders who attempt suicide are bent on success, and choose violent and effective methods when possible. Suicidal threats and talk ("maybe everyone would be better off without me") should be taken seriously, especially when the person shows signs of severe depression, grief, or physical suffering. It is right for the geriatric counselor to view suicide as psychopathological when the patient can hope for recovery and a better life thereafter. However, if the patient certainly faces irreversible deterioration, death may be a preferable alternative rationally selected by the patient. The therapist must then decide if an antisuicide stance is prolonging life or the process of dying (Gonda, 1977).

HYPOCHONDRIASIS

The power of the mind to affect the body has long been noted by both medical science and psychology. Perhaps most patient visits are due to some mental or emotional problem. Many diseases, such as ulcers, are often psychosomatic, although physical symptoms can be detected and treated. Psychosomatic disorders differ from hypochondriacal complaints in that true hypochondriacs complain of a physical problem that has no detectable or treatable physical symptoms. This syndrome is especially prevalent among elders. The hypochondriac is overly concerned with his body, over-reacts at the slightest physiological sensation, and presumes that some gruesome disease is developing. One explanation for the existence of the syndrome among the aged is an impairment of blood flow to the parietal lobes of the brain, resulting in bizarre sensations of pain, as if the pain were localized in different parts of the body (Walsh, 1976). However, the more commonly accepted theory of hypochondriasis is that it is wholly secondary to a psychological condition, specifically, depression (Fenyon, 1965; Biran, 1963; DeAlarcon, 1968).

Hypochondriasis becomes a particular life-style developed by the depressed patient (Chrzanowski, 1974). Sullivan (1940a, 1940b, 1953) viewed this as a kind of security operation in which the self-esteem of the hypochondriac is organized in such a way that bodily phenomena are given a great deal of pessimistic attention. His intense, morbid preoccupation with his body serves as a distraction from an intolerable personal situation. Busse (1976) enumerated three major precipitating factors: first, exposure to a social situation in which the individual suffers from prolonged criticism and lacks opportunities to escape (physical illness shields the elder from criticism or excuses the conduct that motivated it); second, isolation (physical illness obligates others to pay attention to the hypochondriac); and third, deterioration of marital satisfactions, for example, with a wife who must care for a disabled husband (she may mimic his symptoms as a young husband may mimic those of a pregnant wife).

Busse (1976) goes on to cite three key dynamics in hypochondriasis: first, the withdrawal of interest from other persons and objects so that it may be centered on one's own body and its functioning; second, the shifting of anxiety from a psychic area (with which the patient cannot deal) to a physical one (which is less threatening); and third, the use of physical symptoms as a means of self-punishment or atonement. Another possible dynamic would be the motive of using the symptoms to punish those who have criticized or abandoned the hypochondriac. The relationship between the elder and his physician is also capable of exacerbating hypochondriasis. Medical personnel who use technical terminology with suggestible patients or who become annoyed with their inability to help may have an iatrogenic effect, resulting in increased hypochondriacal activity on the part of the patient (Neumarker, 1966; Lipsett, 1974; Busse, 1976).

SENILITY

Senility has become a wastebasket or catchall diagnosis for all the unsolved cases of mental disorder in elders. Many gerontologists prefer to discard the term as prejudicial and useless. Unfortunately, there are some real mental problems that cannot be ignored. Probably 10 to 25% of all elders suffer from some "senile" mental deterioration. Among the institutionalized elders, the estimates vary between 50 and 80%.

The deteriorating short-term memory of elders has been noted down through history. One of Plato's dialogues has the elderly Lysimachus complain that his memory is so bad that he forgets the questions he was going to ask, and also the answers to them, and that he is quite lost if any interruption takes place. Tests of immediate recall demonstrate that this faculty becomes impaired with age in most individuals. Impaired recall may be explained by a principle of memory known as proactive inhibition, which holds that the total of things learned before an attempt to memorize something new can interfere with the learning of the new item. This principle is operative at any age, and it would stand to reason that the older a person gets, the greater the sum total of items he has put into his memory, and therefore, the greater the amount of proactive inhibition.

However, senile dementia is not merely an advanced condition of normal decline. Dorken (1958) referred to it as something qualitatively different, independent of the normal decline in recall. In senile dementia, the order of forgetting is time, place, recognition, and then counting ability. The last thing to be forgotten is the patient's own name (Fishback, 1977). Other mental capacities affected are problem-solving ability, judgment, and emotional response. Kinsbourne (1971) drew a distinction between structure (the fund of information), which is rarely affected by senility, and process (the ability to manipulate new information), which is highly susceptible to impairment.

In addition to recognizing what senility is, it is also important to recognize what senility is not. Senility is frequently compared with childhood, mental retardation, or schizophrenia, especially schizophrenic regression to childish behavior. Childish playfulness stems from a lack of knowledge about proper adult behavior, whereas senile elders manifest such behavior because of impaired memory, confusion, and/or sensory-motor debility. Adult retardates never were completely socialized into adult roles, whereas senile elders were. The behavioral differences between these two groups are known by those who have had experience with both types of patients. Cameron (1938) examined the verbal responses to sentence fragments made by normal children, normal adults, schizophrenics, and senile elders, and concluded that each group had a characteristic pattern of response. Schizophrenics gave long answers that went off on delusional tangents, but the subjects had no inkling of the inappropriateness of their responses. By contrast, the senile elders gave short and evasive answers, most likely to cover up their cognitive deficits.

Another study (Cameron, 1939) involved the use of wooden blocks varying in color, shape, and size. The blocks also had letters of the alphabet written on them. The subjects were instructed to separate the blocks according to a method determined by the experimenter. The schizophrenics failed to accomplish this task because they could not confine themselves to its boundaries; they got carried away with the other properties of the blocks and began using them to make interesting designs. Senile patients failed in the task because they could not remember the instructions.

Both senile elders and psychotics may suffer delusions and experience a return to childish or infantile thought or behavior. However, one simple distinction is that the schizophrenic is delusional because he can only cope with a fantasy world. The senile elder lacks the sensory or cognitive processes to make sense out of the perceived world, and retreats to some delusional thinking as a result. An uncompromising orientation to reality is generally inappropriate for the schizophrenic and will in many cases only produce more anxiety. The same treatment may assist the senile elder in his feeble efforts to make sense out of his phenomenologically perceived world.

If the schizophrenic regresses, it may be because he had an insecure childhood and failed to construct a firm enough emotional or interpersonal foundation to progress beyond that stage. He may need long-term psychotherapy with the therapist functioning almost as a parent surrogate to help him go back and have a "normal" childhood. The senile elder, on the other hand, regresses primarily because he cannot make sense out of the present or cannot cope with it emotionally because of the profound losses he has experienced. He regresses because his long-term memory is operative while his short-term memory has failed, or because childhood coping patterns were more successful than adult ones. For senile regression, in-depth psychotherapy is not required, and usually a reactivation and reinforcement of adult coping behavior is sufficient.

There are two basic theories concerning the origin of senile behavior: a neurological theory and a psychosocial theory. Unfortunately, too often the advocates of these different theories engage in no meaningful dialogue. I would like to reconstruct both sides of the question, as faithfully as possible, and use their strongest respective arguments. The neurological perspective defines senility as the presence of an organic brain syndrome (OBS). There is something wrong with the patient's thought and behavior because there is a physiological abnormality with the patient's central nervous system. The OBS may be due to some acute condition such as infection (pneumonia), dehydration (produced by vomiting, diarrhea), vitamin deficiencies (a product of a poor diet and reduced absorption combined with increased requirements), drug reaction (to be discussed in the fifth chapter), postepileptic confusion, cerebral circulation disorders (hemorrhage, congestion, anemia, hypotension), or brain tumor. In most cases of acute brain syndrome, the basic underlying conditions are reversible or controllable, and so is the concomitant behavior disorder. The possibility of acute brain syndrome is frequently overlooked, and the result is much needless suffering and institutionalization. One study found that most elders admitted for a psychiatric diagnosis were suffering from an acute brain disorder (Simon & Cahan, 1966).

When OBS is due to an enduring physiological condition it is referred to as a chronic brain syndrome (CBS). Again there are several possible causes of this neurological impairment. Some of these gradual deteriorations begin to take their toll in middle age. Syphilitic paresis is still common in individuals who were infected before the discovery of penicillin and neglected subsequent treatment. The spirochete lodges in vital organs such as the heart and brain and destroys tissue over a period of several decades. Years of heavy indulgence in alcohol can also destroy numerous cortical cells by the late forties. Several brain diseases can also become destructive before the seventh decade: Pick's disease, Alzheimer's disease, and Creutzfelt-Jakob disease may be due to a slow-acting virus or perhaps even to a genetically programmed breakdown of the cortical cells. All of the aforementioned types of CBS are irreversible, inasmuch as neural tissue cannot be regenerated. One other presenile dementia—adult hydrocephalus—results from accumulated fluid in the cerebral ventricles. The pressure builds up and impairs the functioning of the brain. This condition is treatable by neurosurgery which shunts the fluid to another part of the body.

All of the above conditions can occur after age 65, but they are most likely to become clinically significant within the decade before that age. Most cases of CBS originating afterward have been diagnosed as cerebral arteriosclerosis. In this condition, cortical cells are either lost or impaired by tiny lesions on cerebral vessels. The correlation between the degree of cerebral arteriosclerosis and pathological behavior is difficult to verify by either measurement of oxygen uptake or postmortem autopsies. In some of the worst cases of senility, the quantity of cerebral vascular disorder is slight. In some cases in which this disorder was verified, behavior had not been that abnormal. Many of the cases of senility which commence in the mid-seventies are due to neurofibrillary plaque formation, which shows up as tiny specks on brain scanners. Specifically, there are neurofibrillary tangles and granuvacular changes in many of the surviving neurons. The similarity to Alzheimer's disease is striking, and some current thinking is that there is no real difference between the syndromes (Angel, 1977). It is not clear whether this plaque is due to a slow-acting virus, to industrial pollution, or to some genetically programmed breakdown of protein. What is clear is the correlation between the appearance of the plaque and pathological behavior (Corsellis, 1962; Malamud, 1965; Blessed, Tomlinson & Roth, 1968). In many cases, both cerebral arteriosclerosis and neurofibrillary plaque are present simultaneously, and perhaps they appear in combination with another CBS or even with an acute syndrome.

One other factor that could produce senile behavior in the very old is hypothermia. Experiments with animals and humans indicate that when body temperature is artificially lowered, the organism has lowered cognitive capabilities. Below a certain level there is a loss of short-term memory, and difficulty in learning new processes. At an even lower temperature, there is no response to the spoken word. Elders have less ability to maintain their body temperatures. When there is a thyroid condition that results in insufficient body heat, the senility can be reversed by treating the thyroid.

The psychosocial perspective on senility views pathological thought and behavior as the result of the stress and deprivation experienced in later life. Various forms of evidence can be mustered to support this stance. First of all, survey evidence focusing on the life histories of senile elders reveals several significant differences when compared to normal elders. The latter group had done a better job of learning social, occupational, and recreational skills in early life (Albrecht, 1951). Rates of senility seem especially high among persons of low socioeconomic status, the poorly educated, immigrants, those not married, and those with few social roles. Experimental evidence indicates that the lack of a sufficiently stimulating environment, as in cases of sensory deprivation, can produce a lack of contact with the environment and hallucination. Many of the environments of elders who are isolated or in institutions lack sufficient stimulation. Furthermore, hypnosis and suggestion can cause neurologically healthy individuals to imitate the symptoms of CBS (Grunewald & Fromm, 1967). Much of what goes on in nursing homes is a systematic process of suggestion: the staff consistently tells the patient that he is too feeble to do anything on his own. After a while, elders provoke protective responses in others because it is the best way for them to get attention (Butler, 1960; Wolff, 1970). Meacher (1972) carefully studied cases of severe senile delusion and concluded that it was essentially an adaptive response, "extraordinarily inventive and original" in some cases, designed to cope with an environment that was painful and totally unlike anything else experienced in adult life.

I believe that the best model of mental illness is one that serves as the foundation for successful cure. Since both medical and psychosocial factors can result in the improvement of senile elders, I prefer a synthetic view. Both neurological impairment and an inauspicious environment can bring on the same symptoms. These two factors may function quite independently of each other, so that some elders suffer from one but not the other. Other elders suffer from both, and the vast majority of elders are normal and suffer from neither. The two factors may also interact in a number of ways. For example, OBS impairs cognitive functioning, and this loss may trigger an emotional (depressive) reaction as the individual becomes aware of it and grieves about it. Most CBS patients also have affective disorders, which are diagnosable and treatable (Ernst, Badash, Beran, Kosovsky & Kleinhauz, 1977). The emotional reaction may exacerbate the mental and behavioral effects (though not the cause) of the CBS (Pinkerton & Kelly, 1952). These depressive reactions are quite common in cerebral arteriosclerosis (Busse & Pfciffer, 1973). On the other hand, a good psychosocial background (good interpersonal relations and educational level) is essential to the later adjustment of brain-injured CBS patients (Stonecypher, 1974).

There are numerous clinical tests for senility, some of which are better able to distinguish between CBS and depression. The more accurate tests for CBS involve the use of sophisticated medical technology: electroencephalography, echoencephalography, computerized tomography, and neumoencephalography (Busse & Pfeiffer, 1973; Angel, 1977). One simple test for senility is the mental status questionnaire (MSQ). First developed by Kahn, Pollack, and Goldfarb (1961), the MSQ asks 10 short questions which evaluate the patient's orientation in space and time. There are now various forms of the MSQ. On the basis of my cross-cultural experience, I prefer the following form for elders who reside in the community.

1. How old are you? (within two years)
2. In which year were you born? (the exact year)
3. What year is it now? (the exact year)
4. Which month are we in? (If he does not know, ask him the season)
5. What was the last meal you had? (breakfast, lunch, or dinner)
6. What is the name of this building? (clinic, hospital, office, nursing home)
7. Count backwards from 10 to zero. (no errors permitted)
8. What is your address? (number and street of present residence)
9. What day of the week is today? (exact day)
10. Who is the president now? (last name is sufficient)

For institutionalized elders, substitute the following questions for the last three.

8.   How long have you been in this institution? (20% error permitted)
9.   Who is the director (or administrator)? (last name is sufficient)
10.   How would we get from here to the dining room? (directions must be accurate)

Less than two errors indicate no impairment. Three to five errors indicate some impairment. More than five errors show severe impairment. Allow one more error for subjects coming from a lower socioeconomic class.

Plutchik and his associates (1970, 1971) added additional tests to the MSQ, including the possibility of rating the patient by the staff. The most comprehensive of these types of rating tests is the Sandoz Clinical Assessment for Geriatric Patients (SCAG), which claims the ability to distinguish between depression and CBS (Shader & Harmatz, 1974). Fishback suggests using the counting test with visual cues (1977). However, CBS does not deplete all the areas of the cortical mantle at the same time, nor is there any regular sequence, nor do all individuals experience uniform effects of CBS. The impact of CBS on a given individual at a given time may affect certain areas of the brain more than others, and thus impair cognitive functions more than others. Hence a truly comprehensive psychometric evaluation should be made of separate functions: perception, memory, spatial relationships, language, reasoning, and so on. These types of tests, although difficult for CBS patients, are usually within the capacity of depressed elders. The two groups have statistically significant score differences on tests of cognitive ability (Hensi, Whitehead & Post 1968; Kendrick & Post, 1967; Friedman, 1964).

Another convenient test for CBS is the face-hand test (FHT) developed by Fink, Green, and Bender (1952). The patient puts his hands on his knees and closes his eyes. The therapist simultaneously strokes the dorsal side of one hand and one side of the face. The patient must then correctly identify both stimuli, either by pointing or indicating verbally. Ten trials are given, and different combinations of right and left are used: four contralateral, four ipsilateral, and two symmetrical combinations of hand-hand and face-face. Two types of errors occur: extinction (reporting only one stimulus) and displacement (locating at least one stimulus incorrectly, and even occasionally outside of the body). Fink, Green, and Bender (1952) reported that less than one-tenth of CBS patients could do 10 trials without errors, but all those subjects with repeated errors had CBS. Normal elders and schizophrenics pass the test. In the latter group, 30% made some errors during the first 10 trials, but not on the second run. The test data were stable for repeated trials on different days. More recent data (Ferris, Crook, Sathananthan & Gershon, 1976) suggest that any test that measures disjunctive reaction time can diagnose CBS. Depression does not reduce the reaction time of elders (Botwinick & Thompson, 1967), nor does it interfere with other perceptual or motor skills (Alvarez, 1962).

Angel (1977) has noticed that the following physiological responses are indicative of CBS: If the palm is lightly stroked, the patient will grasp it firmly, and he may be rather slow to release it, even when instructed to do so. If the palm is scratched, there will be a contraction of the mentalis and the lower lip will be pushed up. Gentle stroking of the lips produces a "rooting" reflex. Percussion of the orbicular oris (the muscle around the mouth) produces a snout and pucker reflex.

Yet another useful instrument is the Rorschach. Depressed elders restrict attention to detail responses and shading responses. They show a marked delay in responding to card VII, and a great deal of response to card X (Orme, 1955). Depression accompanied by feelings of tension produce inanimate movement responses, while hypochondriasis elicits anatomical responses. The senile patterns are quite different (Orme, 1955; Dorken and Kral, 1951; Ames, Learned, Mextraux & Walker, 1954). CBS patients take longer to answer, especially with achromatic cards. They make fewer responses, refuse to respond more often, and make poorer quality (restricted and stereotyped) responses.

Other tests are also available, but they tend to do a poorer job of distinguishing between true CBS and depression. Because CBS is a multifaceted phenomenon, there are many types of tests that some CBS patients will fail, but which depressed patients will pass. For example, some CBS patients will manifest symptoms such as jargon aphasia, which is nonexistent in depression (Kent, 1977).

INCONTINENCE

The loss of bowel and bladder control is found among a third of all elders in institutions. Some were admitted because of the problem, whereas others developed it in the institution. As with senility, there are both neurological and psychosocial perspectives on the disease. Brocklehurst (1972) has outlined three physiological causes of incontinence in elders. Stress incontinence is very common in women and reflects the degeneration of the urogenital tract. It can be treated with a repair operation or with pessaries—forms that support the vagina or uterus. Another approach is to use electricity to produce a response from the muscles responsible for bladder control, and then to follow this with bladder floor exercises. In the more serious cases, an electronic stimulator which maintains bladder control must be left in place, and the current must be turned off whenever micturition is desired. Overflow incontinence is due to fecal impaction, and the most direct solution is to remove the impaction and promote regularity. Low capacity incontinence, which is frequent in cases of arteriosclerotic disease, occurs because a small amount of urine becomes sufficient to trigger micturition. Antidiuretics and hormones can be effective, as can anticholinergic medication, which blocks the sacral reflex micturition arc.

Interestingly enough, the drug most frequently prescribed in these cases is imipramine, a tricyclic compound with antidepressant properties. Perhaps incontinence, like suicide, hypochondriasis, and some senile behavior, can be produced by depression. Schwartz and Stanton (1950) concluded that incontinence was a type of social participation precipitated by conflict, abandonment, isolation, devaluing, or unconstructive relations. On the other hand, incontinence was found to be rare when anxiety and threat were absent and when group participation without censorship or sanction was the norm. In my own experience with bowel and bladder training programs in institutions, alert patients who are convalescing from surgery or CVAs have the greatest success, whereas those who are confused and withdrawn are the most difficult to retrain.

CONCLUSION

Elders run a greater risk of mental disease than any other age group. A history of a personality disorder or of OBS may be background factors, but most of the psychopathology of later life is precipitated by the bio-psycho-social crises of aging. The chief dynamic of mental/emotional disorders is that these crises produce a sense of loss and a feeling of inferiority, followed by reactive depression. Suicidal, hypochondriacal, senile, and incontinent behavior may be secondary to depression, but diagnostic measures should be employed to identify possible organic causes.

Chapter 3

THEORETICAL PERSPECTIVES

So far the major bio-psycho-social crises and psychopathology of aging have been presented. The task of this chapter is to find the theoretical perspective within the psychological study of personality that can best serve as a comprehensive model for psychogeriatrics and as a guideline for the geriatric psychotherapist.

SOMATOTYPOLOGY

One of the earliest theories of the personality, antedating the science of psychology, is the attempt to explain personal qualities as manifestations of the external bodily qualities of the person. For example, popular legend has it that men with prominent chins have forceful personalities, or that close-set eyes signify criminality. Most of these physical traits have no scientifically verifiable connection with their bearer's attitudes, emotions, intelligence, or behavior.

However, Sheldon and Stevens (1942) demonstrated correlations approaching +0.80 between between body type and personality. Most people are somewhere between being totally fat, totally skinny, or totally muscular, so Sheldon and his team categorized human body structure into three ideal forms: endomorph (corpulent); ectomorph (thin), and mesomorph (muscular with broad shoulders and narrow hips). Sheldon selected representative groups of persons on the basis of body type and gave them a series of personality tests. Each of these ideal types demonstrated a certain conglomerate of personality traits. Sheldon referred to the personality of the endomorph as visceratonia, which included being jovial and sociable, and also the love of comfort and ritual. The ectomorph's personality type is cerebratonia, typified by the shy, socially withdrawn, contemplative individual. The mesomorph's personality type is somatotonia, and includes competitiveness, determination, and a strong achievement drive.

There are several explanations for the correlation between body structure and personality. Most of the followers of Sheldon believe that one's body structure from infancy on sets up patterns by which the individual interacts with his environment. For example, the child with little muscle or fat to protect his body (the ectomorph) will be less equipped for rough play, and therefore develops the withdrawn personality of cerebratonia. But if his body structure is later changed through diet or exercise, the effect on his personality patterns is only minimal.

Sheldon and his followers have found that a person's somatotype affects the way he goes through the different life stages. For example, ectomorphs usually go through puberty and develop secondary sexual characteristics later than the other body types. The mesomorphs enjoy the beauty, power, and status that come during the prime of life, and tend to view old age as a threat of loss. Some somatotonics try to deny the process of aging by searching for new quests, competitions, or achievements. Visceraton-ics are happiest in childhood, especially one that is indul-gent. Aging can be difficult for them if there is a loss of physical sensation or socialization. Both the mesomorphs and the endomorphs are more likely to fear death as the end of the good things they have enjoyed on earth (De-Ropp, 1968). The ectomorphs are very uncomfortable in the rough and tumble world of childhood, and also throughout their extended adolescence. Since their con-templativeness makes them well-suited to long years of study, they develop the guiding fiction that better years lie ahead. To a great extent, later life is more satisfying for the ectomorph, especially if there has been intellectual matura-tion and the chance for reflection on life. Ectomorphs also have less anxiety about death, since it is a great mystery which they may calmly reflect on.

Sheldon's typology, fascinating as it is, contains the danger of becoming another intellectual astrology in which a label (Leo, Virgo or endomorph) serves as a complete digest of the personality. Furthermore, it is of limited use to the geriatric counselor because the body forms of later life may change. In addition, the theory lacks any capacity to comprehend the bio-psycho-social crises that arise in later life and account for so much of the psychopathology in elders. Finally, somatotypology offers no guidelines on the best way to perform psychotherapy on a person of a certain body type.

FREUD

Freud developed his school of psychotherapy, known as psychoanalysis, in Vienna during the first part of the cen-tury. In his theory of psychopathology, Freud emphasized two factors: libido (the quantity of sexual energy in the psyche) and childhood development. He also contended

that the first six years were the most formative ones. Freud
thought that senility was due to a sexual disturbance (1966,
I, 188), specifically, to a decrease of libido (1966, III, 101–
102). Psychoanalysis reviews the patient's entire life—both
realities and fantasies—and attempts to train the patient in
new ways of coping with repressed memories and wishes.
Freud had a very negative view on the possibility of successful psychoanalysis with the aged, complaining that persons
over 40 were no longer educable, and that the mass of
material to be dealt with (all the way back to earliest childhood) was simply too great (1966, VII, 254, 264).

One of Freud's earliest followers was Karl Abraham.
While he remained a loyal adherent to psychoanalysis, he
had to disagree with Freud on the point about psychoanalysis for elders. Abraham (1927) had several patients over 50
years of age and concluded that their treatment was aston-
ishingly successful. He was able to work all the way back to
childhood when necessary, but found this to be less essential when the neurosis had been acquired in later life. Indeed, whereas lifelong mental disturbances tended to be
most difficult, those acquired in later life seemed to be
readily treatable. Abraham concluded that the prognosis
should be contingent upon the age of the neurosis, and not
upon the age of the patient.

Later geriatric psychotherapists tried to explain the
psychopathology and the treatment of the aged from a
psychoanalytic point of view, and they have had to go to
some lengths to make the psychoanalytic theory fit. Kaufman (1937, 1940) hypothesized an inverted oedipus complex in which the elders become dependent upon adult
offspring and transfer onto them some of the libido originally cathected on the patient's original, biological parents.
This inverted oedipus complex is paired with a regression
to a pregenital level of psychosexual functioning. Grotjahn
(1940, 1951, 1955) interpreted the crises of later life as a
narcissistic trauma due to castration anxiety. The neuroses

of later life are but the defenses constructed against that castration anxiety. Although several psychoanalytically oriented therapists have had successes working with elders, the vast majority of psychoanalysts have not been inspired by these attempts to apply Freudian insights to geriatrics. As a result, most psychoanalysts have never treated a patient in later life.

Psychoanalysis is inextricably caught up in a hydrodynamic energy model of intrapsychic phenomena: Quantities of libido are cathected around certain love objects. Furthermore, this model is geared to see everything in later life as a reaction to or working out of sexual and/or childhood problems. Clever psychoanalysts may be able to explain the problems of aging in this format by manipulating the meaning and breadth of the terms, but the end products (such as reverse oedipus complexes) are a little esoteric for the nonpsychoanalyst to employ in everyday practice.

Erikson

In 1927 a young portrait painter from Denmark became a client of Anna Freud. He became fascinated with the psychoanalytic movement and joined its inner circle a few years later. Erik Erikson trained in a nonmedical specialty of psychoanalysis: child analysis. He worked diligently within the orthodox Freudian framework to include social as well as psychosexual determinants of development. It was not until Erikson himself was in his forties that he gave any thought to human development beyond adolescence. Previously, Erikson had constructed five developmental stages, each with a specific bio-psycho-social task, to cover human development from birth through adolescence. Now Erikson hypothesized the existence of three phases in adulthood: young adulthood, middle age, and old age. In the middle years, the life task is to secure the triumph of generativity over stagnation. The generative person is constructing something for the future, in fact, something that will outlive him. Erikson first conceived of generativity as involving the procreation and nurturing of the next generation of human beings. Later he realized that there were other ways of being generative: through one's career, volunteer work, or even an artistic or intellectual creation of enduring value. The individuals who do not create and preserve for future generations stagnate. Such individuals will leave nothing in the sense of positive contributions. They vegetate and do little more than the necessary activities of the daily routine and otherwise kill time.

Erikson's eighth and final stage of development is his most poorly developed. Here he identified the life task as securing integrity over despair. Integrity is the acceptance of one's life in its entirety in the face of the physical, social, and perhaps even mental decline of old age, and in the face of the prospect of death itself. The individual who is able to find solace and satisfaction in the way he had led the seven previous stages is the one who succeeds in this last phase. The generativity of the previous stage should assuage death fears by convincing the elder that something of him or from him will live on after he is gone. In other words, the key to having a happy old age is to live one's earlier life with vigorous meaning, making lasting contributions. Individuals who have failed to do so find themselves engulfed in despair. Such despair may be hidden behind disgust and contempt for others or the future generation, or blame of others for one's own failures in life. All of these different symptoms point to the same sad evaluation of one's life. The most profound and final part of despair is that it is now too late to start over and rectify the past.

As the last chapter pointed out, a person's life history is a factor in geriatric mental health, but current developments are of overriding importance. Essentially, Erikson's model is of little use to the geriatric psychotherapist because of its backward gaze, and because of the therapist's need to confront the here and now bio-psycho-social crises of later life. The central psychopathology of later life is not a brooding over the past 30 odd years, but reactive depression triggered by events in the recent past.

The only useful clinical technique inspired by Erikson has been Butler's (1964) life review process. However, Butler himself is most cautious about accepting Erikson's theoretical framework. "His experience with the middle aged and elderly is very meager, and his popular conceptions of generativity versus stagnation and integrity versus despair do not hold up well in my clinical and research experience with patients in middle and later life." (Butler, 1975, p. 255n). Although Erikson does a better job than Freud in taking account of the environmental influences throughout the life cycle, he also falls into the trap of defining old age as a mere reaction to earlier life.

EGO PSYCHOLOGY

Along with Erikson, other progressive psychoanalysts have carried on Freud's work and advanced it beyond their mentor's premature crystallizations of theory. This growth within psychoanalysis has taken the name "ego psychology" because the emphasis has shifted from the libido, drive, instinct, and sex to the ego—the conscious, rational part of the psyche which is in touch with reality and (in mentally healthy individuals) controls behavior. White (1963) has been at the forefront of this movement and introduced the theory that the ego itself had independent sources of psychic energy. White then contended that the organism strives for a feeling of mastery over its environment, in addition to striving for gratification of instinctual needs. The organism feels *effectance* when it can influence its environment, and *competence* when it can control the environment. Danger is sensed when the organism exceeds its competence.

The ego drives introduced by White can be used to describe much of infant behavior. The young child seeks independence, exploration, and experimentation, and eventually draws away from the need for being mothered. White suggested that, instead of focusing on the psychopathology of instinctual drives, the emphasis should be on the ego drives: What went wrong with the growth of the sense of mastery? Self-esteem is deeply rooted in the sense of mastery, and feelings of inferiority arise when mastery is frustrated.

Although White developed his theories from a background of child development, they are applicable to geriatrics. In later life the bio-psycho-social crises pose new threats to the organism's ability to cope with its environment. As a result, feeligs of danger and inferiority arise. The solution is for the therapist to assist the elder in regaining the experience of mastery (Thompson, 1964).

LEWIN

Psychoanalytic thought has been only one influence on modern personality theory. Another central European force has been the Gestalt school, which developed about the same time as psychoanalysis. Instead of the Freudian dissection of the psyche into vying drives and repressing agents, the Gestalt school conceived of the psyche as a unity. The central teaching is that the psyche must be understood as a whole. Kurt Lewin was a student of the Gestalt school, and he carried its holistic perspective into the study of motivation. Lewin attempted to understand a subject's motivation by means of a complex mapping of the goals, means, and barriers which a person perceived in his life, referring to this as *hodological* space, or the life space. For young children, Lewin felt that ambivalence (positive and negative values associated with the same goal) could account for much hesitant and aberrant behavior. Adolescents live in a period of great changes in body, goals, and social roles, and this results in a shifting life space. Adolescent behavior is largely trial and error which is designed to fashioned new patterns of comprehending and coping with the new life space.

Although Lewin did not focus on problems of elders, his system is applicable. The problems in later life are not so much the goals or ambivalence, but the disappearance of means or the development of barriers. Not only do bodily changes contribute to this problem, but body image (the closest dimension of the life space) becomes unknown and confusing. Social expectations also shift. Sometimes society treats elders like responsible, autonomous adults, at other times like a privileged, prestige caste, at others like dependent, irresponsible children, and at other times it ignores them as obsolete, former members of the social order. In such a life space, the degree of confusion is great and individuals come to depend more and more on small and insignificant cues for their orientation. This is the very process that is conducive to the development of paranoia in elders. Depression in elders can be understood in terms of a loss motivation in the face of disappearing goals and means, combined with the appearance of barriers which are perceived as being insurmountable.

There are many ways that Lewin's theory can give bearings to the geriatric counselor. First, he must strive to comprehend the patient's life space as perceived by the patient. Otherwise, the counselor will be giving directions that make little sense to the patient. Furthermore, Lewin's theories focus the therapist and patient together on identifying goals (remotivation), finding means (rehabilitation), and lowering the barriers (environmental manipulation).

ADLER

Alfred Adler was the first of Freud's inner circle to break with the master and establish a competing school of psychotherapy. Adler was also greatly influenced by the Gestalt tradition and the very name of his school, "individual psychology," was selected because each patient's psyche was considered to be an indivisible unit. Adler is most remembered for his theory of the inferiority complex. Originally, Adler attributed all neuroses to inferiority complexes, and all inferiority feeling to physical defects. As Adler's views matured (1956, 1964), he realized that other factors could influence feelings of inferiority: poverty, sibling rivalry, and even unrealistic goals which the patient sets for himself. Probably the most important factors are unwise child-rearing patterns. Specifically, parents who neglect, harshly treat, or pamper their offspring are likely to cause inferiority feelings in them. The child who is ignored or abused by his parents wonders what is so wrong with him that his parents should treat him like that. The pampered child wonders what is so wrong with him that his parents have to take such elaborate care of him and do so much for him. The child who is the apple of his parent's eyes is also in for a big letdown when he gets out of the home and into the school, where he is only one among many children, and enjoys no special favors among adult authorities or peers. Wise upbringing provides parental support and encouragement for the child to assume independent behavior. If the child fails or misbehaves, the adult explains the error, but affirms basic faith in the child and encourages another trial.

Adler finally concluded that all individuals have some inferiority feeling, if for no other reason than that they were once children, and every child is inferior in many ways to adults. The child lacks the speech, mobility, power over his environment, and privileges of adulthood. Granted, some

individuals, by virtue of organic defects or unwise upbringing, are bound to have more inferiority feelings than others. However, Adler finally decided that feelings of
inferiority were not a direct cause of neurosis, but only a
challenge which, if the individual failed to meet, became an
excuse for neurosis. Adler saw that each individual develops his own style of life, which represents his own solution
to the problem of inferiority feeling. A mentally healthy
life-style is one in which there is compensation for inferiority feelings by means of what Adler called *Gemeinschafts-
gefühl.* This term is usually translated as "social interest"
but could also mean taking into account other people's
happiness.

Adler identified three healthy paths for compensation:
friendship, family, and career. A relationship with friends
allows one to gain a sense of significance and counteracts
feelings that one is inferior or unloved. Also, conversations
with friends show us that all people have problems and
worries, and reassure us that we are not "weird" or abnormal. Our family also gives us the opportunity to be someone very important in the lives of others. A career provides
an opportunity for status and achievement, and even real
pride in one's contribution to society. Each of these justified sentiments counteracts inferiority feelings.

Those people who do not attain compensation via socially approved routes may turn to a private logic by which
they can escape the awesome feeling of inferiority. They
may desire to be known as the meanest or the most daring,
and may place a claim on status that way. They may strive
for a sham sense of superiority by having the ability to hurt
others. Adler referred to this path as "masculine protest"
because our culture tends to foster such behavior in males
rather than females.

The second chapter demonstrated that inferiority feeling is widespread among elders. This feeling can be engen-

dered by physical decline, by loss of status, beauty, economic deprivation, or by a combination of these and other factors. Given this fact, there is a special challenge to the mental health of elders. However, their ability to compensate for inferiority feeling has been reduced on each of the three paths. The number of friendships is reduced as old friends die or move away. Gone are the contacts from work and from many forms of recreation. The volume of time spent with friends can also be reduced by problems of mobility. Loss of sensory function exacerbates isolation. Many elders find that these same factors inhibit the development of new friendships. Family life is threatened by the geographical mobility of offspring and by modernization and technology, which reduce the family's interest in the elders. The most serious threat to the compensation afforded by the family role is widowhood. Finally, compensation through one's career is ended by retirement. Therefore old age is an especially difficult period of life, for the factors facilitating the development of inferiority feelings are on the increase, and compensation becomes more difficult to attain.

One other exacerbating factor can be the reversal of parent-child roles. The child or an institution becomes responsible for the elder's care and support. An infirm or senile elder requires extensive care similar to that given to an infant. Within this role reversal lurk the dangers of neglect and/or pampering. If an elder suspects that his family or society have neglected his needs or have forgotten about him, this can only worsen his feeling of inferiority. If the family or the institutional staff resent their work and give care begrudgingly, the problem is compounded. On the other hand, unwise sympathy or a zeal for efficiency can pamper the elder to the point where much of his basic decision-making capacity has been usurped.

Various aspects of geriatric psychopathology may be

explained in Adlerian terms. For example, Adler recounted many cases of children who feigned illness (consciously or unconsciously) to win special status or treatment. This could apply to cases of hypochondriasis in elders. Rigidity may be nothing more than adherence to a private logic which arises as individuals withdraw their social interest. Several gerontologists have attributed the conservatism and rigidity of elders to inferiority feeling (Gilbert, 1952; Cowdry 1939). Adler associated the neurotic life-style with overcautiousness and a hesitancy to make decisions and to commit oneself to them. Perhaps senile behavior can be seen as a neurotic shrinking from the challenges of the world and as a complete submission to dependency needs. Alder, himself a physician in general practice, never denied the impact of the physical on the mental, but he always felt it possible for the strength of will to compensate for the handicaps. He loved to recount how many individuals with weak legs overcompensated and became track stars, or how others with weak eyes devoted much attention to the visual and became great artists. Therefore an Adlerian perspective also gives us hope that the real physical impairments and neurological bases of mental decline can be compensated for by the healthy organism.

Adler also gives geriatric psychotherapists a guideline: Undercut inferiority feelings and neurotic life-styles by helping the patient develop social interests, cultivate independent behavior, and win a sense of achievement. An Adlerian perspective can reinterpret the disengagement issue. The question is not how much social activity a person has, but to what degree his activities are guided by social interest. Disengagement is but a new opportunity for compensation when social interest has been preserved in an individual, but disengagement constitutes a rejection when either the ability or desire to be socially involved has been damaged in the process.

JUNG

Probably no other member of Freud's inner circle wrote more about the second half of life than Jung. In 1913 Jung followed Alder's lead and broke with Freud to set up his own school of psychotherapy, known as "analytical psychology." Even more so than Freud, Jung de-emphasized the environment and sought to explain things in terms of the dynamics of the intrapsychic process. Jung replaced the Freudian focus on childhood with the theory that an individual is born with an inherited capacity to form symbols, and he spoke of this capacity as the collective unconscious. However, like Adler, Jung focused on the individual's own capacity to try to make sense of his world and also to change his behavior by changing his perspective on things.

Jung defined mental health in terms of the individuation process, which is a growth of the conscious part of the psyche in full harmony with the collective unconscious. At birth the psyche contains only the potential for consciousness. This potential is actualized as the individual learns how to relate to his environment. For the first half of life the individual's task is to grow into the roles with which his society provides him. In therapy with young people, Jung felt that it was sufficient to clear away the obstacles to further growth. He followed Freud's techniques to clear away sexual complexes and Adlerian techniques for inferiority feelings. But in the second half of life, the situation changed, for the future no longer beckons with marvelous possibilities. Whereas the younger person has the task of normal adaptation to the world of external necessity, the person in the second half of life has an inward orientation. The elder must devote more attention or psychic energy to the intrapsychic processes so that he can come to an accord with the collective unconscious and prepare himself for death. Two-thirds of Jung's patients were over 35, or as he phrased it, in the second half of life. Therefore Jung's therapeutic techniques were constructed on the basis of what he considered to be most appropriate for the second half of life.

Jung's system for furthering the individuation process centered around the use of symbols. The symbol is distinguished from the sign, which conveys a specific meaning clearly apprehended by consciousness. The symbol, by contrast, conveys a multifaceted and multivalent meaning, only imperfectly intuited by consciousness. Such a symbol serves as a bridge to the unconscious and brings its psychic energy to the disposal of the conscious part of the mind. So the task of all individuals, especially elders, who wish to maintain their mental health is to nurture their capacities for symbolic experience. There are two ways of doing this. The first is to search through one's own religious tradition, contemplate the meaning of its myths, symbols, and rituals, and then allow them to guide one's life. Indeed, Jung was fond of saying that all of his patients had fallen ill because they had lost contact with their religious traditions, and that they recovered only inasmuch as they regained a religious outlook.

The other method of deepening contact with symbols was dream interpretation. Jung criticized psychoanalytic interpretive methods for treating dreams as if they were signs rather than symbols. Instead of finding a precise meaning for each aspect of the dream, Jungian strategy is to use the dream as a channel for establishing more contact with the unconscious. Indeed, the word *interpretation* is misapplied, and Jungians prefer the term *amplification.* The latter term implies that the dream brings something from the unconscious, and it is the task of the patient and the analyst within their psychotherapeutic relationship to get as much as they can out of the dream.

Jungian analysts prefer to consider dreams in a series, rather than as unitary creations. Therefore the amplification of a given dream involves references to other dreams and even to mythological, literary, and religious parallels. Successful amplification convinces the client that his dreams have a profound and universal meaning, and that his very identity, while unique, possesses collective bonds to all humanity throughout history. According to Jung, this is the type of attitude necessary for successful aging and preparation for death.

The Jungian perspective does a good job of accounting for and explaining the potential therapeutic relevance of one aspect of aging: the process of introversion. However, because of its focus on the intrapsychic, it has only a limited capacity to explain the environmental dimensions of the psychopathology of aging.

MASLOW

Another psychologist who expressed great interest in religious experience is Abraham Maslow. He is best remembered for his five levels of needs. First, there is basic body gratification: food, shelter, sleep, and so on. Second, there are safety needs: protection from forces that cause death or injury or pain. Third, there are the needs for status and acceptance. Fourth are the feelings of adequacy and self-esteem. Last is the need for self-actualization, which Maslow defined as the need for creative expression.

Most of his later works focused on this highest level, and Maslow listed numerous differences between the self-actualizer's way of looking at things and those of persons not functioning on this level. Essentially, the actualizers are creative, they feel an underlying kinship with the rest of humanity (even though they may prefer solitude at times), and they have what Maslow refers to as "B-cognition." This is a kind of religious wisdom familiar to the mystical traditions of the world's great religions.

One of Maslow's theories is that the lower needs have priority over the higher. Therefore a hungry individual may risk his life to get food. A person without status or acceptance by a group may find it difficult to maintain feelings of self-esteem. Of course the self-actualization needs are the most vulnerable to the competing demands of all the lower levels. Maslow's perspective allows us to view the bio-psycho-social crises of aging as threats to the lower levels of needs. Basic bodily gratification is threatened by physical deterioration. Safety is threatened by the fear of crime. Status and acceptance are impaired by negative social attitudes on aging, and by the loss of career and social roles. The need for self-esteem is eroded by the feeling of inferiority. Because of these numerous threats to the lower levels, it would seem exceedingly difficult for elders to attain or maintain functioning on the self-actualization level.

Surprisingly, Maslow also noted that the majority of self-actualizers he found were elders. This testifies to the adaptive ability of the human organism to transcend impairments on the lower levels, to treat them as challenges to creative ability and not as obstacles to it. Maslow's description of the self-actualizer is an interesting description of what aging can be, and perhaps should be, if only the threats to the lower levels of needs can be cleared away.

FROMM

Another famous humanistic psychologist is Erich Fromm. His theories have their roots in psychoanalysis, philosophical Marxism, and twentieth century humanism. His personality theory is based on the assumption that humanity has an essential nature: a potential for reason, love, work, and responsibility. However, alienation from that essential nature is also a part of human existence. People experience being cut off from fellows and from their own productive talents, and they experience a subsequent sense of shame, helplessness, and anxiety. There are no real solutions for this condition, only comparatively better means for coping with it. The best solution is for the individual to maintain a productive and loving attitude and relationships. Such individuals are rooted in being, doing, and giving, not in having. However, the personal limitations of individuals and the imperfections of our socioeconomic order cause most individuals to develop a personality somewhat short of Fromm's productive ideal.

Fromm outlined four lower levels of interpersonal and productive relations. The lowest is the receptive (oral-dependent), whose goal is to obtain passively without having to give. The next level is the exploitative (oral-aggressive), which is similar except that it is more active, using force. The hoarding level (anal-retentive) is one in which the individual seeks to construct a protective wall and desires to bring all wealth within. The marketing orientation is a product of the anomie of other-directed, mass society and emphasizes the acquisition of wealth via exchange and manipulation instead of productive relations.

Many elders are in a state of alienation, isolation, and separation from their community and from the opportunity to love and use productive talents. Therefore they experience shame, helplessness, and anxiety. Retirement may be the loss of one's primary productive relationship. If the elder fails to meet these challenges and to develop new loving and productive relations, he will slip back into a lower level. Many elders could be classified as hoarding, clinging to worthless relics of the past. Senile dependency is represented by the lowest, receptive level.

Rogers

No other single theory of psychotherapy has had such a large impact on its practice in the last 25 years. Rogers' understanding of mental health is that each organism has an innate capacity for valuing. The individual who is truly in touch with himself is said to be congruent (mentally healthy). Rogers' theory of psychopathology was that parents and society impose conditions of worth. Individuals who internalize these standards become closed to organismic valuing, and hence, lack congruence. The task of psychotherapy is to subject the client to a situation in which he receives unconditional positive regard, so that he will feel safe enough to trust his own basic organismic valuing process.

Unfortunately, despite the popularity of Rogers' ideas among psychotherapists, it is not readily apparent how his theories explain anything about the bio-psycho-social crisis or the psychopathologies of aging. Are elders more closed to organismic valuing? Is this due to the recrudescence of old parental conditions of worth? Perhaps the conditions of worth are the social attitudes on aging. But, as the first chapter demonstrated, these factors have only a minimal role in geriatric mental health.

Conclusion

The two foremost perspectives on psychotherapy (Freud and Rogers) overload the importance of the parent-child relationship and seem to be the perspectives least applicable to geriatrics. Theories that rely heavily on some prefabricated developmental task which all healthy individuals must successfully complete (Erikson, Jung) ignore the great environmental differences that predispose certain elders to psychopathology. Developmentally preprogramed theories (Freud, Erikson, Sheldon) have little relevance to the geriatric psychotherapist in his quest for effective strategies and techniques for treatment. Those perspectives that describe the crises of aging in environmental terms (Lewin, White, Adler, Fromm, and Maslow) do a good job of describing the second half of life and explaining how they lead to psychopathological thought and behavior. Of all the theories discussed, probably Adler's can be applied most comprehensively to explain the roles of bodily changes and the organism's attitude and will, in addition to the reactions to the environment.

Chapter 4

PROPHYLAXIS

An ounce of prevention is worth a pound of cure. This proverb is especially appropriate for the mental health of elders. Treatment can only take place after the problem has been identified and the patient has been directed into the mental health care delivery system. Even then, treatment may not be appropriate or adequate. It is much more simple, economical, and effective to maintain health, both physical and mental, rather than to attempt to restore it after it has been lost. This chapter is devoted to factors by and large out of the direct control of the mental health professional. It is designed primarily to broaden the vistas of mental health personnel, who occasionally come to believe that they alone must shoulder the problems of individuals.

If one key word can identify those programs that facilitate the maintenance of mental health in elders, that word is *flexibility*. Procrustean programs intimidate elders (and other individuals in need) and fail to provide sufficient resources to help elders cope with bio-psycho-social crises. The more flexible the supportive programs are, the more they can help individual elders with their individual problems.

RELIGION

Church and synagogue attendance takes on some interesting patterns with age. Among highly ritualistic religions, such as the Roman Catholic and Episcopalian churches, attendance at mass increases after age 65. The same trend is found in the Jewish faith, but in this case, the trend may be due to cohort factors. A good percentage of the aged Jewish population is foreign-born and clings to the habits of the old world. In most Protestant denominations, attendance declines after about age 50. In all denominations there is a correlation between health and attendance. Obviously, the infirm elders are more likely to be bedridden or house-bound and not able to go to the services. (One recent Roman Catholic project worthy of note has been the "Eucharistic Ministry," in which lay volunteers bring the consecrated host to the shut-in.)

Leadership in most denominations approaches a gerontocracy, at least among the clergy. Catholic Popes and Mormon Prophets are usually over 65 when selected, and they have a life term. The fact that fewer younger people are being ordained means that the average age of the clergy is getting higher. However, the trend among the lay leadership is still with the middle-aged. The number of church offices held declines after age 60 for the laity of most denominations.

Religious activities such as Bible reading, private prayer, study groups, and listening to broadcasts increase in later life. One religious program on the radio stated that 80% of its mail was received from listeners over 70. This same age group has the highest percentage of opinion poll respondents who state a belief in God, religious conservatism, and life after death. Most elders who are religious to begin with deepen their faith in later life, and tend to find it more rewarding.

It has long been observed that the happiest elders attend church or synagogue the most often, and the saddest the least often. Studies of the rate of mental illness indicate that these rates are lowest in those who frequently attend services and highest in those who rarely attend (Berkman & Lowenthal, 1970). Numerous studies have correlated religion (whether measured by church activity, prayer, Bible reading, or beliefs) with successful adjustment to aging. The only possible exception to this tendency would be fanatical members of fringe sects, especially late-life converts.

One area in which religion helps is in facing death. People with strong religious beliefs tend to have somewhat less death anxiety (Jeffers & Nichols, 1961; Swenson, 1958). Those with lower levels of religious activity usually manifest more fear of death. Again, religious fanatics tend to be an exception, but perhaps they were driven to fringe cults by profound death anxiety or other problems of adjustment. Perhaps the most impressive studies on religion and adjustment to aging were made by Moberg. His initial study (1953) confirmed differences between highly religious and nonreligious groups. His later and more extensive work (1956) used matched pairs to control such variables as physical health, social class, and marital status, and found that significant differences could still be attributed to religion.

It should make no difference what the religious views of the psychotherapist are. An open-minded therapist will use the religious beliefs of the patient to bolster mental health. Jung, with two-thirds of his patients in the second half of life, frequently indicated that they had fallen into mental disturbance because they had lost contact with their religious traditions. He further believed that the solution was to reintegrate the patient into religious life. This does not require that the psychotherapist become an evangelist who is trying to save the patient's soul. However, the psychotherapist should be open and flexible on the topic, question the patient about his spiritual life, show reverence for his faith, and encourage and endorse beliefs and practices that have psychotherapeutic side effects.

ACTIVITY

The great debate between the activity and disengagement theories was aired in the second chapter. The conclusion is that flexibility must be maintained. Specifically, there must be sufficient opportunity for activity so that the only idle elders are the ones who have chosen to be idle and with whom the choice was a rational deliberation and not a withdrawal from reality.

The federal government has responded to this need with a series of geriatric WPAs which recruit and train and then employ older workers with low incomes. The senior companion program puts able-bodied elders with dependent elders. This provides care for the latter, while giving the former income and a sense of usefulness, and hopefully a meaningful interpersonal contact. Green Light is a federally sponsored program that uses older women in an outreach program for shut-ins. Green Thumb uses older men to build, renovate, and beautify parks, rest areas, and historical sites, in a manner reminiscent of the CCC camps of the 1930s. Foster Grandparents is an OEO program for elders who are 60 and older and are below the poverty level. It trains them to work with neglected and deprived children, especially the mentally retarded, physically handicapped, or emotionally disturbed, in or out of institutions.

Although this is one of the larger federal programs for employing elders, only 4500 foster grandparents have been put to work. Many of them have been underutilized, despite the fact that an estimated 40,000 children are inadequately supervised during weekdays.

There are also numerous volunteer programs for elders sponsored by the federal government. The Peace Corps and Vista are the most famous, but few elders have joined these projects. Retired Senior Volunteers (RSVP) is another branch of Action. These retired professionals aid public and nonprofit organizations with their store of skills. They receive no salaries, but are reimbursed for travel and meals. The Service Corps of Retired Executives (SCORE) serves the Small Business Administration by providing expertise to small companies. Unfortunately, these volunteer programs are not much more economical or efficient than the ones that employ the elders. The staff of the House Select Committee on Aging reported in June of 1976 that administrative costs ate up 80% of the RSVP budget, yet over half of the volunteers were never even visited by their supervisors. The staff presented an analysis which showed that costs had been $31.7 million, while benefits were estimated at only $31.1 million.

Federal programs cannot be relied on to provide meaningful activity for all of America's elders, or even for a significant portion of them. Of our over 20 million elders, 13% are gainfully employed and another 14% are volunteering in nonfederal programs. Another 10% (over two million) who are not currently active would like to be. Many who have tried to get into a federal program do not know where to start or are put off by bureaucratic red tape. Many have investigated federal programs only to reject assignments after finding out that the program could not be tailored to their own needs, limitations, and interests.

Elders usually have better luck when volunteering for local government projects or for those sponsored by private organizations, but even here the question is where to begin. Some elders who take the initiative and contact some agencies about the possibility of volunteering become disheartened after several attempts meet with failure. They may even suffer a blow to self-esteem if they conclude that no one needs their skills. The best solution for this problem is for elders to start their own agencies. An interesting case in point would be the retired American community in Guadalajara. They are largely retired military, professionals, and executives. Instead of letting their skills atrophy, they have organized charity relief and fine arts projects throughout the city. Some of them work over 60 hours some weeks, and claim to be busier now than before they retired. Some have devoted themselves to training Mexicans in their skills. For example, Lowell Eisenhower, a retired 74-year-old film maker, has served as a consultant to a group of young Mexicans who started their audiovisual company. He helped them design the proper equipment and buildings and trained them in the art and science of films and slide shows. His efforts helped the company grow to the point where it is now doing several million pesos worth of business a year.

For elders who wish to gain a remunerative position, there are even more obstacles to be overcome. Not only is there a certain prejudice against the older worker, but there is a lot of competition from younger, stronger, better educated workers. Government policies have had a most stifling effect here. The Social Security rate structure penalizes remunerative labor. The minimum wage rates hurt elders along with adolescents. In fact, they hurt any worker when the job is not essential and the productivity is not high. For example, every school, public building, and even city block could use more guards. For a dollar or two an hour it might be worth it for the public and the elder alike, but three or four dollars an hour may be prohibitively expensive.

Again a solution is for the elder to start his own business. Such an enterprise would permit him as much work as he wanted. Colonel Sanders is perhaps the most widely celebrated success among retired individuals going into business. However, starting a company takes capital, and most elders who are in need of remunerative activity do not have that much of a financial reserve. Furthermore, government bureaucracy is there again with a confusing array of regulations and licenses. Finally, any new business started by elders cannot employ very many other elders, or else the problems of unionism and minimum wage crop up again.

What every community needs is some local elders who will establish an agency that puts idle elders into volunteer positions or paid employment. Such an agency does not have to be a national bureau. Federalization first drives out the elders and replaces them with career bureaucrats, and then embroils everything in red tape and forms which only deter elders from using the service. A local agency listing local opportunities for activity is sufficient because few elders would be willing to relocate. The agency staffed by local elders would know the directors of small businesses and local charities, and could encourage them to place their clients. The clients would be assured of personal attention on the local level and could choose from a wide array of opportunities with different requirements of hours, days, length of service, educational level, physical demands, and so on. This is how flexibility can be used to provide activity.

MEDICAL CARE

The first chapter indicated that poor health, especially chronic physical limitations, plagues elders and predisposes them to mental disorder. Another factor emphasized was the unfortunate and unnecessary delay in treatment because all parties concerned, from the patient to the health care professionals, are overly tolerant of gradual deterioration.

The best remedy for this would be a comprehensive and systematic approach to screening. Visual examinations should test for cataracts and glaucoma. Glaucoma blinds 3500 a year, 3000 of whom could be saved by an annual examination. Even if visual examinations did nothing more than prescribe new lenses which made reading more easy, the screening would be worth it. Likewise, audiological testing could detect deafness, a debility which is too frequently overlooked. Blood pressure readings could detect hypertension and lead to lower rates of heart attack and stroke. Diabetes and cancer would be two other conditions warranting screening.

Such yearly examinations would detect many diseases while treatment was still possible, inexpensive, and simple, and before long-term or irreparable damage had been done. Elders now account for a disproportionately high percentage of the nation's medical bills, primarily because of their chronic conditions. Systematic screening would be the best way to reduce this burden, as well as the human suffering involved. But current screening programs are piecemeal, and worse yet, they are not flexible. They usually have one fixed location, or if they are mobile, they are only in a given location for a short time. The elder must try to locate the glaucoma screening project, get there, and go through the same process all over again for the cancer screening project next month.

Another factor that would improve the medical care of elders while saving money would be a greater reliance on self-care. When an elder has to go into a clinic and wait in line to get medication, there is a great incentive to let it slip. Elders can be trained to administer their own medication. There are new automatic syringes that can be used by blind diabetics. However, there are dangers to unsupervised administration, and these are covered in the next chapter.

Cost is one major stumbling block to adequate medical care for elders in America. In fact, medicare now pays for less than half of the elders' medical expenses, with the remainder now being covered by insurance, out-of-pocket expenditures, or some form of public assistance. In fact, as a result of inflation in medical costs, elders pay more for their own medical care today than they did before the medicare program was enacted. These high costs deter elders from seeking medical care immediately for what they hope will prove to be a temporary condition. Unfortunately, many of these conditions worsen, although only gradually, and continue to debilitate the elder. Probably the best solution for this is a reduction in health care costs. Further increases in medicare must wait for the system to root out the fraud and inefficiency that have plagued it. The Senate Special Committee on Aging's Subcommittee on Long-Term Care reported in June 1976 that probably half of all payments made under medicare were inappropriate. Medicaid, a welfare program, has picked up much of the difference. Whereas the program cost only $3.3 billion before medicare, it cost $15 billion in 1976. One way of driving down the cost of drugs—the single most expensive item for which the aged must pay themselves—would be to have consumer cooperative purchases of medication.

One of the most insidious threats to the health of the elders is quackery, with a one-two punch. First, it drains off financial resources that could have gone for legitimate medication. For example, worthless gimmicks for curing arthritis bilk the public out of $25 for each dollar spent on arthritis research. Second, useless nostrums lull their victims into a sense of security and thereby delay effective treatment. In some cases, actual harm is done by the preparation. An all-out war on quackery waged by consumer groups, governmental agencies, and legitimate health care producers is necessary. Such a war can best be waged on the local level by gathering information and educating the elders.

REHABILITATION

Although many of the ravages of geriatric disease are permanent, there are ways of compensating for specific losses and rehabilitating the patient. Debilities of the body lead to mental disturbance for two reasons. First, the patient becomes less able to interact successfully with his environment. Second, the change in body image affects self-image, and the result is a negative impact on mental health. Rehabilitation can be prophylactic by removing these causes of mental disturbance, and also by giving the patient a sense of having overcome difficulties through effort. The feeling remains with him and will help him overcome future difficulties.

Usually the type of rehabilitation required depends on the specific nature of the loss. For the blind and visually handicapped, rehabilitation involves learning new compensatory skills such as Braille reading, typing, cane travel, the development of object sense, or the use of a guide dog. For the hard of hearing there are hearing aids. Some foundations will give free devices and fittings, while others will give free trials and loans. For the more seriously impaired, there are classes in lip reading and manual communication. For patients with lung diseases there are special breathing exercises to help them increase lung capacity. Patients recovering from cancer (especially those who have undergone ostomy, mastectomy, or laryngectomy) may develop special body image problems and may have special rehabilitation requirements.

The loss of teeth is often ignored in most discussions of rehabilitation. Most elders have lost a majority of their natural teeth. Sometimes the false teeth do not fit right and are uncomfortable. This impairs the elder's ability to masticate and perhaps even impedes his speech. There may also be some effect on the elder's self-image. Given the importance of the face in socialization, some elders withdraw from social contact because of the way their mouths look.

One of the most challenging causes of physical debilitation among elders is stroke (cerebrovascular accident, CVA), in which certain parts of the brain are destroyed by thrombosis or hemorrhage. Because of the immediate onset of the condition and the irreversible nature of neural damage, CVA usually leaves the patient with a profound sense of loss, which psychotherapy alone can rarely ameliorate. The real solution is to be found in physical rehabilitation. Physical therapy is necessary to train new neural pathways to take over the functions of the destroyed brain cells. In addition to rehabilitating the body, various devices can compensate for debilities: walkers, bars and rails, and wheelchairs. How these items are introduced to the patient, and how he is trained in their use, has a major impact on how he will come to see them—as symbols of inferiority, or as tools for maintaining normal activity.

POVERTY

About one-third of the income of American elders comes from current employment. Perhaps even more comes from unreported income of bootleg employment. Earlier in this chapter it was indicated that the earning opportunities for elders could be increased by relaxing government regulations on minimum wage and maximum earnings under Social Security eligibility.

The Social Security program itself could stand for some reform as well. First of all, the system is highly inequitable. While it penalizes income earned by labor, it ignores income from investments. A greater problem is that Social Security is headed for bankruptcy because of the great increases in the number of recipients and the level of payments, and the corresponding inability of the fixed-rate Social Security tax to keep pace. Probably the best solution would be to abolish the Social Security tax and finance the program through general revenues, which are gleaned from various sources, including a fairly progressive income tax.

In addition to these problems with Social Security, the adequacy of the funding may be questioned. Since 1965 federal welfare payments to the aged, blind, and disabled (now known as Supplemental Security Income) have trebled despite the Social Security increases. These SSI funds can be used for food or rent, and also for household repairs, necessary appliances, and even moving expenses. Perhaps a consolidation of Social Security and SSI would provide the same level of support with fewer gaps, less duplication, and a lower administration cost.

The other side of the coin in helping the aged financially is to reduce their taxes. Sales and property taxes tend to be regressive. Some states still tax food and medicine. Property taxes average 8% of the income of elders, but in some cities they can go as high as 40%. There are state and federal income tax credits for such taxes, but often the forms are too complex or the waiting period for the refund is too long.

NUTRITION

In the last five years psychiatry has rediscovered the role of nutrition in mental health. The role of B-complex vitamin deficiency in mental illness has been established. Watson (1972) reported cure rates of 80% with megavitamin therapy for patients previously treated unsuccessfully with psychotherapy. In addition to directly causing mental problems in the aged, dietary deficiencies can produce physical debility. For example, lack of calcium in the diets of elders is one of the main factors predisposing them to broken bones and making it so difficult for them to recover. There are several reasons for the inadequate diets of elders. Poverty may cause them to buy food frugally rather than wisely. Poor teeth or poorly fitting dentures prevent proper mastication. The intestinal tract in old age is less capable of thoroughly digesting the food and absorbing nutrients. The dietary limitations of certain elders are unwisely applied so that certain nutrients are excluded from their diets. Finally, there is a great deal of ignorance and much distortion of fact about nutrition among elders.

There are several ways of attacking the food problem. The federal government has tried giving out food stamps to elders. This reduces the financial burden but provides no assurance that the nutritional quality of food consumed will be improved. Nutrition centers have been started by local government agencies and charities in many cities. They can furnish well-balanced, prepared meals at least once a day during weekdays, for free or at minimal cost. At the better nutrition centers, the needs of heart patients, diabetics, and surgery patients can be met. There are special low-sodium, low-cholesterol, and weight-reduction diets that do not short-change nutrition or the palate. However, one of the main problems with nutrition centers is getting the elders down to the center. The Meals on Wheels program solves this problem by bringing the food to the elder. Another and less expensive way of doing this would be to send NASA shelf-stable rations through the mail. This approach assumes that the elders could then prepare the food that the postman brings. As with other aspects of prophylaxis, flexibility is the key, and there must be numerous ways of providing elders with proper nutrition.

Housing

Thirty percent of American elders live in substandard housing, largely in order to save money. Paradoxically, some of these houses and apartments are too large for lone elders. An ideal residence for the independent elder should be constructed in such a way that there are a minimum of barriers, especially steps. It should be safe, environmentally stimulating, and close to necessities: a bank, post office, supermarket, drug store, cleaner, park, clinic, and a spot for socializing. Although relocation is, under certain circumstances, harmful, putting the patient in an environment that he can best cope with is an excellent prophylaxis against mental disturbance. Since the needs, interests, and limitations of elders differ, there must be flexible alternatives for housing.

Transportation

In many cities, the aged and handicapped have special rates on public transportation. Some cities also have special buses for transporting persons in wheelchairs. Another deterrent to greater use of public transportation is the fear of crime. Until this is controlled, many elders will remain housebound. One solution is for young, able-bodied volunteers to serve as escorts.

The city of Palo Alto, California, has a special taxi service for elders, with rates only slightly higher than the bus fare. Some organizations, such as the Red Cross, offer transportation to the physician's office, clinic, or hospital. Some entrepreneurs have started excursion services for elders. Usually operating with small vans equipped to handle wheelchairs, the excursions go to picnics, theatres, museums, shops, religious services, or just sightseeing.

SOCIALIZATION

Sustaining and forging new interpersonal contacts is essential for mental health at any age. Senior clubs and drop-in centers are excellent ways of meeting the social needs of the mobile elders. For shut-ins, there are visiting volunteers. One excellent modification of these visits, which has different names in different cities, is daily telephone reassurance. The volunteer caller and the elder agree on the time of the call, its length, and the steps to be taken if there is no answer. This small bit of interpersonal contact is psychotherapeutic inasmuch as it orients the shut-in elder to time and forces him to communicate.

One of the most interesting experiments in socialization has been the Senior Actualization and Growth Explorations (SAGE) group in Berkeley, California. Beginning in 1974, Gay Luce tried to interest groups of elders in things ranging from Tibetan meditation, to yoga breathing, to Tai Chi, to biofeedback. These techniques were not billed as such, but rather as exercises or relaxation training. In addition to the direct benefits in body building and tension reduction, there are the by-products of self-confidence, taking responsibility for oneself, and socialization. SAGE members report that they have lost the feeling that life is over. They have become increasingly aware that there are many new experiences they could have, if only they will seek them out and strive for them. SAGE members believe that they can overcome pain and boredom, and also the gulf that separates human beings. "We love each other. We touch. We hug."

EDUCATION

Many community colleges and small private colleges are trying to entice elders back into the classroom. Education is valuable for its own sake inasmuch as it provides intrinsic interest. But education for elders can also take the form of practical information: how to retire, how to age success- fully, how to talk back to your doctor, or how to survive with physical debilities. Education can also focus on training elders for some new form of social utilization and thereby facilitate their activity. Taking any course gives an elder a reason for getting out of the house and an opportunity to meet new people.

Libraries can do much to assist in the education of elders. In addition to maintaining books on their needs, libraries can help elders by serving as socialization centers. Scheduled discussions of current events, travelogues, or tables for checkers and cards are excellent catalysts. Librar ies can also develop programs for elders with physical handicaps. For elders with poor mobility, there are book- mobiles and even books delivered by mail. For the visually impaired, there are reading machines and large-type books. For the blind, talking books on records or tapes are necessary.

EUTHANASIA

The first chapter indicated that the fear of death was not a great problem for most elders. What bothers them more is the fear of living beyond usefulness, to the point where life is painful or a burden on others. Clear-cut state laws that permit voluntary euthanasia are required. If the patient is conscious, he could give direct consent. If the patient were in a coma or a confused state, the authorities could perform euthanasia on the basis of a living will signed by the patient while he was of sound mind. On the other hand, euthanasia instituted at the request of the family of the elder patient does not have the same psychotherapeutic effect. Indeed, some elders may become more anxious when they think that their relatives have the power to terminate their lives without their consent.

FACILITATION

There are a maze of programs designed to help American elders. These programs have different purposes, different requirements for eligibility, different administrations. Each agency is not always that well-informed about what the other agencies are doing. What each agency does know is what it itself is not supposed to do. The result is the pat answer, "I'm sorry, we don't do that. Try somewhere else." The result is the runaround.

Some cities have established senior information and referral centers. These offices collect information on all the programs available for elders and try to steer their clients to the agencies most capable of helping them. Elders also need counseling on specific problems: money management, taxes, and the law. In some cities lawyers or accountants will serve needy elders for free or for a reduced fee. One important factor with any kind of counseling is the need for counselors who can communicate with many elders who are poorly educated or who are not fluent in English.

One extension of counseling is advocacy. The counselor tells the elder how to do something or how to go about getting something from a government agency. The advocate or ombudsman goes to the agency and applies whatever pressure he has to get something for the elder. Various federal poverty programs have employed advocates. The danger is that it can result in interagency squabbles that make red tape faster than the advocates can cut through it.

Conclusion

Many programs can help elders cope with their environments more effectively. The psychotherapist must be informed about programs for elders in his locality so that he
can offer them to his patients. A psychotherapist who is
familiar with these programs can also make some suggestions for their improvement.

Chapter 5

PSYCHOPHARMACOLOGY AND RELATED TOPICS

This chapter is written especially for nonmedical personnel in the hope that they may gain a deeper knowledge about one of the most important factors in geriatric mental health: medical intervention by drugs and other means. No one who attempts geriatric counseling can ignore the specter of physical disease and medication. Physicians and nurses keep an up-to-date copy of the American Medical Association's *Physician's Desk Reference* available at all times. This is wise standard operating procedure for all geriatric counselors.

PERILS OF POLYPHARMACOLOGY

Chapter 1 demonstrated that elders are more susceptible to chronic physical debilities, and that combinations of chronic conditions are also frequent. This situation may be referred to as multiple system pathology, and it results in elders using many different types of medication at the same time: one pill for the eyes, one for the heart, one for the kidneys, one for arthritis, one for insomnia, one for pain, one for nervous tension, and so on. Although elders constitute only 10% of the population, they account for 25% of all prescriptions. Hospitalized Medicare patients average 10 different prescription drugs. Nursing homes spend 10% of their budgets on medication.

There are also special limitations on an elder's tolerance to medication. The homeostatic mechanism in the aged is impaired and less able to tolerate some levels of medication. Basically, there is more water, fat, and circulating albumin in the body, and the renal function is diminished (Hollister, 1977). The reduced rate of elimination means that drugs are retained in the body longer, and this makes toxicity reactions more likely. There are more dangers of mental confusion arising as a consequence of sedation. Finally, the older patient has a more unpredictable response to the specific drug. Drug reactions in elders are characterized by a great degree of variability, from patient to patient and from time to time. Unfortunately, the increased levels of medication in elders and the greater risks have not prompted adequate development of the field of geriatric pharmacology. Many physicians, nurses, and pharmacists are woefully ignorant of the specifications for using drugs with elders.

One particular problem in geriatric pharmacology is that patients tend to stockpile unused portions of prescribed medications. Thus pill bottles accumulate in medicine cabinets. There is the danger that these medications will be used indiscriminately at some point in the future. Another problem is that patients visit different doctors simultaneously, without telling either one about the other. This opens the door to the dangers of multiple prescription for the same disease, or possibly of miscombinations and dangerous interactions of medications given for different reasons. The borrowing of medication is another problem. Some elders complain of their symptoms to their friends, who are in turn only too happy to help out by going into their own medicine cabinet stockpile. Deliberate disregard for the medication's instructions is also a possibility. Some patients, who are very upset by the intensity of their condition and seek immediate relief, may be tempted to double the dosage, thinking that this will bring relief twice as fast. Genuine error in drug administration is also a possibility. Numerous studies have been conducted on the percentage of patients or doses in which an error in administration can be found. Between 20 and 60% of patients who self-administer medication make errors. Elders plagued by poor eyesight may have specific problems here.

Unfortunately, the situation is not much better in nursing homes. There are over half a million employees in these homes, but only 80,000 of them are licensed nurses and many of these work part-time. Even though it may be illegal, untrained aides and orderlies give out medication in some institutions. Seven types of medication errors can take place in a nursing home: wrong drug, wrong dose, wrong time, wrong route, wrong patient, missed dose, and multiple dose. Examining each of these categories and the opinions of numerous expert witnesses, the Subcommittee on Long-Term Care of the Senate Special Committee on Aging concluded in January 1975 that 20 to 40% of the drugs administered in U.S. nursing homes had been administered in error.

In addition to these errors in administration, there is the problem that two different drugs may interact in some undesirable way. For example, two drugs might be perfectly safe for a given patient, when that patient takes either of the drugs separately, but together the drugs produce some harmful side effects. Another problem is that one drug's desired effects may be potentiated by the second drug so that the level of the effect becomes undesirably high. Aspirin potentiates the action of Warfarin, a blood thinner, to the point where internal hemorrhaging can occur. Yet another problem is the reverse of this: One drug may nullify another. Laxatives and antacids are major offenders here, interfering with broad classes of other drugs. Again, nursing home patients are not safe from drug interactions. Over half of these elders take drugs which can interact in such a way that they pose a threat to life. At some time during their stay, about one in four nursing home patients requires a physician's attention due to drug miscombination. Unfortunately, the medical attention is too late too often. The Senate Subcommittee on Long-Term Care estimated that 30,000 nursing home deaths a year are caused by drug miscombinations.

Nowlin (1973) reflected that "Perhaps the physician's pad is the most insidious cause for mental aberration in the older person" (p. 151). Lofholm (1976) estimated that almost a million "senile" elders were actually victims of the misuse of medication. Peterson and Thomas (1975) found that the majority of admissions to geriatric wards of general hospitals were due to acute drug reactions.

Against such substantiated indictments of geriatric pharmacology, there is only one defense for the continued medication of the elders: necessity. Many of the chronic and acute physical conditions controlled by drugs would, in the absence of pharmacological treatment, lead to acute brain syndromes and mental confusion. Hyperthyroidism, uremia, and some circulatory, respiratory, and hepatic disorders all fall into this category. Therefore the intelligent solution for the problems of geriatric pharmacology does not lie in withholding all medication from elders, but in realistically appraising the potential dangers of each medication, balancing them against the consequences of alternative therapies, and closely monitoring all medicated elders for evidence of undesirable reactions.

Circulatory compounds are perhaps the most commonly used drug in later life, and they are also prone to causing an adverse reaction. The "dig" group (digitalis, digoxin, digitoxin) should be monitored for various physical reactions (nausea, cardiac arrhythmias, hazy vision, weight loss). From the standpoint of the geriatric counselor, the most important factor is electrolyte balance. There is the danger that heart medications will deplete the body's supply of potassium, resulting in mental confusion and hallucinations. Only systematic monitoring of electrolyte balance can ascertain if potassium levels are within normal bounds. Antihypertensive medication such as the Rauwolfia derivatives or Guanethidine may lead to cerebral vascular insufficiency and a resulting mental depression and confusion. Methyldopa, another hypertensive, depletes the central nervous system of dopamine, norepinephrine, and serotonin, leading to excessive sedation, depression, and dementia. Diuretics (thiazides, furosemide) should also be monitored carefully. They are given to remove the electrolyte sodium from the body. Unfortunately, they sometimes act indiscriminately and take the potassium along with the sodium.

Arthritis is another common debility of later life. The corticosteroids prescribed for relief may alter electrolyte balance and produce personality disturbances such as irritability, depression, and toxic confusional states. Indomethacin can also lead to mental problems. Many of the analgesics (morphine, meperdrine, propoxyphene) depress the central nervous system.

Other types of medication with possible mental effects are the anticonvulsants, especially primidone, which can lead to visual hallucinations. Antihistamines can lead to drowsiness, blurred vision, and central nervous system depression. Long-term use of levodopa for Parkinson's disease can also bring on depression.

PSYCHOTROPICS

As part of the American Bicentennial, the American Chemical Society announced the greatest discoveries of the past 100 years. One of those was the use of psychochemicals for treatment of mental illness. Up until 1955 the mental hospital population had grown year after year until the majority of the nation's hospital beds were occupied by mental patients. The mental hospitals were characterized by noise and filth, and bars on windows and straitjackets were common sights. The widespread use of psychotropic (mind-altering) drugs for alleviating the symptoms of mental illness has changed all this. The number of institutionalized mental patients has gone down year after year. Many hospitals have closed. These measures have been prompted by budgetary considerations and also the fact that the new medication restores the patient's ability to function so that he can remain in the community and be treated as an outpatient. Psychotropics have permitted the humanization of mental institutions. Now patients can be trusted with tools, mirrors, and razors, instead of being treated like dirty animals. Finally, psychotherapy itself has been benefited immeasurably by the use of psychotropics. Patients who were too hyperactive, despondent, or delirious to communicate can, under medication, enter into a dialogue with a therapist.

But, as with modern medical miracles for physical diseases, each drug has certain contraindications, warnings, precautions, and adverse reactions, not to mention rules for dosage, administration, and combination. Everyone involved in the mental health team should have a basic knowledge of the workings and dangers of psychotropics. One source of information is the *Physician's Desk Reference* mentioned above. Another source is the fine print in the drug advertisements in most psychiatric journals. Each drug and each patient are somewhat different, but there are basic similarities within classes of drugs.

The tricyclic compounds include imipramine (Tofranil), which is the most popular, desipramine (Norpramine, Pertofane), amitriptyline (Elavil), nortriptyline (Aventyl), protriptyline (Vivactil), which is probably the most potent and potentially toxic, and doxepin (Sinequan), which has both antidepressive and antianxiety agents. The rest of the tricyclics are used almost exclusively for antidepressive purposes, though they are sometimes used for childhood enuresis. The most common side effect of the tricyclics is dryness of the mouth, which occurs in about one-quarter of all adult patients. Other reactions reported with a frequency of less than 10% are drowsiness, constipation, dizziness, tremulousness, restlessness, weakness, epigastric distress, paralytic ileus, sweating, and a peculiar taste in the mouth. Cardiac arrhythmias are somewhat rare, but a possibility in elders. Tricyclics are contraindicated in the acute recovery period of myocardial infarction. Blurred vision is a side effect which usually indicates the presence of glaucoma. The administration of the drug should cease in such cases.

The chief susceptibility of patients of advanced years is a mentally confused state. This may take place in two ways: by hypotension or by anticholinergic poisoning. Hypotension means low blood pressure. The tricyclics bring on cerebral vascular insufficiency by reducing perfusion of blood to the brain. Along with some of the other psychotropic medications, they are part of a large class of drugs that have anticholinergic actions. In elders there is the danger that a toxicity buildup will result in a central anticholinergic syndrome characterized by a delirium which may mimic some symptoms of psychosis, mania, paranoia, and/or senility. Short-term memory becomes impaired, as does the patient's capacity for attention and orientation. Anxiety may increase along with auditory and visual hallucinations. This syndrome can be noted on the EEG as a slowing of the alpha waves from the normal 9 to 12 cycles per second down to 6 to 8 cycles per second. Detoxification returns the EEGs to normal and removes psychiatric symptoms due to anticholinergic poisoning. One rapid way of countering toxicity is to use physostigmine salicylate (Antilirium Ampules). It can even reverse the coma and tachycardia brought about by extreme anticholinergic toxicity. Physostigmine is the only commonly used cholinesterase inhibitor that readily penetrates the blood-brain barrier. However, it should only be used after a thorough medical evaluation of the patient, because if the physostigmine is overdone, there is the danger of excessive cholinergic-parasympathetic stimulation.

Another class of antidepressant medication is the monoamine oxidase inhibitors, MAOIs. These include phenelzine, isocarboxid, and tranylcypromine sulphate (Parnate Sulphate). The level of monoamine oxidase increases in the aged central nervous system, and this may be a biochemical explanation for the high incidence of depression in elders (Nies, Robinson, Davis & Ravaris, 1973). This factor has convinced some psychiatrists that MAOI is the logical prescription. However, the consensus is that, especially with elders, the MAOI drugs are less effective than tricyclics and pose higher risks (Whanger & Busse, 1976). The MAOIs can bring about confusion, irritability, and psychotic symptoms, and are definitely contraindicated in patients with cerebral vascular insufficiency. Liver damage is a potential danger. The biggest practical problem with the MAOIs is dietary restriction. The patient must avoid pressor agents, cheese, beer, wine, pickled herring, decongestants, cold medications, anorexiants, pods of broad beans, chicken liver, and other foods with tyramine.

Stimulants are rarely appropriate for geriatric depressions. The amphetamines can lead to addiction, confusion, irritability, insomnia, and psychosis. They are contraindicated in glaucoma patients. Methylphenidate (Titalin) can also result in confusion, paranoia, and a lowered convulsive threshold. It is less useful than placebo in combating fatigue, and may even decrease vigor in males.

Lithium carbonate is especially appropriate for manic depression in younger adults. However, this type of depression is uncommon among elders. Furthermore, the decreased renal function of elders makes them more vulnerable to lithium toxicity. Electrolyte balances must be monitored carefully, especially when used in combination with the diuretics. (Some physicians refuse to put an elder on lithium if he is already on a diuretic.) The symptoms of lithium toxicity are nausea, stomach pain, vomiting, weakness, diarrhea, thirst, frequent urination, and sleepiness.

Hypnotics, or somnifacients, are drugs used to induce sleep. These prescription drugs and their over-the-counter cousins are frequently used by elders because insomnia seems to be a recurrent problem in later life. All of these may cause daytime drowsiness and hangover, especially in elder patients. Some of the over-the-counter drugs are contraindicated in glaucoma patients. Some examples of prescription hypnotics are ethchlorvynol (Placydil), methaqualone (Quaalude), methyprylon (Noludar), and flurazepam (Dalmane), which may cause an arthritic type of allergic reaction. The barbiturates are probably the most potent somnifacients, but they are habit forming. They may bring on hypotension, cerebral anoxia, and delirium in some patients. They also diminish sleeping time and produce numerous vivid dreams when the patient is taken off the drug. Chloral hydrate (Noctic) is the drug of choice for many physicians, but it can cause gastric irritations, miosis, and a dangerous interaction with Warfarin.

The minor tranquilizers, or antianxiety drugs, are barbiturates and the glycol derivatives: meprobamate (probably the mildest), bromides, paraldehyde, chlordiazepoxin, and the benzodiazepines (Librium and Valium). These drugs are muscle relaxants and sedatives and have no real antipsychotic effect. However, they may dull cortical function to the point where confusion may be induced, especially in aged women. They are potentiated by alcohol and are habit forming. Withdrawal may produce vivid dreams and convulsions. This class of drugs is probably the most overprescribed geriatric medication in America today.

The major tranquilizers, or antipsychotics, are mostly phenothiazine derivatives: chlorpromazine (Thorazine) and thioridazine (Mellaril). These drugs are used to secure temporary remission of schizophrenic symptoms: agitation, hallucination, and psychotic thinking. In elders, the phenothiazines may cause drowsiness or a hypotension leading to a delirium. The most frequent side effects are extrapyramidal symptoms and tardive dyskinesia, which develop in most elders who have been on regular dosage for several months. These symptoms involve involuntary movements of the mouth, tongue, and occasionally the eyes, or a peculiar gait or rocking stance. Probably the best treatment for tardive dyskinesia is lowering the phenothiazine dosage, though this may not reverse the symptoms in many cases. Antiparkinson agents, such as diphenhydramine (Benadryl), benzotropine, and trihexyphenydyl can, can be used. Some researchers report that 50 milligrams of diphenhydramine intravenously can control some gross symptoms in a matter of minutes. Unfortunately, such counter-medications may not be effective in long-term phenothiazine users. The phenothiazines themselves, and the drugs used to control tardive dyskinesia, are anticholinergics. Simultaneous use of these medications may lead to central nervous system poisoning—the anticholinergic syndrome, which can mimic psychosis and result in the prescription of more phenothiazines, which only exacerbates the problem.

Somewhat less effective than the phenothiazines are the Rauwolfia derivatives, particularly reserpine, which is also used for hypertension. Unfortunately, prolonged use of this drug may deplete the brain's catacholamines and result in depression. Haloperidol (Haldol) is a new antipsychotic which has won widespread acceptance by geriatric physicians who seek to spare their patients from tardive dyskinesia. It also causes less of a drop in blood pressure. However, haloperidol can bring about lethargy, thirst, jaundice, and even some extrapyramidal reactions. On the other hand, some patients find haloperidol stimulating. Most of the aforementioned side effects are not very common. The biggest problem is that it can bring on the symptoms of dementia and depression, especially when used in combination with methyldopa (Thornton, 1976). There are many other new antipsychotic drugs coming onto the market, but most are just new phenothiazine compounds that carry the same old dangers, though perhaps somewhat reduced in degree.

The most helpful development in geriatric psychopharmacology in the last decade has been the use of antisenility medications. Perhaps the best known of these is dihydroergotoxine (Hydergine). It has been effective in 30 to 50% of patients. The only contraindication is a known allergy to the drug. Adverse reactions are usually limited to mild nasal congestion and nausea. In addition to dihydroergotoxine, there are other vasodilators: papaverine, isoxuprine, cinnarizine, and cyclandelate. They appear to have few contraindications or adverse reactions (usually flushing and gastrointestinal disturbances). One potential difficulty is that such drugs also dilate blood vessels in other parts of the body, and in fact are often prescribed to increase peripheral circulation. This could divert more blood from the brain and exacerbate the cerebral vascular insufficiency.

Anticoagulants have been used to help circulation and have been quite effective when combined with psychotherapy (Walsh & Walsh, 1972; Walsh, 1976). The most recent quest has been for a general brain stimulant, and some experiments with pentylenetetrazol and also with physo-

stigmine have been encouraging. In eastern Europe procaine hydrochloride (Gerovital) has been used for 20 years.
From behind the Iron Curtain there are exaggerated reports of reversing leathery skin, gray hair, depression, and
dementia. This drug is currently under investigation in the
U.S.

No discussion of psychotropics would be complete
without mention of the oldest: alcohol. Galen, who recognized its tranquilizing, somnifacient, analgesic, social, and
euphorient effects, referred to it as "the nurse of old age."
Another important factor is that it is a vasodilator. Used in
moderation, it seems to improve morale, sleep, communication, and perhaps even circulation. However, it can
potentiate many other psychoactive drugs and result in
confusion and unsteadiness. There is also the danger that
depressed patients will turn into alcoholics as they habitu-
ally turn to it to seek relief.

Most of the psychotropics have an effectiveness ranging from 70 to 95%. In other words, these drugs can secure
temporary remissions of psychiatric symptoms in the vast
majority of the cases. Therefore the potential dangers of
these drugs should call for careful screening and consideration of alternatives before prescription, and for careful
monitoring of symptoms afterward, but not for a blanket
ban on the use of psychotropics with elders.

There is substantial abuse of psychotropics with geriatric patients today. The principle problems are with the
hypnotics and the tranquilizers, both major and minor. The
biggest offenders are the nursing homes, which spend 37%
of their pharmaceutical budgets on drugs that deaden the
central nervous system. Senile elders are on heavy phenothiazine regimens just to keep them quiet and immobile,
because that way the they require less time from the staff.
Geriatric use of psychotropics outside of nursing homes is
also a threat to mental health. Half of all geriatric admissions to the psychiatric wards of acute hospitals are due to

drug reactions, and 80% of these involve a legally manufactured and distributed psychotropic (Peterson & Thomas, 1975).

INDICATIONS AND REGIMENS

The purpose of this section is to discuss some typical problems of elder patients and to discuss the various alternative therapies which psychologists and physicians dealing with the elders usually recommend. When a patient complains of *insomnia* or *anxiety,* the first alternative would be to manipulate the environment and try to provide a calmer or quieter place for relaxation. Another alternative for insomniacs is to make them more active during the day and early evening. If this is found to be impractical or ineffective, brief psychotherapy may be tried. Training in deep muscle relaxation techniques should be most useful. Some physicians prescribe a mild analgesic (aspirin or acetaminophen) or a small amount of alcohol just before retiring. Only after these measures have failed should hypnotic medication be considered, and then only if sleeplessness has produced physical or mental stress. Most geriatric physicians then select chloral hydrate. In general, the prescription of antianxiety agents should follow the same procedure, unless the anxiety can be identified as the product of a new and temporary situation that will not require long-term use of these drugs.

For *paranoid* or *psychotic* thinking, there is no real value in prescribing the minor tranquilizers (Pfeiffer, 1975). In fact, there is a considerable risk because they act on the cortex and further reduce the patient's ability to comprehend his environment. The first thing to check for would be an acute brain syndrome, especially one induced by anticholinergics or vitamin or mineral deficiency (such as potassium). If the paranoia or psychosis is severe enough, and if the patient is unresponsive to psychotherapy, he should be started on a major tranquilizer. The initial dosage recommended by most geriatric psychiatrists is a low one: 25 milligrams of chlorpromazine administered three to four times a day. The dosage is then increased gradually until the agitation stops or the side effects set in. The phenothiazines and haloperidol secure remissions in about 80% of the cases.

If the agitation cannot be controlled within the safe ranges of the phenothiazines, psychosurgery is one alternative to consider, especially for institutionalized patients who have demonstrated long-term disturbance. Lobotomies have been performed for 40 years and are a proven way to diminish irritability, reaction to frustration, and obsessional thinking. Psychosurgery does not cure schizophrenic thinking per se, but it does result in a considerably less agitated and more manageable patient 80% of the time (Sweet, 1973). Many lay persons have argued that such operations are dangerous and cruel, but there is little evidence to back up either of these charges. I have worked with lobotomized patients and consider their lot to be better than some of those who have been maintained for years on heavy phenothiazine regimens.

Depression is the most widespread psychiatric problem in later life. Uncomplicated reactive depression can usually be handled with brief, supportive psychotherapy. Even endogenous depressions may respond well to this approach. Other innovative treatments include such measures as sleep deprivation (Cole & Mueller, 1976). There is a slight risk of mania, but sleep deprivation is contraindicated only in schizophrenia or manic-depression. The prognosis is determined by the immediate response to the initial treatment. (Because sleeplessness may be a natural antidepressive mechanism, physicians should be very cautious about giving hypnotic medication unless insomnia involves a clear threat to physical or mental health.)

When the depression does not respond to these treatments, most geriatric psychiatrists considered tricyclic medication. The starting dosage is usually quite low, about 75 milligrams total per day. Twice a week, the daily dose is raised by 25 milligrams until the 200 to 300 milligram level is reached. A four-week trial is necessary to assess effectiveness with tricyclics. In those cases in which the trial period has not shown the tricyclic to be effective, the physician may try another tricyclic compound. An alternative would be to stop tricyclic medication for two weeks, and then to use an MAOI. The latter drugs also need about four weeks for a trial period. During the trial periods for either drug, brief psychotherapy should be continued.

Of all the treatments for depression, electroconvulsive therapy (ECT) has the highest rate of effectiveness, securing remission of symptoms in about 90% of all cases. One disadvantage is that the patient must be hospitalized. Usually three to six treatments are effective, and the patient can be out of the hospital in a week or so. The treatment is not so popular in lay circles, where ECT is viewed as something cruel and dangerous, and inappropriate for frail elders. Actually, the only known contraindication for ECT is brain tumor. Cardiovascular disease may require special preparation, but the actual danger involved is minimal. In fact, for patients with heart problems, ECT may be preferable to tricyclic medication (Cole & Stotsky, 1974).

The most serious side-effect of ECT is memory loss, but the preponderance of experimental evidence is that such effects are temporary and insignificant. The modern technique of using ECT on only one side of the brain (the nondominant hemisphere) has greatly reduced the extent of this side effect. Unilateral ECT is, however, equally effective in treatment. Not only does ECT have the advantage of effectiveness, rapidity, and fewer side effects, but it can be helpful in cases in which depression is mixed with schizophrenic or paranoid features (Goldfarb, 1971). All things considered, many geriatric psychiatrists consider ECT to be the best treatment for depression (Rosenthal, 1968; Wilson & Major, 1973). However, ECT should never be the sole treatment. It can and should be combined with psychotherapy before and after ECT (Pfeiffer, 1968).

Psychosurgery may also be considered in cases of depression that has been severe and prolonged or recurrent. Post, Rees, and Schurr (1968) reported the beneficial effects of bimedial leucotomies on geriatric depressives. Improvement rates of 96% have been cited in geriatric cases (Thorpe, 1958). A more recent technique of psychosurgery is stereotactic tractotomy of the substantia innominata by implantation of radioactive yttrium seeds. Knight (1966) considered depressed elders to be good candidates for this procedure.

In dealing with the *suicidal* elder, it must be kept in mind that such a condition is usually secondary to depression. However, antidepressives are inappropriate in such cases because they are slow acting and because of the potential for abuse. Hospitalization is generally the most appropriate solution once the geriatric counselor has become convinced that the suicidal dangers are real. Hospitalization prevents the patient from acting on suicidal impulses and also affords the opportunity for ECT, which gets to the depression which is at the root of the suicidal impulse (Kopell, 1977). The effectiveness and rapidity of ECT usually make the hospitalization short. Psychotherapy should continue.

In *hypochondriasis* the only generally agreed upon principle is that it is ineffective and unwise to confront the patient and accuse him of being an impostor. Pfeiffer (1975) recommends a placebo, or as he calls it, "supportive medication." This legitimizes the patient's need to be sick and establishes the therapeutic relationship. Busse (1976) thought that informal psychotherapy was perhaps the best treatment. Unfortunately, there seems to be little evidence of the effectiveness of either placebo or psychotherapy with hypochondriacs. Even though hypochondriasis is usually secondary to depression, ECT has not been effective (Chrzanowski, 1974). Tricyclic medication is the treatment of choice according to many geriatric psychiatrists. Doxepin is usually selected because it is the best tolerated compound, and therefore gives the hypochondriac fewer side effects to complain about. Doxepin has been found particularly effective in hypochondriasis (Grof, 1974). Sulpiride, a newer drug, is also remarkably effective in hypochondriasis (Muzio, Cicchetti & Gabrielli, 1973). Walsh (1976) demonstrated that hypochondriasis can be secondary to cerebral vascular insufficiency. The impaired flow of blood to the parietal lobes of the brain causes bizarre physical sensations. Walsh found that a regimen of anticoagulants in combination with psychotherapy is effective.

For *chronic brain syndrome,* antisenility medication is usually the treatment of choice. When cerebral vascular insufficiency is suspected, the vasodilators are usually considered. Dihydroergotoxine is prescribed in a sublingual dose of 0.5 milligram given four to six times a day. A three-month trial period is necessary to assess effectiveness. Starting in the late 1960s there was great interest in hyperbaric oxygenation as a means of getting more oxygen to the brain. Now most authorities are doubtful about any long-term benefits (Eisner, 1975). When neurofibrillary plaque is suspected as the primary cause of the CBS, a general brain stimulant may be more appropriate, but there is no hard evidence that any medication can be effective in these cases. The possibility of CBS due to high pressure in the ventricular fluid should not be overlooked. If diagnosed, surgery for a ventricular shunt is highly effective. ECT is not contraindicated by the presence of CBS, but consequent memory losses due to treatment may be more severe and enduring. Nevertheless, Whanger and Busse (1976) often use ECT several times on a CBS patient as a kind of diagnostic test for depression masking its symptoms as CBS. With all of these treatments of CBS, psychotherapy is a welcome addition.

Conclusion

Even the nonmedically trained geriatric counselor must know about geriatric pharmacology and other somatic treatments for mental disorder. The polypharmacology of elders combined with their increased vulnerability to adverse reactions means that all forms of medication, including psychotropics and over-the-counter drugs, can result in acute brain syndromes. Each one of the psychotropics has certain contraindications and the potential for dangerous adverse reactions. The only solution is to look at each case carefully, and to consider the needs and limitations of the patient, along with alternatives to psychopharmacology. When a psychotropic is selected, careful and systematic monitoring for symptoms is the task of all professionals on the treatment team.

Chapter 6

BEHAVIORAL MODIFICATION

Along with drugs, lobotomy, and ECT, behavioral modification is a useful tool in geriatric mental health, but one that is poorly understood and even feared by many non-professionals. Unfortunately, many psychologists oriented toward counseling are also poorly informed about it. One of the reasons for this is that the behavioralists and those interested in psychotherapy have different approaches and terminologies. The psychotherapist begins his training by studying the different theories of the human personality. The behavioral specialist does not concern himself with elaborate theories of intrapsychic forces and interpersonal relations, nor with neurochemistry. His concern is with learning in general, and specifically, with its simplest form: conditioning, which focuses on the stimulus-response relationship resulting from practice. Whereas the psychotherapist studies the interactions between conscious and unconscious, the behavior specialist ignores these distinctions and focuses on what can be measured: behavior.

As researchers, behaviorists usually use experiments rather than case studies or surveys. They study the application of their principles to normal human beings, and also to retardates, CBS patients, neurotics, psychotics, psychopaths, children, and even animals. Because nonhuman subjects are the least expensive and the most expendable, behaviorists do most of their experimental work on rats, monkeys, pigeons, cats, dogs, planaria, and even cockroaches. Although certain patterns of responses are unique to a given genus or species, there is a great deal of similarity in conditioning across all species, even those that do not have highly developed central nervous systems.

CONDITIONING AND AGING

Ivan Pavlov, a Nobel Prize winning Russian physiologist, and John Watson of the U.S. independently developed a model of *classical* conditioning early in this century. In this type of conditioning, the experimenter observes a naturally occurring stimulus-response relationship in the organism; for example, the way that the stimulus of food elicits the response of salivation in dogs. The experimenter then selects a new stimulus, quite unrelated to the first and not eliciting the same response: for example, dogs do not normally salivate at the sound of a bell. By pairing the two different stimuli on a number of trials, the organism comes to associate the two stimuli, so that the sound of a bell is eventually capable of eliciting the response of salivation. The organism responds not only to the new stimuli selected by the experimenter, but also to other stimuli that bear some resemblance. For example, a dog conditioned to salivate at the sound of a bell might also salivate when a metal pan is dropped.

Watson's famous "Little Albert" experiment involved showing a white mouse to a baby and then making a loud noise, which produced the response of fear in the baby. After that, Little Albert was fearful when he saw the mouse, even though the noise was not made. In fact, Little Albert also became afraid when exposed to other small furry animals, stuffed toys, and even a man with a beard.

This is the theory of neurosis according to classical conditioning: Real life situations have, perhaps by accident, paired certain stimuli so that the organism now responds with fear to a stimulus that would not normally produce fear. The way to extinguish a conditioned response is to present the stimulus repeatedly without subjecting the organism to other stimuli which naturally elicit the response. If the bell is rung many times but the dog is not fed, the dog's salivation response to the bell is gradually extinguished. When the conditioning involves the response of fear, extinction is not likely because the organism will avoid the conditioned stimulus. Therefore specific treatment is indicated in this type of case.

Neither Pavlov nor Watson made much direct mention of aged organisms. Cautela (1969) attempted to apply classical conditioning to the behavior of elders. Pavlov believed that the process of conditioning was influenced by the efficiency of the cortical cells, and that the aging process gradually reduced the efficiency of these cells. Pavlov performed numerous experiments with brain-damaged animals, and found that monotonous stimulation eventually taxed the organism's ability to respond. Cautela contends that much of the environment of the human aged presents monotonous stimuli, and since a significant minority of elders have some degree of CBS, their limited cortical capacities are rapidly taxed, and the result is a low behavioral output.

Pavlov used various techniques to help increase behavioral output in lethargic animals. Any type of stroking or tactile stimulation seemed to facilitate response. More recent experiments with aged animals demonstrate that tactile stimulation can improve performance. Experiments with institutionalized elders also demonstrate that these patients can acquire and maintain a higher level of response if they are hugged, kissed, or otherwise stimulated beforehand. However, with all species and individuals there appears to be a point beyond which the intensity or variability of such extra stimulation produces confusion, disorganization, and inhibition of response. So geriatric technicians must be careful not to exceed the optimum level of stimulation.

Another problem Pavlov noted in conditioning the aged was that lifelong responses become inconsistent in brain-damaged individuals. These same organisms also exhibit great difficulty in forming new conditioned reflexes. Behavioral researchers have found that the learning and relearning of responses by brain-damaged organisms can be improved in three ways. First, paced learning is preferable to massed practice, which easily fatigues the brain-injured organism. Paced learning also results in responses that are more resistant to extinction. Second, because brain-injured organisms are easily distracted, training sessions should take place in special rooms where extraneous stimuli have been controlled. Third, because high anxiety can impair the acquisition of a response, training should be preceded by relaxation and the reduction of tension.

A later American behaviorist, B. F. Skinner, developed *operant* conditioning. Here the experimenter waits for the organism to emit particular responses, and then the experimenter gives reinforcement to the organism. Reinforcement can be either positive (reward) or negative (punishment). Nonreinforcement means that the organism's response receives neither reward nor punishment. A positive reinforcement makes the organism more likely to repeat the response it made just before reinforcement took place. For example, if a pigeon receives food (positive reinforcement) every time the bird turns around, it will soon become conditioned to turn around whenever it wants food. Punishment makes an organism less likely to emit the response it made just before being punished.

Some general rules of operant (and classical) conditioning are that the shorter the time between response and the reinforcing stimuli, the stronger the association. Another factor is that classical and operant conditioning may be used together, so that an initially neutral stimulus is paired with the reinforcement. After the acquisition of the conditioned response, this new conditioned stimulus serves as reinforcement even in the absence of the original reinforcement. The best example is money, which the economy has conditioned us to associate with more direct forms of gratification. Therefore money is a highly effective reinforcer. Hitting the back of one's hand with newspaper to punish the dog is another.

One other aspect of operant conditioning is that responses which are reinforced on every trial are the ones that are most easily acquired and most easily extinguished. When reinforcement ceases, the organism quickly gives up making the conditioned response. Intermittent reinforcement, that is, reinforcement not given each time the organism makes the response, means that the process of conditioning takes longer, but after the acquisition phase, the response is highly resistant to extinction. Gamblers are excellent examples of the power of intermittent reinforcement. The gambler wins occasionally (that is, he receives intermittent reinforcement) and will keep on betting even though he is on a losing streak. This is because intermittent reinforcement has conditioned him to expect an eventual reward after much persistence. The power of intermittent reinforcement can promote virtue as well as vice, as is demonstrated by the persistence of writers, artists, entrepreneurs, and investors in the face of short-term failure.

The possible applications of these types of conditioning to geriatrics will be discussed below, in later sections and chapters. At this point, a few general guidelines should be given. First, the positive reinforcement should be wholly appropriate to the wants and needs of the organism being conditioned. For example, a monkey should be rewarded with a banana and a dog with a steak. With memory-disordered CBS geriatric patients, the most dominant independent variable in successful conditioning is the appropriateness of the reward (Ankus & Quarrington, 1972). Second, punishment should be used sparingly. When it is effective in inhibiting undesirable responses, there is the danger that it will also inhibit other responses as well, and thereby lower the output of behavior. Third, the initial requirements for reinforcement should be within the organism's normal ability. For example, to encourage a patient to ambulate, begin by giving reinforcement for sitting up. As the reflex is being acquired, the reinforcement requirements can be gradually increased. With the same example of getting the patient to ambulate, make the next step reinforcement for getting out of bed, then for taking one step, then for walking around the room, and so forth. Finally, the entire staff must consistently adhere to the same schedule of reinforcement. If not, the purpose of the project is lost, and patients and staff alike feel hurt because expectations were not met.

BEHAVIOR THERAPY

The principles of conditioning have become welded together into a system of treatment for mental and emotional problems known as behavior therapy. The foremost book in the field is still *The Practice of Behavior Therapy* by Wolpe (1969). Behavior therapy views all disorders as problems of maladaptive behavior. The focus is on the patient's conduct, not on his thoughts or feelings, although they too play a part in behavior therapy. The expressed purpose of behavior therapy is to weaken or eliminate these maladaptive habits, and when appropriate, simultaneously to train the patient to behave adaptively.

Behavior therapists, like other psychologists, usually begin treatment by taking a clinical history of the patient. The behavior therapist does this to establish the origin of the conditioned response that led to maladaptive behavior. The therapist assures the patient that the symptoms can be understood within the context of conditioning, and that such behavior can be deconditioned. The therapist is firm, confident, optimistic, objective, and nonjudmental. (In this respect, he is a good model for geriatric psychotherapists.) The behavior therapist reassures the patient that he is not crazy, but merely the victim of some unfortunate process of conditioning. The therapist does not speak of reconstructing the patient's personality or about some vague concept of "growth." The therapist and the patient came to an agreement early in the treatment about what the problem is and what needs to be changed.

Unfortunately, there are many unfair criticisms of behavioral modification (as behavior therapy is called). Perhaps the most unfair is that behavioral modification is brainwashing. It is true that brainwashers employ some of the techniques developed by behavioral researchers, but they also employ some of the techniques employed by depth psychology and social psychology, not to mention the techniques of psychopharmacology. In the relationship between therapist and patient, behavioral modification involves the changing of undesired behavior, and not changing the patient's religious or political attitudes. In this respect, psychoanalysis or some of the contemporary "growth" psychotherapies are much closer to brainwashing, compared with behavioral modification. Another objection is that behavioral modification, like ECT and lobotomy, is cruel and inhuman. Not all forms of this type of therapy involve physical pain or confrontation of feared situations, but some do. However, behavior therapists are cautious to operate with the patient's full consent and never inflict pain beyond his tolerance level.

Many psychologists who are partial to dynamic theories of personality object to behavioral modification because they say it treats the symptoms (the maladaptive behavior) while it ignores the real underlying causes (a personality defect such as an unresolved oedipus complex). These critics of behavioral treatment further argue that if it does succeed in treating one symptom, the underlying and untreated maladjusted personality will just produce another. Such symptom substitution is, in fact, quite rare, as most successfully treated patients stay that way, and neither relapse nor develop new pathologies. Indeed, the behavior therapists contend that when undesirable habits are rectified, the personality is relieved of a great burden and will improve.

Wolpe (1969) cited numerous studies which placed the effectiveness of behavioral modification at about 90% for most symptoms. Some of these were controlled studies comparing the effectiveness of behavioral techniques versus those of psychotherapy, and the former consistently showed superiority. Although we cannot accept the findings of these studies as a final verdict on the ineffectiveness of psychotherapy (because there are many different types of psychotherapy, varying greatly in appropriateness and effectiveness), I do believe that the weight of the evidence is that behavioral modification is effective in various classes of psychopathology. However, the combined use of behavioral modification and psychotherapy, even simultaneously, is not impossible. Lazarus (1971) found that the combination of the two treatments was more effective and had more enduring results than either one used separately.

Many treatment techniques are used in behavioral modification. Most of them were derived from the basic research on conditioning. Usually, each technique is indicated in certain specific pathologies, irrelevant to others, and contraindicated in some. Positive reinforcement techniques are taken directly from Skinner's experiments. The objective is to establish a workable schedule of reinforcement that will condition the patient to engage in some new and desirable behavior.

Negative reinforcement is used in aversive conditioning. The chief type of punishment used in behavioral modification is physical pain in the form of an electric shock applied to the forearm. Such treatment is usually prescribed for a patient who has a bad habit: alcoholism, smoking, overeating, or some sexual abnormality. The pain is administered in the presence of some stimulus (such as alcohol) to which a change in response is desired. The stimulus can be presented by having the subject sit back and imagine it, or by having the image represented pictorially or on a screen, or in a real life situation.

For example, some treatments for homosexuality use the following technique. The patient looks at a number of slides of males, and then ranks them according to their attractiveness. These slides are then presented to the patient in ascending order. The patient is instructed that he will be shocked if the picture is on the screen for eight seconds or more. Furthermore, the patient is instructed to keep the slide on the screen as long as he finds it sexually attractive, but that he can turn it off before the shock becomes painful. After a while, the patient becomes conditioned to escape the shock by leaving the slides on the screen for less time. When a male homosexual is also nervous in the presence of women, the termination of the shock can be accompanied by the picture of a woman, so that "woman" would be associated with anxiety relief.

For alcoholism, a common technique is to give the patient an emetic and then permit him to indulge in his favorite drink. The result is that the ingestion of alcohol becomes associated with nausea and vomiting. This produces a strong aversion to drink.

The general principles for aversion therapy are that the punishment should be sufficiently intense, that the frequency of administration with the paired stimulus should be high, that there should be no delay between stimulus and punishment, and that the only way to avoid or escape punishment should be a turning away from the stimulus. Such therapy sounds simple, but it must be administered by a professional especially trained in behavioral modification if some serious side effects are to be avoided. For example, the length of the session is very important. If sessions are too long, the patient becomes too used to the pain. If the negative reinforcement is too strong, the subject might develop a strong anxiety instead of elimination of a bad habit.

Another way of getting rid of some bad habits is by massed practice, also known as negative practice. In these cases no reinforcement (punishment or reward) is given to the patient. When the organism emits a response over and over again, within a brief period of time, and without reinforcement, the response is more likely to become extinguished than if the same number of trials were completed over a much longer period of time. In massed practice, the patient practices the bad habit from which he is trying to be relieved to the point of exhaustion. This technique has proved especially effective for treatment of tics.

There are also behavioral techniques useful for controlling anxiety. The most basic is deep muscle relaxation. This can usually be accomplished in several sessions. The therapist works on one part of the body at a time, usually starting with the arms or the head. The patient practices tensing and relaxing his muscles, being encouraged to go beyond the furthest point of "letting go." Deep muscle relaxation can be combined with presentations of the feared stimuli in a process known as systematic desensitization. As with aversion therapy, systematic desensitization presents stimuli through imagination, pictures, or in actuality, and works up through a series in ascending order. The end result is to break down the neurotic anxiety response habits in a piecemeal fashion.

The patient is first taught to relax fully, then the least feared stimulus is presented. For example, if the patient fears snakes, perhaps the first stimulus would be a rope. As soon as the patient, aided by deep muscle relaxation, learns to tolerate the weak stimulus, he is advanced, step by step, in ascending order until he is rid of the anxiety. One precaution generally employed is that the patient must be given a button which, if pushed, will immediately terminate the stimulus if it becomes too anxiety provoking.

The procedure sounds simple, but it requires a professional trained in behavioral techniques to make sure that the relaxation is adequate, that the ascending hierarchies are well constructed, and that the imagery is effective. Wolpe (1969) reported that systematic desensitization averaged 12.3 sessions per hierarchy worked through successfully. In his reports of 39 patients receiving this treatment, there were three patients over age 50. Two were treated successfully: a 50-year-old woman with phobias, and a 68-year-old man with two problems. Both patients were treated in less than the average number of sessions per hierarchy. The lone failure was a 52-year-old woman whose therapy was terminated in less than the average number of sessions because she did not cooperate by imagining herself to be in the situation, as directed by the therapist.

Another useful technique for overcoming anxiety is assertiveness training. This technique has been used as part of behavioral modification decades before its recent popularity. Behaviorists developed assertiveness training by reasoning that conditioning a new response to an anxiety producing situation can inhibit the anxiety response. Once such a new response is acquired, it is reinforced each time it is employed, because the patient receives a reduction of anxiety when he responds assertively. One way of seeing if assertiveness training is necessary is to ask the patient what he would do in several hypothetical cases in which strangers take advantage of him. This is followed by having the patient rehearse alternative responses that are more assertive. Such behavioral rehearsal can take place first in the imagination and later in psychodrama. After a while, the patient feels sufficiently confident to attempt these responses in real situations.

There are two contraindications to assertiveness training. One is that the patient should not be conditioned to perform an assertive act that is likely to provoke severe punishment when practiced in real life. The second is that such therapy cannot be used when the patient is still phobic to his own aggression or some other aspect of the training.

In the past few years, assertiveness training has become a virtual fad. Although the treatment is very useful, its widespread popularity has opened the doors so wide that a few poorly qualified therapists now masquerade as experts in assertiveness training. These unqualified individuals do not always observe the necessary precautions and contraindications involve in assertiveness training. Furthermore, some of them have confused assertiveness with being hostile, aggressive, or otherwise venting emotions. The true purpose of such training, if it is to be therapeutic, is to train the patient to behave more effectively in his interpersonal environment, not to abreact.

Similar to assertiveness training is another antianxiety treatment known as reciprocal inhibition. The idea here is to pair the anxiety-producing stimulus with another stimulus or response which inhibits the anxiety. This approach is similar to systematic desensitization. The patient is exposed to an anxiety-producing stimulus, usually in a ranked hierarchy, but he is simultaneously given another stimulus which is associated with pleasure, comfort, security, or the sense of help. The feelings aroused by the second stimulus inhibit the anxiety which the first stimulus used to bring about. The other way of practicing reciprocal inhibition is to train the patient to do something that inhibits anxiety whenever he is in the presence of an anxiety-producing stimulus. Assertiveness training can be considered a form of this technique, but there are many other types of responses that an organism can make to cope with the anxiety by reducing it or by removing its cause.

There are other techniques for the behavioral modification of anxiety. Perhaps the simplest and most direct is "thought stopping." This is especially useful when the patient has the bad habit of ruminating over anxiety-provoking ideas. The therapist instructs the patient to begin thinking such thoughts to himself, and then the therapist breaks the thoughts by saying "stop." The patient is then distracted and his attention is called to the fact that his thoughts have stopped. Then the patient tries it for himself, and tells these disturbing thoughts to stop when he notices them. The thoughts continue to return, but slowly the practice becomes more effective and the thoughts return less readily. The effectiveness of this technique can be increased by pairing the command "stop" with an aversive stimulus. Another useful technique is modeling, in which the patients are shown pictures, slides, movies, or live demonstrations of other subjects performing well in the anxiety-producing situation, for example, handling snakes. When such modeling is followed by guided participation, it is even more effective.

One last-resort technique for overcoming anxiety is known as emotional flooding. This is the exact opposite of systematic desensitization's step-by-step approach. Here the patient is forcibly placed in the situations that provoke strong anxiety. Although a high level of anxiety is the immediate result, it is usually not enduring, because the patient slowly realizes that there is no real danger in the situation. Existentialist therapists have used similar techniques known as paradoxical intension or implosive therapy. The basic technique is the same: a direct encounter with the most dreaded situation, in the absense of any other anxiety-producing stimuli. This technique of flooding usually works, even after systematic desensitization and reciprocal inhibition have failed. However, with some patients flooding exacerbates the anxiety, and for this reason, most behavior therapists consider flooding only when all other techniques have been exhausted.

Specific Applications to Elders

The previous section outlined some of the basic techniques of behavioral modification. In general, the same techniques are applicable to elders. The best reviews of the literature concerning behavioral modification and elders has been Cautela (1966, 1969). For anxiety, deep muscle relaxation followed by systematic desensitization is probably the best treatment, and it can be supplemented with thought stopping and modeling. In my opinion, behavioral modification is the treatment of choice in geriatrics, especially when the patient has a specific anxiety or phobia. I am somewhat less enthusiastic about the use of aversion therapy or emotional flooding with elders, and definitely prefer the use of positive reinforcement to condition alternate or competing responses.

Thought stopping is extremely useful and is easily employed with elders suffering from obsessive reveries. It is useful for controlling fearful thoughts, the buildup of anger, or the degeneration into hopelessness that accompanies depression. Abraham Low (1950) was a pioneer in the development of this method and of its use in the group context. His idea was that the patient could be trained to spot the onset of disturbing thought patterns, and could then order himself to stop working himself up. Novaco (1975) also emphasized cognitive control skills for dealing with chronic anger problems. Therapy consisted of educating the patients about their anger patterns, and then teaching them methods for self-monitoring. Lion (1972) used self-monitoring techniques which encouraged the patient to contemplate the undesirable consequences of his actions (or inaction). The use of self-monitoring techniques has also been applied to depressive thinking (Burgess, 1967; Tharp, Watson & Kaya, 1974).

The use of positive reinforcement occurred to me in the case of one patient who suffered from anorexia nervosa. She was down to about 70 pounds when I first saw her. She had been discharged from an acute-care hospital and was residing with her oldest daughter, who had provided the patient with a special full-time attendant. The first thing to do was to figure out what the patient would consider rewarding. We finally decided that conversation, verbal reinforcement, would be most effective. With the cooperation of the attendant and the family, it was possible to arrange for a schedule of reinforcement. Conversation was initiated only in the presence of food. After that, the conversation was continued only if the patient had an adequate eating response. For example, when she moved close to her food or talked about how she wanted to eat, she was verbally reinforced. Later, the required response level was increased so that she had to go after the food with a fork or grasp it in her hand. Later she had to put the food in her mouth to be reinforced, and so on. This tactic was effective in reversing her anorexia nervosa. The most difficult aspect of the treatment was keeping the family and the attendant on the reinforcement schedule, especially after the patient had improved slightly and gained some weight. Another geriatric pathology treatable to some degree by operant conditioning is rigidity (Coleman, 1963). Perhaps operant conditioning is most useful in institutions, where schedules can be strictly adhered to. Chapter 14 on milieu therapy will return to the potentials of behavioral modification.

CONCLUSIONS

Behavioral theory is a useful perspective on some of the pathologies of aging. Behavioral modification techniques are useful tools in dealing with disturbed behavior in geriatric patients. Geriatric counselors should employ some of the basic insights and techniques of behaviorism in their own practices. For some of the more difficult or dangerous methods, referral should be made to a psychologist specializing in behavioral modification. The administrators and other personnel of long-term care institutions should also consider the use of behavioral modification.

Chapter 7

PERSPECTIVES ON GERIATRIC PSYCHOTHERAPY

This chapter focuses on several questions involving geriatric psychotherapy, including the historical development of the practice and data on rates of effectiveness. I have also included my own theoretical perspective on psychotherapy.

HISTORICAL DEVELOPMENT

The great American pioneer in geriatric psychotherapy was Lillien J. Martin, a psychologist remembered for her boundless energy and contagious enthusiasm. After her retirement from a successful academic career, she established the San Francisco Old Age Counseling Center in 1929. During the next two decades she wrote three books in which she outlined the "Martin method" in geriatric counseling (Martin & DeGruchy, 1930, 1933; Martin, 1944). The approach had little to do with the techniques of Freud or Rogers. Martin herself boasted that she had a rule that psychoanalysis and hypnosis were not to be used at the center (Martin, 1944).

The Martin method involved a series of structured interviews. For the successful cases, five interviews were sufficient 87% of the time. The treatment was a three-pronged attack of discussion, suggestion, and slogans. In the the first interview the client related his life history. This was followed by some psychodiagnostic testing, after which the counselor reviewed the patient's life history and ascertained his physical, mental, and social capacities. Next the client was admonished to banish all resistance to the therapist's authority and to cooperate fully with all suggestions. The counselor then discussed his analysis of the data on the client and pointed out maladjustive patterns of coping. At the close of the session, the client was given some self-improvement slogans which he was required to learn and repeat to himself.

The remaining sessions explored the client's daily program, goals, means, and socialization. The counselor also worked behind the scenes to find more opportunities for the client: employment, housing, social service, interpersonal networks, and so on. The sessions eventually became a sort of running progress report for the client. The therapist responded with praise, encouragement, and new suggestions.

The sparse evidence we have to go on indicates that Martin's project was quite successful. Unfortunately, the Martin method did not become part of the mainstream of psychotherapy. Although Martin had written extensively before founding of project, she wrote no more journal articles afterward. Her three books were not read by psychologists. Part of the problem was that neither Martin nor her colleagues were that interested in hard empirical data to demonstrate the effectiveness of their methods, or in a theoretical foundation to undergird the method and give it some academic status. Nevertheless, a large share of the

blame also falls on the medical and psychological professionals who ignored Martin's work. As a result, the concept
of the Martin method and the old age counseling center
never traveled beyond San Francisco, and Martin's contributions were not built upon. Interestingly enough, her basic techniques have been rediscovered by most of the
persons who entered the practice of geriatric psychotherapy, regardless of their initial psychotherapeutic orientation.

The views of Freud on geriatric psychotherapy were
discussed in the third chapter: He thought it to be a most
difficult, if not impossible task. Fortunately for elders,
Freud's followers proved to be less pessimistic. Karl
Abraham (1927) worked with elders who were depressed,
neurotic, and even psychotic. He found it possible to work
all the way back to the patient's earliest childhood, if necessary. However, Abraham began to doubt if this traditional
psychoanalytic technique was always essential in geriatric
cases. He found that the prognosis was extremely favorable
in those cases in which the psychopathological condition
had broken out only recently, and that these cases could be
treated without a long and drawn out analysis. Another of
Abraham's modifications of psychoanalytic procedure was
that the physician had to offer more direction and provide
more stimuli for the patient during the sessions.

Other members of Freud's psychoanalytic school who
worked with elders included Jelliffee (1925), who published
some psychoanalyses of elders and reported successful
conclusions. However, Jelliffee was quite selective about
accepting aged candidates for therapy. If he did not consider orthodox analysis appropriate for a given patient, he
refused treatment rather than modify the therapy. He also
advanced the idea that some geriatric neuroses were superior coping strategies when compared to what psychoanalysis could offer. A similar view was advanced by Kaufman
(1937, 1940), who viewed rigidity as a geriatric ego de-

fense. He developed a rather complicated theory about geriatric depression: He saw it as a psychoneurosis of a pregenital type combined with an inverted oedipus complex. However, in his analytic practice, Kaufman was highly successful with uncomplicated methods that were effective in short periods of time.

Other psychoanalysts have suggested minor modifications of Freudian procedure with elders. Alexander (1944) evaluated each patient on the basis of ego strength. When such strength was sufficient, he proceeded with analysis that sought to develop insight. However, when ego strength was lacking, Alexander preferred to modify therapy so that it was primarily supportive, so that the ego was not subjected to demands it was unable to control. In supportive therapy, the therapist takes a more direct role, gives the patient guidance and reassurance, and even assumes a protective role.

Fenichel (1945) although remaining loyal to Freud's general view that analysis in elders was difficult, thought that it could be useful for more specific goals, such as the removal of symptoms. Like Jelliffee, Fenichel thought that analysis was contraindicated when the patient was so physically or mentally debilitated that he was largely incapable of developing a new coping strategy, and hence the existing neurosis itself was possibly the best coping strategy available for the patient.

Grotjahn (1940, 1951, 1955) understood geriatric pathology in modified psychoanalytic terms, as a defense against a narcissistic trauma and castration threat. Grotjahn's therapeutic innovations included a type of life review as a way of finding meaning in one's past and also as a way of preparing for the the end of life. This life review is combined with a focus on the real and immediate needs of the patient.

Meerloo (1953, 1955a, 1955b) suggested that the therapist, primarily a social worker, should go directly to the patient's home and attempt to modify the patient's environment. Wayne (1952, 1953) outlined eight modifications of psychoanalysis appropriate for use with geriatric patients.

1. Particularly in the early interviews, the therapist must play an active role, using direct suggestions to guide the patient, raising certain points, and limiting patient response on irrelevant material.
2. The goals of therapy must be limited and agreed upon by both therapist and patient at the beginning.
3. Each session should focus on a current problem which the patient faces, and older problems, even those that have not been resolved healthily, are not brought up.
4. The therapist is active, directing the therapy and providing guidance, reassurance, and environmental modification.
5. The face-to-face position is used during the sessions.
6. The therapist can directly re-educate the patient on how to live more successfully.
7. The patient must have some direct part in improving his life, participate in the process of solving his problems.
8. Scheduling must be flexible, and the number of sessions are gradually decreased.

The contributions of Alvin Goldfarb and Kurt Wolff in the 1950s are certainly noteworthy, pioneering efforts, but these major figures and their writings belong more to a consideration of present issues than to historical development. As such, they will be discussed topically in later chapters.

WHY PSYCHOTHERAPY WORKS

This is the place where I will present my own theoretical perspective on psychotherapy in general, and on geriatric psychotherapy in particular. Ultimately, I reject the reductionist stances of behaviorism and psychoanalysis, which view current behavior as the mere product of the influences of the dead weight of the past. Rather than consider the human organism as a set of effects of environmental and genetic causes, I see it as a set of purposes, or coping strategies. The essential nature of the living organism is to cope with its environment. This essential nature is not changed by a shifting environment or even by CBS. Even neurotics and psychotics are coping with their environments. Granted, their coping may be maladjusted from an objective or social point of view, and it may be ineffective or counterproductive, but it is probably the best that the patient can do given his environment, neurological condition, childhood training, attitudes, and expectations. If treatment is to work (and that means to facilitate the development of a superior coping strategy) it can do so only by changing one or more of the given circumstances. The previous chapters have demonstrated that treatments other than psychotherapy do have a definite value in geriatric mental health. Psychotropic medication, ECT, and lobotomy work by altering the prevailing neurological condition. Behavioral modification works by altering previous conditioning, or by establishing new conditioning which enables the organism to behave in a more mentally healthy way. If psychotherapy is to work, it must effect a change in one or more of the given circumstances.

Psychotherapists from different schools agree on only one thing: Psychotherapy can be a positive force for mental health. On the other issues, there is a great disagreement from one school to the next. They disagree on the preferred techniques of treatment and the ways of viewing the psychodynamics involved in cure. They even disagree as to what "cure" is. However, I believe that the different theories of psychotherapy can be categorized into three basic types, depending upon whether they emphasize thinking (insight), feeling (emotion), or doing (training). These categories cut across many of the artificial divisions between psychotherapeutic schools.

The insight theory of psychotherapeutic cure is based on the belief, deeply ingrained in Western civilization, that knowledge is power. The seven wise men engraved "know thyself" on the temple of Apollo. Socrates taught that self-knowledge was the key to the good life. Jesus told his disciples, "The truth shall make you free." The scientific tradition in the West has advocated a ceaseless quest for understanding the origins and dynamics of all natural phenomena. Technology has demonstrated that knowledge of nature enables us to control nature. Beginning with Freud, many psychotherapists have assumed that knowledge of the origins of a mental complex can be the key to liberation from it. Many laypersons assume that psychotherapy works because it provides knowledge of why we think and feel and behave the way we do, and that armed with such knowledge, we can control ourselves better. The psychotherapist helps the patient to go back and discover the source of his disturbances, and thereby establishes insight with its creative results.

The efficacy of insight is a popular myth. Most therapists know patients who have developed deep and comprehensive insights without any perceptible reduction in their pathological symptoms. There are numerous other cases of total remission or significant improvement in patients who have gained no insight. Surveys and experimental studies of cure rates of insight-oriented therapies frequently show no advantage over no-therapy control groups (Paul, 1966, 1967; Eysenck, 1953; Levinson & Sereny, 1959; Whitehorn & Betts, 1955). The most probable explanation for failure of insight is that most patients seeking psychotherapy do not have the ego strength to make effective use of insight. On the contrary, Fierman (1965) noted that insight frequently caused, or at least fostered, the development of intellectualization, rationalization, dependency, and immaturity in patients. Insight is a tool, and in these cases, the perverse temperament of the patient uses the tool to reinforce the neurosis. Wolberg (1943a) concurred with this view and found that deep introspection relating to the origin or the genetic determinant of their problems facilitated patients in their wish to avoid responsibility for their actions by scapegoating their parents or environment.

An emphasis on insight is contraindicated in certain types of patients. For example, it is best not to emphasize introspection with adolescents (Masterson, 1958; Nichols & Rutledge, 1965). Depressed patients can be worsened by introspection (Huston, 1966). This is especially the case in reactive depressions found in elders, the bereaved, and the terminally ill (Reid & Finesinger, 1952). Insight is also a real danger when the neurotic symptoms represent the best defense that the patient is capable of erecting (Wolberg, 1943b).

"Know thyself" is not really a cure in psychotherapy. However, it can be of value in preserving mental health. Individuals with good mental hygiene can use insights as prophylaxis against mental illness. But this is not the type of insight that relates to the origin and dynamics of mental illness. The type of insight that is valuable is insight related to one's true goals and abilities, especially one's limitations. Insight thus prevents the well-balanced person from unwise or excessive striving. Perhaps this was what the Greeks meant by "know thyself," for the same temple had another inscription reading "nothing in excess."

The next theory is that psychotherapy works on the emotional level. The origin of the psychotherapeutic use of catharsis or abreaction antedates the origins of Western civilization, and can be found in primitive magicoreligious systems such as shamanism. In the last decade there has been a rebirth of interest in folk psychiatry, and the concensus of its reviewers is a healthy respect. Shamanism may be curative in a tribal society, but this does not say anything about its specific ability to restore mental health in modern technological societies. Both the shaman and his "patient" have a *Weltanschauung* that does not include scientific causation. Furthermore, their socialization forces are significantly different, and probably much stronger, than those operative in contemporary Western society. Modern man has shed the supports of communal life and has established a tradition of socioeconomic-geographic mobility.

Cathartic techniques were employed in modern psychiatry by Charcot, in the late nineteenth century. Using hypnosis with hysterics, Charcot was moderately successful. His student, Freud, developed other methods for discharging of pent-up emotions. Foremost among these was free association. However, it would be inaccurate to say that psychoanalysis pursued a path of cure exclusively along abreactive lines, for psychoanalysis includes insight and other curative elements as well. Janov's primal scream therapy is perhaps the best example of treatment by emotional discharge (1970, 1971, 1972, 1973, 1976). This system has failed to become integrated into the mainstream of academic psychology.

My basic reason for rejecting the abreactive model is that it presumes that mental disorder is caused by some sort of infection of the emotions which must be excised in quasi-surgical fashion. There may be a correlation between pent-up emotion and mental illness, but I doubt that the first is the cause of the second. Mental disturbance must be construed as the use of coping patterns which are maladjustive or socially unacceptable. Poorly developed channels for expressing emotion will result in poor adjustment to an interpersonal environment that requires a certain type and degree of emotional expression. Certain difficulties in the expression of emotions may also cause these individuals to develop pent-up emotions. Therefore I prefer to see the correlation between pent-up emotion and mental disturbance as two relatively independent results stemming from the same precondition: poorly developed channels for emotional expression.

However, the correlation appears to be a weak one, because not all people who have difficulty in properly expressing their emotions necessarily develop pent-up emotions. Take the example of the person who displays his emotions too freely or liberally. Instead of suffering from emotional constipation, his disease is emotional diarrhea. He falls madly in love at the spur of the moment, or goes into a blind rage at the most minor provocation. This person's problem is not that he is keeping his emotions inside, but that he can never prevent them from coming out in full force. Such an individual may be another example of how poor habits of emotional expression lead to mental disturbance, but he is not an example of pent-up emotion.

Another objection I have to the abreaction theory is that it presumes a sort of hydraulic model of the psyche. Freud's model is similar to a water-balloon. The instinctual drive, frustration, anger, and other tensions accumulate and need to be released. Neurosis occurs when the psyche gets stretched out of shape by the increasing pressure of the instinctual drives. Normal, healthy individuals maintain a safe pressure (homeostasis) via socially accepted outlets. "Fixated" individuals develop leaks, or outlets that are not socially sanctioned. The psychotic has totally burst his containing surface and has no capacity to maintain homeostasis. Abreaction in psychotherapy is a radical intervention which seeks to lower emotional pressure. Most schools of

psychotherapy do not accept this hydraulic model, but prefer one that interprets human emotions less mechanisti-
cally and permits consciousness a wide latitude of creative
possibilities in dealing with them.

A less dramatic theory of emotional cure is that the
patient is ill because he is out of touch with his feelings, and
therefore cannot live up to his potential as an integrated,
complete, holistic, good, and loving person. Therapy from
this perspective tries to get the patient in touch with his
feelings, in the hope that this will prove efficacious. This
idea was first clearly enunciated by Carl Rogers (1961). It
has become the mainstay of most contemporary eclectic
and humanistic therapy. The most recent example of a
comprehensive and systematic approach to psychotherapy
with this perspective goes under the name of "feeling
therapy" (Hart, Corriere & Binder, 1975). Basically, the
same kind of objections that applied to abreactive therapy
would also apply here.

Essentially, the neurotic develops poor methods of
coping with emotion (such as repression) because it is the
best way he has of preventing that emotion from threatening consciousness. The repression is not the cause of the
neurosis, but the result. The phobic patient is perhaps the
best example of this. He knows that a certain situation
exceeds his capacities for coping emotionally, and therefore develops a fear that keeps him far away from the situation. The obsessive-compulsive patient also deals with a
fear that he cannot cope with. His solution is to repeat over
and over again an action which may only have symbolic
utility as a solution for the real problem, for example, hand-
washing. All neuroses are attempted solutions, although in
the final analysis they may be ineffective, disadvantageous,
or unwise. Being totally aware of one's feelings is a luxury
for the strong, and only a plague for the weak. The solution
is not to put the patient in touch with his feelings, especially
with those feelings that he is not ready to deal with, but to

help make him strong enough so that the feelings no longer need to be repressed.

Another variant of the emotion theory is that psychotherapy must focus on how the patient feels about himself. Psychiatric symptoms often do reflect and reinforce a low self-concept, and mentally healthy individuals usually have a good sense of self-esteem. Probably Alfred Adler (1956, 1964) was the first psychologist to emphasize self-concept, in the form of inferiority feeling. His central psychotherapeutic endeavor was focused around the elimination of this complex. However, the role of self-concept in adjustment can be questioned, as can the correlation between a positive change in self-concept and improved adjustment (Farhner, 1970). I concur with Wolberg (1943a) that improvement in self-concept is usually necessary, though not sufficient for cure. Rather than focus on elevating self-concept as a means of initiating progress, I believe that self-concept will improve fairly automatically if the patient can see himself making progress. This improvement in self-concept consolidates the improvement, facilitates the maintenance of cure, and encourages greater improvement.

The foregoing theories of psychotherapeutic cure seek a clear-cut cause for mental disturbance. Many preconditions go into any patient's condition at any one time, and the attempt to identify a certain memory or feeling or low self-concept as the "cause" often proves fruitless. On the other hand, the training model of psychotherapeutic cure starts with the assumption of the behaviorists that mental illness is maladaptive learning. The solution is to unlearn the old methods and to learn new adaptive methods rather than focusing on some presumed cause. Applied to psychotherapy, the training model indicates that effective psychotherapy must in some way train the patient to deal more effectively with his environments: physical, interpersonal, and intrapsychic. Sanity is defined as the sum total of all functional considerations: Does the person function in each of his environments? If not, frustration and neurotic behavior may develop. No one functions perfectly, just as no one is ever in a state of perfect mental health. When the patient's functioning is not on a sufficient level, more training is necessary.

Instead of trying to deal with the presumed causes of mental disorder, the training model focuses on constructing healthy behavior. Insight therapy tries to show the patient why he is behaving maladaptively. Training shows him how to behave adaptively. Emotion therapy tries to put the patient in touch with his feelings. Training shows him how to cope with those feelings. After training has enabled a change in behavior, the patient's self-concept rises. In a study on psychotherapeutic effectiveness with chronic schizophrenics, Whitehorn and Betts (1955) found that successful therapists assisted their patients to modify behavior patterns by getting them to participate actively in mastering new interpersonal and reality testing skills.

I would never claim that such systems as Rogerian therapy are ineffective because they do not consciously employ the training model. What I do contend is that if any cure comes from psychotherapy, it is due to some training in mentally healthy coping techniques, whether this is the conscious intention of the therapist or not. Frank (1971, 1974) advanced a similar view, that all systems of psychotherapy, if they are effective, enable the patient to do something and provide him with a sense of mastery. In the psychotherapeutic dyad, the patient is being trained in effective interpersonal skills by receiving immediate feedback from the therapist (Coons, 1967). Group psychotherapy is training in interpersonal relations rather than an opportunity for insight (Sager, 1964; Wolff, 1957).

Psychoanalysis, although it strives for insight and abreaction, can also be an effective tool for training. Freud's "working through" is a type of re-education and training in how to deal with memories, wishes, and fantasy along lines that pose less threat to reality testing or the social order. Jungian analysis provides re-education via mythological parallels that enable the patient to cope better with the unconscious. Dream interpretation along Jungian lines constitutes training in how to derive creative products from the frequent incursions of unconscious contents. Transactional analysis does not work very well when people read a book and try to get insight about interpersonal relations, but it can be an effective modification of interpersonal relations when people are trained in its precepts in a supervised trial-and-error practice.

The entire scope of behavior therapy can be incorporated into the training model. This is an important plus, because of the proven effectiveness of that type of therapy. The fact that the insight theory and the emotion theory reject behavioral modification and contend that it cannot work because the "true cause" of the mental illness has not been alleviated only goes to demonstrate the inappropriateness of those theories.

EFFECTIVENESS OF GERIATRIC PSYCHOTHERAPY

Probably the most ubiquitous myth in geriatric mental health is that elders cannot be treated effectively with psychotherapy. I remember one lecture I gave at an acute-care hospital. My first point was that psychotherapy was an effective tool. Several physicians came in late to the meeting and did not hear the first few minutes of my presentation. When it came time for questions and answers, one of the latecomers was recognized and said, "Dr. Brink, this is all very interesting, but nothing can be done for the aged. After all, it is fairly well-established that psychotherapy is not effective with them."

One of the most difficult issues in any evaluation of

psychotherapy is the cure rate. Numerous studies have attempted to identify the rate of significant improvement among all the patients accepted for treatment. Lobotomies are 95% effective for most operable disorders. ECT and behavioral modification approach 90% effectiveness, as do some of the more effective psychotropics. Talk-oriented psychotherapy is not really in the same league, as far as batting averages go. Most comprehensive studies indicate that about two-thirds of the patients in psychotherapy get better without adjunctive treatments (Chance, 1977). This is not very encouraging, especially when it is remembered that about 40% of untreated patients usually improve on their own in the same length of time. About the most important thing that can be said about psychotherapy is that it is responsible for cure in one-quarter of the cases, and that psychotherapy plus any other treatment modality (drugs, ECT, etc.) is more effective than that modality used without psychotherapy.

However, when we consider geriatric psychotherapy, let us keep one thing in mind. The baseline for cures achieved without any treatment is much lower. The 25-year-old man who loses his job, his wife, and his physical health will suffer mental sequela, but he can find a new job, marry again, and regain his health. When a 75-year-old loses these same things, and realizes that these losses are permanent, mental health is more difficult to re-establish. Therefore, even if geriatric psychotherapy secured improvement in one-fourth or one-third of the cases, but the baseline was only 10%, the improvement differential would be about the same for the population at large.

But the facts are much more encouraging. The Strupp, Fox, and Lessler survey (1969) carefully analyzed psychotherapeutic cures and tried to identify those types of patients who were most likely to achieve success. On the basis of age, the most over-represented group among the failures was not composed of the elders, but of the young college students. The elders were the group most over-represented among the psychotherapeutic successes. Furthermore, they were more reliable about keeping appointments and seeing treatment through to completion. Therefore geriatric psychotherapy is more effective than most psychotherapy, boasting a higher cure rate even with the handicap of a lower baseline!

Those who have worked closely with elders in counseling have been uniformly optimistic. Karl Abraham (1927) concluded his discussion of his geriatric patients by saying, "To my surprise, a considerable number of them reacted very well to the treatment. I might add that I count some of those cures as among my most successful results" (p. 313). Effective use of psychotherapy has also been reported by primary care physicians (Sheps, 1955), social workers (Herkimer & Meerloo, 1951), and other mental health professionals. Estimates of recovery rates run from a low of 55% (Straker, 1963) to a high of 80% (Stonecypher, 1974).

Another way of looking at the total effectiveness of psychiatric treatment of geriatric patients is to look at their rates of discharge and readmission to mental hospitals. Gibson (1970) reviewed several studies of geriatric hospitalization. Even though the initial prognoses were poor in about 80% of the cases, one survey reported that 60% of the patients were discharged to their homes within three months. Another survey showed a discharge rate of 54% with a median stay of 42 days. The final survey, involving 49 private hospitals and over 6400 geriatric patients, showed that over 75% returned to their homes within two months. A 14-year survey by Clow and Allen (1951) found that geriatric patients averaged three and one-half months of treatment, compared to five months for the younger patients admitted during the same time period. The readmission rates of mental patients who were initially admitted after age 65 are about 10%, substantially lower than those for younger age groups.

The uninformed critics of geriatric psychotherapy consistently cite the CBS patient as one who is untreatable by psychotherapy. Certainly it is difficult to gain much insight with such a patient, and it is likewise difficult to develop sophisticated feelings. However, psychotherapy is very useful in training CBS patients to behave more adaptively within the confines of their limitations. Goldfarb (1955b) noticed that CBS should not be taken as a contraindication for psychotherapy. Indeed, he found that many of the behavioral symptoms of CBS could be reduced by psychotherapy. Meerloo estimated that active psychotherapy is effective in about half of all senile cases, even when ECT has been tried unsuccessfully (Stonecypher, 1974). Using modified psychoanalytic techniques with 18 CBS patients, Wolff (1963) reported that one had completely recovered, five had improved moderately, four had improved slightly, and only a minority of the patients had experienced no improvement. The final chapter will demonstrate the efficacy of milieu therapy with CBS patients.

Another target for the critics of geriatric psychotherapy has been the long-term mental patient, for example, the schizophrenic who was hospitalized 50 years ago. Abraham (1927) considered the prognosis most unfavorable in these cases. My experience is that geriatric patients who have been mentally disturbed in early life are more difficult to work with than those who have demonstrated prior patterns of effective coping. Nevertheless, Goldfarb (1955b) and Safirstein (1972) have reported good results in treating geriatric patients with long-term neuroses. True, the psychoses are more difficult. Hypochondriasis is also resistant to treatment by psychotherapy because the patient is unwilling to define the problem in mental terms (Garner & Korzeniowski, 1971).

Why are the cure rates for geriatric treatment so high when the baselines are so low? There are several reasons, but I think that the basic one is the length of life itself. Experience in living is an asset in mental health. The child, the adolescent, the young adult have the task of fashioning something new. They have not had much experience with successful coping. The elder has been through other crises, and he has learned how to adapt. The crises of old age are probably more numerous and severe than those of any other point in life, but the elder is probably the person best prepared to cope with these crises. He has experience in effective coping with crises. If he can be remotivated and rehabilitated, and the dimensions of the crises somewhat reduced, effective coping can be restored. This is the proper and realistic goal of geriatric psychotherapy.

A more important question is why the cure rates aren't higher than they are. The attitudes of mental health professionals are to blame (Oberleder, 1966; Rossman, 1976). Most psychotherapists have chosen that profession because they loved the "heavy rap sessions" they were exposed to in college. They love to treat clients who are young, attractive, verbal, intelligent, and successful (Schofield, 1974). It takes a different set of skills and attitudes to be a geriatric psychotherapist.

CONCLUSION

Psychotherapy designed specifically for elders began with the ideas and efforts of Lillien Martin. Although her direct influence was small, the later pioneers in geriatric psychotherapy replicated her emphasis on brief, problem-centered therapy. In contrast, Freud's early speculations on the topic have not proved accurate or useful, and did not guide his disciples who entered into geriatrics.

The mechanism of psychotherapeutic efficacy lies not in insight, abreaction, feelings, or self-concept, but in training the patient to think and act nonpathologically. Any particular method, technique, or approach results in improvement only inasmuch as it is effective in this training.

Rates of psychotherapeutic efficacy are quite high in geriatrics. This is true for divers measurements of success. There are several reasons for this, the most important being that a long life constitutes valuable experience in effective coping. Brief, problem-centered therapy gives the patient that additional training he needs to cope with the present problems of aging.

Chapter 8

BASIC STRATEGY

This chapter deals with such questions as the desired approach to therapy, transference, the authority of the therapist, and the coordination of the treatment team's efforts.

Psychotherapy is a process of interaction between patient and therapist. It is distinguished from some of the other treatment modes previously discussed in that it focuses on communication between patient and therapist (Reisman, 1971; Banaka, 1971). Other therapies may also involve communication, but it is not the focus of the treatment. I contend that there is no hard and fast division between psychotherapy and the other forms of treatment for mental disorders, since the question of focus on communication is a question of degree, and not one of absolute, clear-cut categories. Both the surgeon and the behavior therapist talk with the patient to prepare their treatments. Such talk might have additional benefits, above and beyond its role in making possible the treatment being consciously employed. The surgeon and behavior therapist know that a good discussion with the patient can go a long way toward reducing his anxieties. Indeed, the same can be said about communication between the patient and the other members of the staff, and even with volunteers, friends, and family. The mental health of elders is significantly improved if they have a confidant with whom they can regularly converse (Lowenthal & Haven, 1968). Any interpersonal communication can have a psychotherapeutic dimension.

Another important point about psychotherapy is that although it does focus on communication between patient and therapist as a treatment modality, communication is but the means of facilitating treatment, and not an end in itself. If there is one error that is all too common among contemporary, inexperienced psychotherapists, it is that they forget this point and tend to elevate the inherent importance of the quality of the communication between patient and therapist. Therefore many therapists prefer patients who are college-educated, intelligent, and fluent, for these are the best conversationalists (Schofield, 1974). The psychotherapist, especially if he is dealing with elders, must remember that the dialogue is merely a road to treatment, and not a mutual joyride.

BRIEF THERAPY

The previous chapter, in its review of geriatric psychotherapy, showed that those therapists who have done pioneer work in geriatrics have independently come to the conclusion that therapy should be brief and problem-centered. The experience of geriatric therapists in the last two decades further confirms this approach as the treatment of choice. Two early social gerontologists, Havighurst and Albrecht (1953), recommended informal counseling to help elders comprehend their own situations better and master their resources in order to cope more effectively. Goldfarb (1956), a physician and psychiatrist at the Home for Aged and Infirm Hebrews, concluded that the entire rationale for psychotherapy with elders had to be based on the assumption that their behavior was goal-directed and problem-solving. Seegal enunciated the minimum interference principle for all aspects of geriatric medicine.

> The principle of minimal interference is paramount to the management of the elderly. The older a patient, the less his way of life should be disturbed. Destruction of an established pattern of life may result in confusion and tragedy. The young amorphous personality can usually be vigorously moulded without danger. In contrast, the older, more rigid personality is like crystal, easily shattered by unwise impact. (1956, p. 101)

Safirstein (1972) used the analogy of surgery when he advised that the geriatric therapist move quickly, take care of a specific problem, and then get out. Pfeiffer (1971) listed several characteristics of psychotherapy with elders, the most important of them being limited and specific goals. The problem-solving approach has also been reported by Godbole and Verinis (1974), Garner and Korzeniowski (1971), and Lazarus and Fay (1975).

The basic steps in any problem-solving task are (1) to define the problem; (2) to collect the facts; (3) to gather alternative solutions; (4) to pick the best solution; (5) to act. Therefore therapy becomes focused on the here and now, and not on the abuses of the past or worries about the distant future. The task of the therapist in this problem-solving endeavor is to do more than just be a stimulating conversationalist. The therapist has to wear many hats and serve many roles: social planner, community consultant, vocational rehabilitator, recreational facilitator, family counselor, and friend (Zinberg, 1964). However, his foremost responsibility is to use his counseling sessions to motivate the patient to participate even more in solving his own problems. In psychodynamic terms, the therapist is taking account of the patient's total psyche, trying to get through to those areas where the ego is yet capable of dealing with the environment, and strengthening those ego areas by training in effective coping. There is a danger that the therapist will push the patient too fast, beyond the patient's developing capacities for confronting reality (Hammer, 1972). This is why the counselor must never retreat to the role of the inspirer who does not also train the patient and facilitate the patient's activity.

Some case studies of the effectiveness of brief psychotherapy are now in order. Hammer (1972) reported the case of Mr. M, a 68-year-old man suffering from a persistent depression. He had worked as a piano player in musical combos. His failing eyesight and chronic arthritis made it impossible for him to play to the satisfaction of his professional musical colleagues, and as a result, he found it difficult to get and keep a job. This deprived him of meaningful activity and a source of income. His problems were complicated by the fact that his other main support in life, his wife, had recently died. Now he had no friends, no children, no career, and poor health.

In the course of the early sessions, the patient revealed many long-standing personality deficits: chronic dependency, inability to make friends, inferiority feelings with respect to a sibling, and high anxiety over death. Many therapists would have been tempted to try to work through some of these problems in a long-term analytic relationship. Fortunately, the therapist did not permit the content of his sessions to become fixated on the past. Mr. M began to feel that there might be some hope in his life. With the therapist's guidance, other vocational possibilities were considered. Specifically there was one section of town that had no piano teacher, and the therapist recalled that several women had expressed a desire to find someone who would give their children music lessons. This prospect sufficiently motivated the patient. The new role of music teacher provided Mr. M with income, status, human contact, and artistic expression. After the sixth session, the patient's life had become more meaningful, and he ceased his broodings over the past injustices at the hands of his brother, the death of his wife, his present problems, and fears of death. He declared that he felt able to carry on without further immediate assistance.

Blau and Berezin (1975) report the case of a 75-year-old man. The patient suffered from intense body anxieties, specifically, a fear of dying of cancer. Early in the therapy, the patient made the connection that some of the symptoms were like those that his brother had during a terminal illness. The patient then reflected that his older brother had been a wonderful protector throughout his life, and that now the patient felt somewhat vulnerable. These disclosures gave the therapist an opportunity to go back and do some heavy analysis of sibling relations. Fortunately, this course was not pursued. Instead, the patient altered his living arrangements so that he could live with a younger relative who could assume that protective role once filled by his brother. This had a calming effect on the patient and his symptoms subsided after a total of four sessions.

One of my cases involved time-limited therapy necessitated by a commitment I had to leave the country in 15 days. Nevertheless, I began seeing a slender 64-year-old widow who complained of insomnia, feelings of uselessness, and suicidal thoughts. I have discussed this case in depth elsewhere (Brink, 1977). This patient had a very real long-standing problem: a self-punishing tendency acquired early in childhood. Her medical history correlated very closely with emotional disturbances, so that definite psychosomatic patterns were apparent. The death of her husband and youngest son several years earlier had been most difficult for her. The most recent aggravating factor had been the decision of her 34-year-old daughter to marry and move away to another city. This exacerbated not only the patient's psychological problems, but also her ulcer and epilepsy. In addition, there was now some intrafamilial anxiety about who would take care of the patient after the daughter had departed.

Since there was no way I would have had time to work through the patient's long-standing tendency to punish herself with physical illnesses, I had to focus on her active problem-solving abilities. Throughout her life she had been an active and religious woman. Since her mind showed no signs of organic impairment, and her body was in no way chronically debilitated, activity was still an option. Her desire was to remain in her own large home, rent out the rooms to medical students, and take care of them. She was fully capable of doing this work, and the major stumbling block had been the disapproval of her family on the basis that she was too sick, or that it would not be dignified for a woman of such a position to do such work. I endorsed her position and helped her convince her family of its wisdom.

The patient had used religion as a defense against suicidal thought. She reported prayer to be effective in breaking the reveries. I helped her work out some of the practical problems (such as transportation) that she faced in once again becoming more active in the church. Significant improvement was seen from one session to the next, and there was no need for antidepressant medication or ECT. The total treatment time was four hour-long sessions completed within 15 days.

TRANSFERENCE

One reason for brief psychotherapy with elders is that it avoids thorny problems of transference, particularly de-

pendency (Safirstein, 1972). However, transference is not
something that always can or should be avoided. Freud
suggested that classical psychoanalysis encouraged the patient to project, or transfer, his unresolved parental conflicts and their emotions onto the therapist. Therefore the
patient begins to experience the therapist with the same
emotional affect previously reserved for the parent. Freud
hypothesized that the process of transference could play a
curative role in liberating the patient from the burdens of
these conflicts, and that perhaps it could eventually facilitate their resolution. Since Freud, various therapists from
different schools have identified transference as the dynamic force that produces cure (Braccland, 1966).

The important thing to remember about transference
with geriatric patients is that it is most likely to be different
from traditional transference relations. There are several
reasons for this. One is that the therapist is likely to be
about 20 to 30 years younger than the patient, and not the
other way around. Another reason is that the elder has a
mental history in which the parents are only one of many
significant others (Hiatt, 1966). Hiatt listed four possible
transference relations in geriatric psychotherapy: parental,
peer, son or daughter, and sexual, although he admitted
that in practice there is a considerable overlap in each case.
Surprisingly, Hiatt found that the most common pattern is
parental transference, and he presented the case study of
a 62-year-old convalescing from a myocardial infarction
who needed some father figure to give him permission to
be a man.

In peer transference, the patient comes to view the
therapist as a colleague, confidant, or sibling. These patients look to the therapist as someone who can confirm
reality and help them with decision making. Reverse transference, in which the therapist is viewed as a son or daughter, son-in-law, nephew, grandson, and so on, can take
various forms. In some cases the therapist is the dutiful son

who continues to respect and provide for an aging parent. (Interestingly enough, I have found this type of transference most prominent in a therapy group in which the chief complaint was that the sons and daughters had neglected the elders.) When the reverse transference is sexualized, we may speak of a reverse oedipus complex (Hiatt, 1966; Hammer, 1972). Hammer found that this situation played havoc with the therapist's attempts to bring the patient's oedipus complex to resolution.

In addition to the dynamics of transference, there are those of countertransference, which consist of the affects that the therapist projects onto the patient. Most therapists are not comfortable with the traditional transference relationship, which assigns them the role of being a good parent. Meerloo (1955b) and Grotjahn (1955) have discussed the anxiety found in therapists who deal with the sexual problems of elders. This anxiety is due first of all to our society's prevalent notion that elders should not be sexually active or even interested. This problem becomes most severe when the transference follows the pattern of the reversed oedipus complex. When the therapist and the patient are both male, the therapist's unresolved hostility toward his own father can get in the way of treatment (Wayne, 1952). Grotjahn (1955) believed that this potential conflict could be resolved within the context of therapy. The elder may try to make the young therapist feel guilty about being young, but if the latter resists this ploy, he can help the elder come to a resolution of his hostility.

When the patient and therapist are of opposite sexes, the problem is that the therapist may not be able to deal with the seductiveness of the patient. This problem seems to be greatest among inexperienced therapists, and it may even cause them some anguish outside of the counseling sessions. Such a therapist may feel guilty or horribly ill at ease because he is violating the societal taboos against incest. The problem is often exacerbated by widowed patients who feel that they must have their sexual attractiveness confirmed (Hammer, 1972). The best solution for this problem is prophylaxis: careful screening of the patients and therapists. Another helpful technique is for the patient and therapist to get the patient's seductiveness out in the open. I never miss an opportunity to praise the attractiveness of my female patients, but likewise I make clear my devotion to my wife. In this way, the woman's seductiveness is not directed against the therapist, but it is not stifled. It can be refined and used constructively as a means for resocializing the patient.

Other possible contributions to countertransference could be the therapist's early relationship with his grandparents (Grotjahn, 1955). Another potential stumbling block for good countertransference is therapist identification with a patient who is helpless and feeble (Stern, Smith & Frank, 1953). A similar problem arises when the patient's hopeless, irreversible condition wounds the therapist's narcissism (Meerloo, 1955b). Such a wound can also be made when, in the reverse situation, the patient treats the therapist like a child and fails to accord the proper respect due to a mental health professional.

Goldfarb advanced a slightly different concept of geriatric transference (Goldfarb & Turner, 1953; Goldfarb & Sheps, 1954; Goldfarb, 1955b, 1956, 1964). The basic theory is that elders have great dependency needs, and that these can be manipulated psychotherapeutically within the context of transference. The therapist assumes the role of protective parent and fosters the illusion that the therapist is omnipotent and has magical powers on which the patient can rely. Within the course of the therapy, which uses 15-minute sessions twice a week and then tapers off, the patient tries to usurp some of this power. Success of treatment rests on the patient's conviction that he has tricked the doctor and overtaken his magical powers. Therefore, according to Goldfarb, it is good for the therapist to promote a transference relationship in which the patient sees the therapist as an authority figure on whom the patient may depend, and whose power the patient may later usurp.

In one case study cited by Goldfarb (1956), the patient had been a 20-year resident of the Home. Recently she had suffered from increased disability, forgetfulness, and the paranoid thinking that other patients and staff were stealing her clothes and jewels. She spoke warmly of a fatherly former administrator who, she said, would not have allowed those things to have happened to her. The therapist received some of this transference and used it to reduce the patient's panic and anger. Another patient idolized her late husband, who was a physician. This greatly facilitated the transference of her devotion to the wise protector and magical healer to her physician-therapist. A third patient viewed her scientist son as her protector, and transfered these qualities to her therapist. Goldfarb's brief therapy technique also involved problem-solving, but he insisted that the dynamics of dependency-protector transference were essential to cure.

I am not sure how much I agree with Goldfarb on this point. It is helpful that the patient view the geriatric psychotherapist as a type of authority figure having some special powers which are beyond the patient's comprehension. (This makes physicians and the clergy excellent candidates for geriatric therapists, because they begin the therapeutic relationship with the position of an authority possessing quasi-magical powers.) The value of authority in psychotherapy was defended by Worden (1951) and more recently by Osmond and Siegler (1975). Research indicates that the patients with the best prognoses are those who have had a good previous relationship with authority figures (Lesse, 1966). One thing is for certain, if a psychotherapist is to be effective with a patient, the relationship must be one in which the patient is not allowed to resist by means of his usual neurotic maneuvers (Braceland, 1966). An excellent way of preventing this resistance is to convince the patient that he is now facing somebody who is qualitatively different from the ordinary, by virtue of office and knowledge.

A case study is illustrative here. When I visited some asylums for the indigent in Mexico, I was presented to the patients as "the expert from the United States." The lower class, poorly educated residents suffered from excessive disability. In many cases this was reduced by administering placebos and by sharing the expectation of more activity with the patient. The fact that local physicians and psychotherapists had not achieved such striking and rapid results can probably be explained by the difference in the degree of transference.

Another item to discuss in relationship to transference is Safirstein's (1967, 1968, 1973) theory of institutional transference. If the topic of religion is considered, it can be seen that the church itself is accorded high respect, independent of the fact that priests can be found there. Likewise, the hospital has a charismatic influence, and hospitalized patients develop institutional transference. They may not care much about which particular doctor treats them but they feel dependent and seek the magical power of the hospital. Safirstein concluded that a close personal relationship with the therapist was not necessary if institutional transference could be provided.

SUPPORTIVE THERAPY

Not all psychotherapy with elders can be brief or problem-centered. Sometimes there is no real solution to the underlying problems. All that can be done is to extend to the patient a genuine human relationship in which he can find some solace. Supportive therapy does not strive for insight or abreaction, nor does it always strive to train the patient in some specific skill, although it might be argued that the training in effective coping comes about as a by-product. Supportive psychotherapy is appropriate in terminal illness, and also immediately after some great irremediable loss such as widowhood or paralysis. Such therapy can also be appropriate if it is used to manage the patient to a baseline level of functioning in the community, but remains dependent on the transference relationship.

Safirstein (1972) presented several examples of such maintenance therapy. A 61-year-old woman who had devoted her life to her family showed extreme anxiety bordering on schizophrenia. This was a reaction to the facts that her 32-year-old daughter had been rehospitalized as a schizophrenic, that the 27-year-old son had been keeping bad company and "running wild," and that the husband (a schizophrenic in his own right) had a chronic heart problem. The patient's life had focused around her problems in the family, she had never advanced herself educationally or in a career, and she did not have a good friendship. Although the family traumas waxed and waned over eight years, she was sustained by a long-term psychotherapeutic relationship. In one sense the relationship was somewhat of an addiction, but the patient continued to find it beneficial and did not wish to terminate.

In another example cited by Safirstein (1972), the patient was a 62-year-old male homosexual. He initiated the therapy because of impotence. He then revealed life-long patterns of poor adjustment, especially depression. Years of classical psychoanalytic treatment and ECT had secured only temporary remissions of that depression. Added to all these problems, he was currently addicted to sleeping pills and constantly fantasized about taking an overdose. Therapy was successful in detoxifying the patient, and also in reducing his impotence and the frequency and depth of his depression. However, the chronic dependency of the patient meant that he had become addicted to the therapy in place of the drugs.

In a final example, Safirstein presented the case of a highly dependent woman who turned to sexual promiscuity and alcoholism after her husband left her. During the 14-year therapy, she has given up promiscuity, drinking, smoking, and the use of sleeping pills. At the same time she has found gainful employment for the first time in her life. Safirstein referred to her as the kind of person who can function only when emotionally supported by someone else, and he has accepted her as a patient for life.

The therapist can never know beforehand which patients will be capable of functioning after a few sessions and which patients will require long-term supportive therapy. For this reason, it is generally wise to avoid a hard and fast ending to therapy. Instead the sessions can be tapered off, or they can be changed from regular sessions and given the status of patient progress reports. Even when the patient is totally ready to go it alone, always remind him that the therapist is available for future psychotherapy if necessary. Other techniques for reducing the patient's dependency on the therapist would be to use surrogate supports, such as institutional transference, group therapy, or networks of friendship.

TEAM THERAPY

It is obvious that institutional life requires a coordination of all the different departments. The last chapter focuses on the possibility of milieu therapy in long-term care facilities. Unfortunately, this same type of teamwork, which is so obviously necessary in institutional environments, is rarely duplicated outside of an institution. Elders living in the community who are treated as outpatients at the local clinic and the local counseling center do not have this advantage.

The following round table discussion is purely fictitious. I am part of several geriatric treatment teams, but
none of them conforms to the ideal represented by this
discussion.

Counselor: I was referred a new patient this morning.
Mr. Q, a 62-year-old, was arrested for shoplifting from a
drug store. The arresting officer found him to be quite
confused and called me. Have we had enough time to process him?

Physician: We ran a physical on him early this afternoon. He suffers from diabetes and arthritis. Neither of
these conditions has received any treatment. I also found
high blood pressure and evidence of arteriosclerosis.

Counselor: His scores on the MSQ and FHT indicate
a moderate degree of impairment. Does it look like a case
of CBS due to cerebral arteriosclerosis?

Psychometrist: His performance on several tests would
be consistent with CBS. However, I also think that there is
some depression there.

Physician: There was no trace of brain tumor or neurofibrillary plaque on the brain scan.

Nurse: He was confused all right, but he was aware
enough to ask me where he could get some whiskey.

Employment Counselor: He had no history of alcohol
abuse, at least up until several years ago. The report from
his last employer indicates that he was a good and reliable
worker. Then he started making more errors on the job and
became irritable, and was forcibly retired six months ago.

Ophthalmologist: I checked his vision, and it is pretty
bad because of cataracts. What kind of work did he do?

Employment Counselor: A printer.

Ophthalmologist: No, there's no way he could see fine
type.

Counselor: After he lost his job, what other problems did he have?

Social Worker: He was pressured to leave his former residence, and now he lives in a flophouse.

Counselor: Who does he have: wife, siblings, children, friends?

Social Worker: According to my records, no one now. He was the youngest child, and all his brothers and sisters are now deceased. He lost his wife and two children in a fire 30 years ago.

Ophthalmologist: It's not too late to operate. I think we can still save his sight.

Employment Counselor: That would do him a world of good. Our records show that he was a most diligent worker until recently. Apparently, after he lost his family, he really poured himself into his work and wanted to be known as "old reliable" down at the shop.

Occupational Therapist: I think we could provide him with some things to keep him active after his sight returns, but arthritis will be an enduring limitation. Just how serious is the CBS?

Psychometrist: His computational and language abilities are the most impaired. He is pretty good in the other areas, although he demonstrates some space-time disorientation.

Ophthalmologist: But a good deal of that might be due to the cataracts, and perhaps even the diabetes.

Psychometrist: And the depression.

Social Worker: We can get him a better residence over at the Shelter Care Home. That will at least get him away from skid row and the habits of that subculture.

Ophthalmologist: We also have a group therapy program for the visually impaired, operating out of the Shelter Care Home. I will prescribe that he attend.

Physician: That sounds excellent. If we are done with Mr. Q, I have another case that's been worrying me, Mrs.

R. This is a case I've been working on for the past two years. She's a 71-year-old widow, and quite affluent, but she has deteriorated markedly over the last few months. She has become greatly withdrawn and somewhat more confused. Yesterday she fell and fractured her hip.

Psychometrist: I suspect an OBS. How about a potassium deficiency?

Physician: She has been on antihypertensive and diuretic medication for two years, but we've carefully monitored her electrolyte balance, and she's doing all right.

Pharmacist: Sometimes I doubt if she is taking her medication properly. I've noticed the confusion increasing over the last two months. She doesn't seem to be concerned about her medication, and if she had been taking it daily, she would have been in for refills more often.

Physician: But her blood pressure and serum cholesterol have declined.

Counselor: How is she doing socially?

Nurse: She doesn't say very much, but she did ask when her daughter would be in to visit her.

Social Worker: That daughter is the only person Mrs. R has now. Mr. R died 15 years ago, and although Mrs. R made a satisfactory recovery from the grief, she hasn't built up a sufficient array of compensations. She's lived alone for three years. The daughter is married, and just moved to Thailand with her husband who is stationed there.

Priest: She was once active in the Catholic Youth Organization as a volunteer. She helped develop a program to teach ballet to ghetto children. That was over 12 years ago. In the last year I haven't seen her at mass or confession.

Counselor: I wonder how much her confusion, physical debilitation, and this latest accident may be serving the unconscious purpose of provoking her daughter's return?

Social Worker: It is very possible that Mrs. R's deterioration is a way of saying, as boldly as she can, "Come back and help me!" I have sent a telegram to the daughter, but she hasn't answered yet.

Nurse: One other point: I get the impression that she feels a little guilty about being a burden on others.

Psychometrist: I also picked up a little guilt. Maybe Father should see her, if she is ready to see anyone yet.

Physical Therapist: I've already spoken with her at her bedside. I found her quite subdued, not confused or dependent. I explained some of the rehabilitation exercises we would be doing. She told me she used to teach ballet. She seemed almost eager and certainly cooperative.

Counselor: You may be picking up some transference. Maybe you remind her of the dancing teacher she had when she was a girl, or you may remind her of a dancing partner she had as a performer, or a prize pupil she had as a teacher.

Priest: I have an idea. One of her old students is really starting to make it big in ballet. I think I could get him to drop by also.

Counselor: That would help relieve her of the nagging doubts about the worth of her life. It would also give her a link with the future, and possibly inspiration to try to recover.

Dentist: I would like to mention one other requisite for recovery. Her old dentures no longer fit well. I think it must be quite difficult for her to chew anything.

Dietician: I asked about her daily food intake, and she seemed quite hesitant to give me some specific answers. I think her regular diet has been tea, toast, juice, and bananas.

Social Worker: That fits in with something else she said, that it was too much trouble to cook for just one person.

Physician: That type of diet would explain several things. First of all it would explain her weight loss. It could also account for the lowered pressure and serum choles-

terol, perhaps even in the absence of the prescribed medication. The bananas are high in potassium and would keep
her away from hypokalemia in any case.

Dietician: But that diet was very low in calcium and B
vitamins.

Physician: Which ties in with her hip fracture.

Physician: And the vitamin deficiency could account
for the OBS picked up on the psychometric tests. I'll consider megavitamin therapy.

The foregoing panel discussions never took place, yet
they are very typical of the way that geriatric patients are
referred to counseling, and also of all the professionals who
must be involved in the treatment. Because the entire
health care delivery system and the elders themselves have
rejected the ideal of early detection and treatment for
geriatric patients, usually intervention is not made until
there is an emergency. The police officer or physician is
called in first, and they usually call in the geriatric counselor (Stenbäck, 1973).

Because geriatric counseling should take a problem-
solving approach, the counselor must go to the other professionals who can give information on both the
dimensions of the problem and the scope of the potential
solutions. All of the professionals mentioned above in the
fictitious dialogue made a definite contribution. When the
geriatric counselor can get in touch with professionals who
have worked closely with the patient, it is the counselor's
duty to do so. Because one great round table conference,
involving all of the professionals simultaneously, is usually
impossible to schedule, the counselor must do a lot of work
behind the scenes. When these other informed professionals do not exist or are not accessible, the geriatric counselor
has the duty of filling as many roles as he can, and then
bringing in new, competent professionals on the case
whenever his own competence is exceeded. Each geriatric

counselor should have a list of physicians, psychologists, social workers, nurses, physical therapists, occupational therapists, recreation directors, family counselors, clergy, lawyers, dentists, dieticians, eye doctors, and homemakers who understand the special problems of elders and have a good rapport with them. The list should also include the names of reliable extended-care facilities.

The geriatric counselor's job is made markedly easier when there is an established, ongoing team, perhaps at an acute-care hospital, clinic, or long-term care facility. The team is rarely as large or comprehensive as the one presented above. Therefore even the team must be pulling in outside professionals for given cases. When there is no established team working on a given case, one of the professionals working on that case must try to put a team together and coordinate its efforts. The physician probably wields the greatest authority and is in many ways the logical "head" of the team. He is also the therapist of choice for individual psychotherapy, especially when the problem has its origins in reaction to a real loss (primarily physical), or when the patient demonstrates rigidity and would be likely to resist most other professionals (Siegler et al., 1963). Unfortunately, most physicians are so busy with their other cases that they do not have time to give the patient much in the way of individual psychotherapy, let alone to do all the homework it takes to put together and manage a team.

The geriatric counselor who is not a physician faces a different problem. Even if he has the time and good fortune to be able to organize a treatment team for a given patient, he may not be able to coordinate it. The central stumbling block is authority. How can the nonphysician tell the physician what to do with his patient? Many physicians are especially touchy about this type of situation. Furthermore, the geriatric counselor must be extremely cautious and diplomatic about making suggestions with physicians. Not only will the physician's ruffled feathers mean that the management of the particular case will be poor, but perhaps the physician will not refer any further cases to the counselor. The best approach is for the counselor to be very respectful of the physician's knowledge and power, but slowly to expose the physician to the modern psychotherapeutic aspects of geriatrics. It is probably better to compromise one's ideals on a particular case, rather than to alienate the physician and lose all possibility of striving for one's ideals on all of that physician's future cases.

The following case study is an example of therapeutic failure. The patient was a 66-year-old divorcee. I was called in on the case by the patient's psychiatrist. The patient had just returned home after several weeks in an acute-care hospital for myocardial infarction. She had had high blood pressure since 1960, and had several previous heart attacks. But after this one she was much weaker and confused. Her weight dropped steadily during the last five years and was down to 80 pounds, although she was a tall woman of 5'8". Psychometric testing ruled out CBS and depression. She was lucid and alert in both of the sessions that I had with her, although she trembled and complained of being very weak.

Her employment history was exemplary: long, hard, reliable service in several different office positions. That and her devotion to her son, an only child, compensated for a rather poor marriage to a ne'er-do-well alcoholic, who was finally divorced 10 years ago. A corporate merger induced the patient to retire voluntarily at age 60. She then moved in with her bachelor son, and together they fixed up apartments and duplexes. They went on several vacations to foreign countries. But after retirement, the physical problems began to mount: the weight loss, the return of the migraines, arthritis, backache, and within the last year, three hospitalizations for her heart condition.

The patient had no current interpersonal complaints.

She blamed her weakness for her inability to do anything. She had been an avid reader, but now found that her vision was blurred. She complained that she just could not eat. The son prepared food for her, and even came home from work to help her eat. But many times, especially in his absence, she ate little or not at all. She was under numerous dietary restrictions from her cardiologist and complained that she found most health food unappetizing.

Some of her medications' side effects could have accounted for her mental symptoms. The particular type of digoxin she was using can result in anorexia (the lack of a desire to eat), apathy, and visual disturbance. In fact, it is sometimes prescribed to treat obesity. The diuretic could have depleted potassium, and perhaps this was responsible for her lethargy, mental confusion, and anorexia. Her primary physician, a cardiologist, insisted that electrolyte balance was being maintained, and rejected the idea of taking the patient off of digoxin. The psychiatrist had been called in on the case when the hospitalized patient became confused and agitated. He had prescribed haloperidol. The patient believed that this "calming medicine" was appropriate as a bedtime sedative, and took two capsules before retiring. Some of the side effects of haloperidol can be lethargy, visual blurring, and anorexia. The psychiatrist refused to consider my suggestion of discontinuing the haloperidol. He recounted the extreme delirium and agitation that the patient had experienced in the hospital, and feared that it would return. He was convinced that the best treatment was to push the patient to be more active, and he urged me to pursue that course.

The patient's optometrist was a most valuable source of information. He previously recalled her as a jolly old girl. He had just examined the eyes of the patient and noted a dramatic drop in visual acuity and spirits. He had diagnosed the poor vision as an entirely somatic problem, and had prepared a new pair of glasses which would improve her vision somewhat. However, he also noticed cataracts that would require surgery.

In my second session, the patient expressed a real desire to be more active and perhaps eventually to return to her work of fixing up apartments. I presented her with numerous opportunities for social, religious, and political activities in the local area, and she seemed genuinely interested, but she was obviously still too weak. For the immediate future, her goals were more limited: She wanted to be able to read again and to be able to eat better so that she could gain strength. I concurred that this was the immediate task. Meanwhile, the patient had seen another medical specialist, this time an endocrinologist, who suspected her problems were related to the thyroid.

There was never a third session. When I showed up, the patient was simply too weak to see me. Her condition was becoming a great burden on the son, who had neglected his job somewhat to take care of his mother. I recommended a live-in housekeeper and a behavioral modification program for increasing the patient's food consumption. The son was unenthusiastic about having someone else in the home and had more or less made up his mind that a nursing home was the next step.

Why did this team fail this patient? Did the physicians fail to notice the side effects of their medication? Was the son too quick to take the last step? Did I fail to uncover and improve some pathological interpersonal processes between mother and son? Such cases of failure do not always leave the counselor with a ready-made answer about who let the patient down. Neither should the geriatric counselor dwell on this type of question. It can only shake his self-confidence and thereby diminish his effectiveness in other cases. Reflection should focus on what could have been done differently, which sometimes leads to useful insights that can be employed on future cases. In the above case, however, I did not gain such an insight. There is no way that I could have overruled the decisions of the other professionals or the son. The two sessions did not allow enough time to diagnose or work through any problems in the mother-son relationship.

I have introduced this case of therapeutic failure to illustrate the problems of a breakdown in the team, and also to share with other geriatric counselors the fact that some failures do happen. Other failures leave fewer doubts, such as when the patient dies shortly after counseling begins. Working with elders, especially elders who require the services of a geriatric counselor, necessitates exposure to failure. Anyone who cannot accept this cannot become an experienced geriatric counselor.

SUMMARY

The preferred form of geriatric psychotherapy is one that emphasizes brief and problem-centered discussion backed by a coordinated team of professionals. The counselor must be more directive, active, and oriented to the present needs of the patient when working with elders. Long-term therapy is appropriate in only a few cases. The dynamics of transference and countertransference in geriatric psychotherapy are diverse and complicated, but with the proper understanding and attitudes on the part of the therapist, transference problems can be avoided.

Chapter 9

SPECIFIC TECHNIQUES

The purpose of this chapter is to suggest some useful tactics in geriatric psychotherapy. Too often therapists assume that geriatric psychotherapy differs only in overall strategy, but that once the therapist is face-to-face with the patient, the same old counseling techniques are just as appropriate. This is often a serious error. Part of the problem stems from the fact that most psychotherapists do not begin to practice therapy until they are far along in their graduate education. In most undergraduate courses in counseling, and in the type of workshops that spring up on weekends, one student practices on another. The traditional training in the Freudian and Jungian institutes is to teach practical therapeutic techniques by having the therapist candidates undergo several years of analysis with a master therapist or senior analyst. Even when the student is given a patient of his own at the university counseling center, the patient is usually another student, or someone within the confines of the extended university community.

These types of training condition the therapist to use techniques that will be appropriate to young and fluent patients. Usually these patients love techniques that bring them insight or some deeper contact with their emotions. Therefore these are often the very techniques developed by the practice. When the therapist is given a patient who is old, poorly educated, or from a different social class, the same techniques may not be appreciated by the new patient, who is less likely to view therapy as a introspective journey designed to foster psychic growth.

The best way to train students in geriatric psychotherapy is to give them field experience that provides them with one-to-one contact with elders. Long-term care institutions, acute-care hospital intake, or community mental health intake are possible training environments. The important thing is to give the students experience in talking to elders in a clinical context. The student must learn how to develop and sustain empathy and also how to get to the root of the problem quickly.

QUESTIONING

The opening remarks of the counselor should set a tone for the rest of therapy. If the basic strategy is therapy which is brief and problem-centered, the tone must be a realistic evaluation of resources accompanied by assessment of the magnitude of the problems. Usually a formal introduction and the maintenance of formal address are appreciated by elders. For example, introduce yourself as "Dr. X," "Father Y," or "Mrs. Z." If the doctorate is not an MD it is best to clarify this at the same time. For example, "I am Dr. X, the psychologist." Most elders enjoy being addressed as "Mrs. A," "Professor B," or "Deacon C." Of course, if there is any indication of a preference for informal address rather than their official titles and surnames, do oblige them.

Another good move is to ask the patient at the very beginning how he came to you. Not all contact with a mental health professional is voluntary. Perhaps the elder was referred by his physician or social worker and came voluntarily, though it may be with some reservations. In other cases, the patient has been more or less commanded to go by the family, physician, directors of a residential care facility, or even the police. Such patients often come in with a built-in resistance that cannot be ignored.

The patient's expectations must be assessed early in the initial contact with the therapist. The patient can be asked to describe his hopes about the course and result of the therapy: "Why are you here?" "How do you think I could help?" "What kind of results can we hope for?" Then ask the elder for his commitment to the joint enterprise: "Will you work with me on that?" The response to this last question is a good indication of resistance and depression. Some patients' answers indicate a great deal of suspicion of the therapist, even when the therapist claims to be working on the goals enunciated by the patient. Depressed patients respond that they are not able to help. The best response to any such answer is an imperturbable and unvoiced confidence, and perhaps a faint smile.

Next explain to the patient that you must take a history, and that to do it you must ask many questions. Reassure the elder that your purpose is not to try to embarrass or psychoanalyze him, but simply to get the information you need. Questions should cover basic life data, interpersonal relations, activities, religion, geography, and medical status. The following questions are usually sufficient to fill up the initial interview.

What is your full name? Maiden name?

When were you born? Married?

Are you married now? (Follow up by asking when the spouse was divorced or died.)

What happened to you as the result (of the death or divorce)?

How many children do you have?

Which do you see regularly? (Digression on this point is often helpful.)

Where have you lived in the past 10 years? With whom?

Do you visit many friends regularly? Why not?

What was your occupation? Did you like it?

When did you retire? Why? Have you enjoyed retirement? Were there any changes in your life-style as the result of retirement?

What have your hobbies been? Reading? Physical exercise? Charitable work?

Which of these are you active in now? Why not?

Which would you like to do if you could?

Do you attend mass (church services, synagogue, temple) regularly?

When was the last time you had a chance to speak with your priest (rabbi, minister, clergyman)?

Do you suffer from heart disease? Arthritis? Severe pain?

How well do you see? Hear? Eat? Sleep? Get around?

Do you ever worry about anything? What? How often? What do you do when you worry?

What has been your greatest physical problem?

What medication are you taking? How do you take it (dosage and frequency)?

These questions do not have to be asked in this particular order. In fact, it is probably best for the therapist not to be seen running down a list. The purpose of these questions is not just to assist the therapist in understanding the extent of the problem and the available resources, but also to establish rapport. In cases of depression, direct and precise questioning is often the best way to establish empathy (Regan, 1965).

One thing must be remembered about the use of questions in psychotherapy. By and large, to ask a question is to limit the answer. The more specific and here-and-now the question, the more the answer is limited. This is probably the best technique for the initial interview, especially with depressed patients (Regan, 1965). However, as therapy progresses, questions that do a little more than get chartable information are required. When the patient seems to want more contact with his feelings, and when he seems to respond well to that technique, he may be asked directly, "How do you feel when situation X occurs?" But if the therapy is brief and problem-centered, this type of question should be followed by, "What do you do when you feel this way?"

When the patient seems to respond well to insight, the following questions may be useful: "What do you tell yourself in situation X?" "How would you interpret your actions?" Many times the patient will respond with insight, but this will not be expressed in the kind of language that the therapist is familiar with. The patient may use the language of folk wisdom or proverbs. Whenever possible, the therapist should endorse such insight and explain to the patient that although psychology uses different terms, the essential meaning is the same. It is not necessary to educate the patient in psychological terms. The important thing is that whatever insight the patient is able to arrive at should be translated into an improvement in his behavior or thought patterns. Therefore the therapist must encourage and help the patient to incorporate insight into the total life-style.

However, it is a mistake to assume that insight is always necessary for treatment, or that insight is always beneficial.

Huston (1966) contended that too much introspection makes depressed patients worse. Depression can be treated by brief, active psychotherapy (Hammer, 1972) or by supportive psychotherapy (Lesse, 1974) without insight.

One final point needs to be brought out. The counselor should never ignore any suicidal symptom or comment from the patient. In fact, when the patient is extremely depressed, it does not hurt to ask directly if he has contemplated suicide. Take elders seriously when they speak about suicide. More than any other age group, they are successful in their suicide attempts. Furthermore, when the counselor acknowledges the suicidal thoughts of the patient, the patient has at last found someone who is taking him seriously. This can go a long way in establishing trust. The therapist can offer a promise of help, and make it good by providing a flexible schedule and frequent visits (Resnick & Kantor, 1970).

Even more so than with nonsuicidal elders, the therapist must be decisive and authoritative when dealing with potential geriatric suicides. If possible, he should remove all firearms and potentially lethal medications from the patient's home. The interpersonal relationship between patient and therapist can be used as a motive for the patient to maintain his life. The therapist can say, "We have an appointment next week, promise me that you will not do anything before then" (Soulen, 1975). But such a measure is merely a desperate attempt to buy time. When the diagnosis is depression, this time buying may be justified because the condition can be treated and the patient restored to a happier life, which the therapist may presume that the patient will later appreciate. However, when the patient has a terminal illness and is enduring great suffering, the therapist should not string the patient along. If the patient is sufficiently rational in his desire for the termination of his life, the therapist may have to accept this.

In no case should the therapist respond to the suicidal

thoughts judgmentally. This will only compound whatever condition lies behind the thoughts with guilt feelings or the feeling of rejection, and will further deter the patient from expressing his innermost thoughts to the therapist in the future. However, sometimes the patient himself will offer a moral judgment on the suicidal feelings. The follow-up should be for the therapist to ask the patient if he agrees with that moral judgment. If he does not, and the therapist has not taken a judgmental stance, this little interchange on the subject might be enough to relieve the patient of a guilt complex. If the patient does agree with the moral judgment, he is really saying that he does not want to commit suicide, and is attracted to the course of action only because it has appeared to be the only way out. This interpretation can be shared with the patient, along with the promise that the therapist will work with the patient to find another way. One final point on suicidal tendencies in the aged: Usually the condition is secondary to a depression, and as soon as the depression is being lifted, the suicidal danger is lessened, but may not disappear.

PROBING THE PAST AND PRESENT

Direct questioning is not the only way of gathering information or of bringing about a therapeutic relationship. At the end of the initial interview, it is a good tactic to give the patient some homework. One thing to work on would be an autobiography, which can be written or tape-recorded. It is not necessary for the patient to bring this in to the next session with the therapist, but such autobiographies are often very helpful in providing information. Getting the autobiography before the next session would help the therapist review it and would prepare him for the next session. However, this is not the sole purpose of the autobiography.

It also has a psychotherapeutic use.

Butler (1964) outlined the "life review" as a therapeutic tool in geriatric cases. The rationale is that the key to successful aging lies in one's review of his own past (Livson, Reichard & Peterson, 1962). Reconstructing the past can give an elder a sense of achievement, the feeling that life has been worth living. An autobiography is not the only useful means for this. Pilgrimages, reunions, genealogies, scrapbooks, albums, and interest in ethnicity can all serve this function.

There are at least two ways of interpreting the usefulness of the life review. One is Eriksonian and conceives of the life review as the fulfillment of the life task of the last phase of life, a warding off of despair which permits the elder to go to his grave with a good feeling about his life. My perspective on the life review is somewhat Adlerian. The life review, when it is helpful, is helpful because it has reminded the patient that life is a series of crises and protracted struggles, and that he has persevered in the past and triumphed. Such an interpretation of one's past serves as a powerful motivation for one to try to cope with the new demands of the present. When the therapist debriefs the patient on his autobiography, the therapist must emphasize enthusiastically this interpretation of the patient's life. If not, the life review can become counterproductive and convince the patient that life has been one failure after another, and that he is now just too weak to keep on struggling.

Thinking about the past, by itself, is not necessarily therapeutic. Martin and DeGruchy (1933) contended that fixation on the past could become the cause of the loss of short-term memory. They reasoned that concern with the present could become crowded out by the old, useless, and even painful memories of the past. As a solution, Martin and DeGruchy recommended a systematic program of forgetting the useless, "sweeping out the mental cobwebs," and filling the mind with the new. So, before he can decide how to use the patient's past, the therapist must answer the question, "Is the past a firm foundation for present coping, or is it an impediment?" The initial interview should give the therapist enough information to answer this question. When the patient has been successful in meeting life's problems, a life review is a good tactic. When the patient's entire life has been a failure, a life review is contraindicated.

In addition to the past, the patient can be given homework about his present. A daily journal describing his activity is useful for the therapist as a source of descriptive information about how the patient spends his time, and also for demonstrating to the patient that he is too inactive in his present life-style. Another piece of homework is to have the patient write down his desires and goals for the present. This helps to motivate him and also to direct the psychotherapist's intervention. One benefit of the journal and the life review is that they get the patient doing something other than sitting around and brooding.

EMPATHY

Freud discovered the importance of the patient-therapist relationship in psychotherapy and attempted to explain this in terms of transference. Rogers offered the concept of empathy as an explanation of how this interpersonal relationship functions to secure improvement. Empathy is the therapist's ability to go beyond an objective understanding of the patient's thoughts, feelings, and behavior, and to experience the patient's world phenomenologically, as the patient does. The therapist must convey to the client that his behavior is understood and yet accepted. When this takes place, psychotherapeutic communication at an emotional level begins.

Various studies have supported Rogers on the importance of empathy, warmth, and genuineness in successful psychotherapy (Shapiro, 1969). Other studies have directly challenged the role of these factors in cure (Lesser, 1961; Garfield & Bergin, 1971). Ferreira (1961) doubted the very ability of the therapist to measure empathy. Indeed, therapists may assume that they are empathetic when the client does not perceive it. Kurtz and Grummon (1972) found no relationship between objectively measured empathy and psychotherapeutic success, but they did find a strong correlation between successful outcome and empathy as perceived by the client. Whitehorn and Betts (1955) compared the physicians having the highest cure rates with those having the lowest. This study, which was confined to institutionalized schizophrenics, found that the effective therapists exhibited some grasp of the personal meaning of the patients' behavior. Stone (1971) interviewed a group of therapists who had been unexpectedly successful with long-term schizophrenics; he concluded that most of these therapists had experienced countertransference patterns that made them extremely empathetic with the patient in question. We have no reason to doubt that empathy is a desirable technique in psychotherapy with elders.

While it seems that empathy is psychotherapeutic, the precise mechanism through which patient behavior is changed is a matter of debate. Rogers (1961) explained that the therapeutic nature of empathy derived from the fact that it was capable of releasing the patient from "conditions of worth" that had been imposed by significant others, and thereby allowed the patient to value his own experience "organismically." Rogers' explanation leaves much to be desired. His terms are so vague that they virtually preclude empirical research to establish the validity of his theory. Furthermore, I find it most difficult to conceive of the problems of elders in Rogerian terms. Most geriatric cases involve adjusting to real privations, and conditions of worth imposed by others are at best secondary.

Another way of explaining the curative role of empathy is to recognize that unconditional positive regard can generate a healthier self-concept, which in turn serves as a foundation for healthier thinking and behavior. Religion is an excellent example of this. The proselytizing sects of Christianity frequently emphasize God as an accepting, forgiving father. When someone begins to look at God from this perspective, he can replace his old self-concept (unworthy sinner) with a new healthy one (child of God). As a result, not only his thinking, but his conduct change (sanctification). Probably Adler (1956, 1964) was the first psychotherapist to emphasize self-concept in treatment and to use empathetic techniques in helping patients shed themselves of inferiority feelings. Butler and Haight (1954) concluded that self-concept was the factor responsible for improvement in empathy-oriented therapy.

Yet another explanation for the curative power of empathy is that it can serve as a positive reinforcer for training the patient in healthy behavior. In the psychotherapeutic dyad, the patient receives an empathetic reaction from the therapist, and this reinforces the patient's efforts to communicate empathetically and genuinely (Coons, 1967). One bit of caution must be noted. In any type of operant conditioning, if the positive reinforcement is available for whatever the subject does, the subject is not conditioned to perform any specific act to get the positive reinforcement. In fact, if empathy is consistently provided when the patient demonstrates maladaptive behavior and confused or self-defeating thought, empathy only reinforces mental illness. When used selectively to reinforce good reality testing or competent interpersonal skills, empathy can turn off the flow of meaningless babblings and condition the patient to function in a more adaptive fashion (Rickard, Dignam & Horner, 1960).

One other precaution regarding empathy should be given. Many therapists think that they are striving for empathy when they ask the patient prying questions or attempt to establish an intimate relationship. Often attempts to establish closeness can backfire, especially with a patient who is prone to fear close relationships. This fear may be expressed by direct resistance to the therapist, missing sessions, arriving late, talking about irrelevancies, or do anything else that puts distance between him and the therapist (Safirstein, 1967). Many so-called cold fish therapists who respect distance, do not ask unnecessarily prying questions (especially about sex life and fantasies), and treat their patients in a professional way have excellent results with adults (Safirstein, 1967). The use of formal address and keeping the therapy focused on concrete problems are good ways of preventing this type of destructive empathy.

SYMPTOM REMOVAL

In addition to whatever major psychopathology a patient may have (depression, CBS, paranoia), many elders also have several symptoms which cause them great distress. These symptoms may or may not be related to the pathologies diagnosed. They may have originated in later life or may be life-long conditions. One of the purposes of psychotherapy is to remove or modify as much as possible these distressing symptoms. Specific examples of these symptoms are anxiety phobias, letting other people take advantage, uncontrolled anger, or any type of bad habit from swearing to overeating. As the chapter on behavioral techniques indicated, these symptoms, even if they are long-standing and tied in with the personality structure, can be removed by a variety of techniques without the development of new symptoms.

With elders, a surprisingly effective solution to many symptoms is a direct request from a firm, but fair and understanding, authority figure (Poe, 1969). Adolescents may tend to resist such advice, but many elders will abandon a bad habit of many years on the advice of a physician or clergyman. If the psychotherapist is viewed as a comparable authority figure, similar results may be anticipated. The exception is the elder who is rigid in his defiance of all authority, whether wielded with the scepter or the stethoscope. This type of elder loves to continue in bad habits (for example, diet or drink) and to brag about how he knows more than the doctors.

Suggestions can become more effective if they are given when the patient is relaxed. This is the foundation for hypnosis: relaxation followed by suggestion. In brief psychotherapy, hypnosis is often the treatment of choice for symptom removal (Wolberg, 1972). The prerequisite for hypnosis is a willing, cooperative, and relaxed patient. The hypnotist then suggests that the patient relax more and more, until the patient is in a trance state in which conscious control of his body has been temporarily surrendered to the hypnotist. Age has a great deal to do with hypnotizability. Children are the easiest to hypnotize; the older one gets, the more difficult it is to be put into a deep trance. Elders tend to be more tense and suspicious, and therefore resist the hypnotist. Also, hypnotism is more difficult when patients are easily distracted. Therefore hypnotism is quite difficult with retardates and patients with brain injuries. Nevertheless, hypnosis can be used with elders (Brenman & Knight, 1943). Estabrooks (1957) claimed that it could be profitably used in elders with CBS senility to remove such symptoms as anxiety and irritability. Successful applications to the problems of incontinence and inadequate self-care would be a major breakthrough in treatment. However, my own efforts along these lines have not been fruitful. I suspect that CBS reduces not only hypnotizability, but also the utility of the posthypnotic suggestion, which may not be remembered.

Hypnosis can also be used as a diagnostic tool, to

recover repressed ideas and memories. Freud and Jung began using hypnosis as a means for exploring the childhoods of their patients. Although both of these pioneer psychotherapists later developed other techniques and abandoned hypnosis, its ability to help people recover memories should not be forgotten. The one caution is that asking questions which are too emotional, too early in the psychotherapy may upset the patient, make him suspicious of the therapist, and impair the patient's ability to return to a trance (Estabrooks, 1957). Brenman and Knight (1943) used hypnosis with a 71-year-old woman who had proved unresponsive to all other techniques. Via hypnosis, memories were recovered and insights were gained, and presumably this brought about the patient's improvement. Posthypnotic suggestion can also be used to get CVA (stroke) patients to practice their physical and speech therapy exercises (Shires, Peters & Krout, 1954).

One distressing symptom which the therapist should try to remove is persistent pain. Meares (1967) suggested an approach based on relaxation. It bears similarities to hypnotic suggestion and also to the systematic desensitization used in phobias by the behavior therapists. Hypnosis can be used to a certain extent, with certain patients, to remove pain or at least reduce it. One excellent book providing a theological as well as a neurological and psychological perspective on pain is *Pain and Religion* by Brena (1972).

Self-Help

Another useful technique in symptom removal is self-help. The use of self-monitoring was discussed in Chapter 6, but there are many other self-help techniques which therapists can pass along to their patients. Probably the best book in this area is *Psychiatric Self-Help* by Forrer (1973). His approach is based on six steps. First, *stop complaining.* Forrer is referring to the type of complaining that is repetitious and serves no useful purpose. Such complaining is a negative influence on all interpersonal relations and fixes the mind on the useless. Second, *give up raptus,* the strong, staring, mindblown state that babies indulge in while nursing. Adults should not just stare and think of nothing; it only wastes time and weakens ego control. Third, *stop churning.* By this, Forrer means that the patient should learn to control his thought reveries and stop the repetitious rehashings of fears, injustices, and worry. If possible, a good habit should be substituted whenever one finds himself engaged in churning. Fourth, *churn* intentionally at regularly scheduled short periods, for example, three intense periods of five minutes during the day. This step relies on massed practice, and the result is that churning becomes boring and ceases to fascinate the mind. Fifth, *write down your stream of consciousness.* The person should simply write whatever is in his head, and not think or plan or organize. This is somewhat similar to the free association of psychoanalysis. After being written, the material should be destroyed. One should not show the material to anyone else, or even let it be known that he is engaging in the process. The author should not even reread his old material. The purpose of such writing is to desensitize people to their own fantasy lives. Sixth, *do a daily good deed* for which you receive no material gain. Forrer urges his readers to stick to his suggestions for at least three months before they pass judgment on their utility.

Another excellent book with a self-help theme is *I Can If I Want To* by Lazarus and Fay (1975). They advise their readers to keep a notebook, define the basic psychological problem, try to see it as a learned behavior pattern which can be unlearned, devise a way to measure the problem, and then devise a way of lessening the problem while simultaneously increasing positive and adaptive responses. The patient makes an entry in his notebook whenever he engages in faulty or unhealthy thinking, for example, attributing his own feelings to external events. For the self-denying patient who believes that happiness must be earned, Lazarus and Fay recommend that he devise a point system for pleasure, and that he try to get a minimum number each day. For the overly timid patient, the recommendation is that he should keep a notebook that records all of the opportunities for human contact and then grades his use of these opportunities. For the overly independent patient who is too proud to ask for help, the notebook should record situations in which assistance should be asked for. The last type of patient also needs practice saying thank you.

THREE DIFFICULT POINTS TO PONDER

There are at least three very thorny problems that crop up frequently in questions about technique in geriatric psychotherapy. Each of these problems requires the therapist to walk the razor's edge and respond in such a way that he is doing the right thing, at the right time, and to the right degree.

The first of these problems is the question of pushing the patient. Elders frequently need directive authority to get them living actively again. Depressed patients may need forcible exposure to behavior that is reinforcing. This exposure may be to behavior that provides escape, avoidance, or tension reduction (Seligman, 1974). On the other hand, there is the danger that the patient will be pushed too far too fast, especially in the areas of re-establishing interpersonal relationships before he is truly capable of doing so (Huston, 1966). The same can be said about pushing the patient in his religious life. Many times a return to religion, via church attendance, scripture reading, fellowship, or a resumption of prayer is a real boon to the patient's total mental health. It can give a sense of purpose, a feeling of special strength and courage, and relief from the pains of the temporal world. Nevertheless, too much religious exhortation too soon can cause some patients to feel that they were sinful for neglecting their religious lives so long.

A second problem that requires cautious resolution and management is resistance. Elders do have a propensity to be rigid, and like adolescents, once they are alienated, they stop listening. However, with most elders there is an abiding respect for authority figures, especially physicians and clergy. The best bet for the therapist is, in most cases, to assume a comparable authoritative posture at the outset. When resistance does rear its ugly head, I found that the best thing to do is not to fight the patient's strength of will, but to respect it fully. Directly concede that the patient has a strong will and that even with all your professional tricks it would be impossible for you to overcome him and to change his thinking on a certain point. Therefore, tell the patient you will not try. This makes the patient feel a little bit better about himself, and even favorably disposes him to the therapist.

The task is now to use that will power to help the patient follow up on his rehabilitation, and to secure the removal of specific symptoms. Life review can tie in here. When the therapist gives the patient the interpretation of the life review as a series of crises met and problems endured, this helps to give the patient enough motivation and self-concept to use his will power to help himself. Attempts to overcome resistance to the therapist by breaking the patient's will or by reminding him of his dependent nature are usually unsuccessful. If the patient's behavior is totally untenable, he can only be reminded that if he does persist, the forces of external reality will eventually see to it that such and such will happen to him.

One last difficult point is the question of allowing the

patient to ventilate feelings of grief, hostility, inferiority, hopelessness, and so on. Currently, there is a fad in pop therapy that it is good to express one's feelings, to let it all hang out, to get it out of one's system. This catharsis theory of emotion can be traced back to Aristotle's theory of tragic drama: that the actors and audience could be somehow purged of emotions while watching a play. However, neither Aristotle nor the other major figures in Greek, Christian, or Oriental philosophy considered the direct expression of anger, hostility, or aggression to be therapeutic. The great theological minds, East and West, have stressed the virtue of self-control of emotions.

The basic question is, does the expression of an undesirable emotion, such as anger, cause a discharge in which the patient is relieved of that emotion, or does it merely train the patient to express anger, and indeed to be angry? There may be very well a relationship between anger and other types of mental illness, but it is not correct to assume that anger that has not been expressed has caused these diseases, or that expression is therapeutic or prophylactic. Rather, the difficulties in managing any emotion are symptomatic of poor mental health. The best solution is training in constructive ways to manage one's emotions so that they cause a minimum of intrapsychic stress or disturbance to interpersonal relations. The expression of anger via verbal or physical aggression does not improve the aggressor's self-concept (Dichter, 1965). In various experiments, those subjects allowed to strike back at their frustrators were not more likely to be on friendly terms with their frustrators in the future. In fact, catharsis, whether verbal or physical, direct or displaced, is more likely to increase the subject's future levels of anger and aggression (Freeman, 1962; Nighswander & Mayer, 1969).

Despite this experimental evidence and the advice of 2500 years of world philosophy, some psychodynamic theories hold that depression is the result of an introversion of agression against the self, and that the externalization of aggression is a therapeutic agent (Galton, 1975; Stamey, 1971). Kleban, Brody, and Lawton (1971) found aggression to be a reliable predicter of improvement in patients with diagnosed excess disabilities. Nevertheless, there is some evidence to indicate that aggression will mask depressive symptoms, without resolving underlying problems (Spiegel, 1967, 1968; McCranie, 1971). At best, depressive symptoms have been eclipsed by competing responses of aggression and anger, which may not be therapeutically superior.

Of course, assertiveness should not be confused with aggression. The former expresses wants and defends rights rationally and effectively, while the latter is more concerned with the discharge of an emotion, rather than the effect of that discharge. Assertiveness training can also give the patient new responses that eclipse the depressive symptoms and simultaneously make him a more capable coper, whereas aggression only trades one symptom for another. The ability to distinguish between assertiveness and aggressiveness, and the ability to train the patient in the first, while not encouraging the second, is something that the therapist must learn.

When the patient expresses anger, grief, inferiority, or hopelessness, the therapist must be careful not to give too much reinforcement, because this will only condition those thoughts so that the patient will continue to think, feel, and behave pathologically in hopes of getting some warm human contact. On the other hand, the therapist cannot ignore such feelings, because this does not lead to a therapeutic outcome. Either the patient loses rapport with the therapist, or the patient learns to ignore his feelings (without learning how to deal with them). The trick is for the therapist to acknowledge the patient's emotions without reinforcing them. This can allow the patient to face such emotions without becoming addicted to them.

SUMMARY

Precise and authoritative questioning is a good technique in geriatric psychotherapy. There are several uses of the life review, and it seems to be contraindicated only in patients whose lives and memories are, on the balance, unsuccessful and painful. The daily journal is helpful from a diagnostic and prognostic point of view. Empathy is an essential aspect for effective therapy, but Rogerian theory is not necessarily the best way to comprehend the nature and use of empathy. Specific symptoms can be removed by direct suggestion, hypnosis, and behavioral modification. Self-help techniques are often very useful as adjunctive therapy. Three difficult areas for the geriatric psychotherapist are the questions of how much to push the patient, how to cope with resistance, and how much to permit ventilation of distressing feelings.

Chapter 10

DREAM THERAPY

Freud was the first psychotherapist to express a great deal of interest in dreams as a diagnostic and therapeutic tool. In the intervening decades, certain changes have been wrought in dream theory and dream therapy. First of all, dreams are not considered as products of a liberated un-conscious, but of a somewhat limited or altered state of consciousness (Ullman, 1955, 1958a, 1958b). Freud's piecemeal interpretation of dream symbols has been replaced by a theory which considers the dream as a holistic production and attempts to establish the context of the dream, usually by considering a series of dreams (Kelman, 1944, 1965; Hall, 1966; Ullman, 1959). Nevertheless, there is much agreement with Freud that the dream is a product of the dreamer's mental state and reflects his perception of phenomena (Bonime, 1962, 1969; Spanijaard, 1969; Hall, 1966; Gershman, 1973).

Dreams can be used as sensitive diagnostic and prognostic instruments that zero in on the patient's central conflicts (Gershman, 1973). For example, dream analysis is very useful as a tool for getting an assessment of suicidal risk (Hammer, 1972). Dreams can be useful in long-term therapy that revolves around transference relations, because they are especially revealing of the changing quality of that relationship (Snyder & Snyder, 1961). Dreams can also be used in brief therapy, but in these cases the interpretation should be close to the manifest level and help catalyze meaningful relevance to current experience (Merrill & Cary, 1974).

Dreams can also be used in problem-centered therapy. One theory of dreaming is that the dream is a rehearsal for action, or an attempted solution of a problem, and consequently the purpose of psychotherapy is to help the patient better understand his creative attempts at problem-solving (Adler, 1956, 1964; Jung, 1966; Wolff, 1952). Experiments with laboratory animals indicate that when they are deprived of dreams, but not sleep, their performance on daytime tests is subsequently impaired. Likewise, human subjects who are experimentally deprived of dreaming develop irritability, loss of concentration, and even some hallucinations (Dement & Fischer, 1960; Greenberg, Pillard & Pearlman, 1968). This evidence of dream deprivation would be consistent with the theory that dreaming is an aid to coping with life's problems.

The aged exhibit distinctive patterns of dreaming. They are less likely to remember their dreams (Kahn & Fischer, 1968). Experimental investigation of sleeping elders indicates that they do in fact dream regularly, though for much shorter periods (Kahn & Fischer, 1969). These differences between age groups hold even when such factors as CBS are taken into account (Kahn, Fischer, & Lieberman, 1969; Kramer, Roth & Trinder, 1975). Investigation of the dream content of elders reveals a preoccupation with diminished resources and loss (Barad, Altschuler & Goldfarb, 1961; Altschuler, Barad & Goldfarb,

1963; Hall, 1966). This is directly related to their life situations. Two examples of these types of dreams follow.

> I was driving my truck up a mountain road to visit my daughter's house. The road was very bumpy and a jar of jam spilled off the shelf and onto my neck. At the house there was a big party. I started to bake some bread but then went upstairs to tidy up. When I came down, the bread was burned. I was very angry at my daughter for allowing this.

> I noticed a thread in my mouth. I started to pull it out. Then I felt a twinge of pain and saw a piece of flesh attached to the thread. I kept pulling and noticed several feet of it come out. Then I thought that it must be my tongue. It looked like a salami and had the texture of a balloon. I was a little worried that someone would see me, and so I tried to put the tongue back into my mouth. It made my mouth feel too full, and I thought that I would have trouble talking.

The important thing for the geriatric psychotherapist is not the specific patterns of dreaming in elders, but the degree to which dreams can be used as a diagnostic, prognostic, and therapeutic tool. Reduced dream recall and dream content associated with loss, misfortune, and incompetence are not very encouraging indications. Barad, Altschuler and Goldfarb's conclusion is worth repeating: "The findings leave little doubt that the aged person is capable of sensitive emotional response, even in the presence of organic brain damage" (1961, p. 424).

To initiate dream therapy with a patient, the method of Mahrer (1971) is useful. It includes seven steps.

1. The patient selects a dream that is recent, clear, and intense.
2. The dream is one that was recorded in the morning upon awakening.
3. In the therapeutic session, associations are made to recent events.

4. The patient and the therapist together attempt to identify the motivation.
5. The critical life event is identified.
6. The patient experiences the motivation.
7. New behavior is facilitated.

In following these steps, try to get the patient to alter his dream content via suggestion. The result is that the patient will recycle his attitudes, dream experiences, and even his behavior (Garfield, 1975; Corriere & Hart 1977). The suggestion helps to alter dream content, and this leads to changes in the dreamer's self-concept and experience.

The approach outlined above is not the only one that can be used with the elders. Grotjahn (1955) used the old psychoanalytic method to interpret the following dream of a 70-year-old woman.

> I went with you in my garden and we walked into the part with the strawberries. They were big, juicy, just ripe, and ready to be picked. We admired them, we picked every one up singly, looked at them, and wrapped one up in white tissue paper. Then we put them into a little box to eat later.

Grotjahn's interpretation of this dream is that it showed "undisguised sexual symbolism" and commented on the evolving transference relationship. Rosenthal (1959) used psychoanalytic techniques, including dream interpretation, successfully with geriatric patients.

In practice, different types of dreams and patients require different approaches. One type of dream told by some patients is the distressing dream. These patients need reassurance that the dream does not portend anything bad, and that they are not morally culpable for having had the dream. An 81-year-old woman had the following dream and was extremely ashamed of it.

> I was in bed with my sister. We wanted to have sex together, but did not have a rubber. Finally I saw another couple in bed, and while they were not looking, I stole a large yellow rubber from them.

The dreamer felt very guilty about this dream. She swore that she and her sister had never had any type of erotic relationship and denied any lesbian desires. Her greatest fear was that the dream meant that she was really homosexual, and she feared that this would cause her much suffering in divine judgment. This patient needed a little reassurance that dreams often embellish or disguise our true fears and desires with symbols. The patient did feel very close to her sister, but had not seen her in a month, even though she lived on the same side of town. Two days before the dream, the patient noticed a sale on bananas at a market near her sister's house. The patient really wanted to visit the sister and use her shopping as an excuse. The therapist explained to the patient that the banana was the tool which was used to facilitate contact with her sister, and perhaps the dream symbolized that into a rubber, a device for facilitating sexual contact. The patient was greatly relieved upon hearing these explanations.

Another example of a distressing dream comes from a 62-year-old man who recently converted to a fundamentalist sect.

> I was urinating on little children who were in diapers. Whomever was urinated upon was the Antichrist. I then turned to the scriptures and read that people should shit thin, like the noses of foxes.

The dreamer, who was not in therapy either during or after this dream report, reacted to this dream in different ways. On the one hand, he felt it was a dirty dream, and was somewhat embarassed to reveal it, while on the other, he seemed to hope that it was an inspired prophecy, and wanted someone else to aid in its proper interpretation. This dreamer was instructed that bodily states (hunger, thirst, the need for elimination) during sleep could influence dream content, and also that presleep activities (in this case, scripture reading) tended to recur in dreams. This interpretation was especially likely in this case, because the dream was poorly developed in theme, and loosely connected. The dreamer was simultaneously relieved and disappointed upon hearing this, but he did not get over his obsession with the dream.

Distressing dreams tend to be produced when patients are taken off a minor tranquilizer that has been suppressing dreams. the amount of dream time then greatly increases, and sometimes the dreams become more intense and colorful. An 80-year-old man had the following dream.

> I saw Arizona state troopers, dressed in cowboy outfits, on horseback riding around in a circle. They were firing shots in the air and making noises like Indians. They were riding around a farmhouse as if they were holding it in siege. Then the house rose into the sky. It became two dimensional and whirled about, like a kite made of paper or plastic. Then my son and I ran into a church, but the Mafia men followed us. My son told me that I should go back to Chicago, because Daley would give me asylum there, but I thought that the Mafia was too powerful in that city. Then we got in my old car and drove away. Then the Russian army came and shot at us, killing my son. At this time, we were stopped off the road. I got back into the car and drove away, just as it started to rain very heavily, like Chicago in the spring. Helicopters and old World War I biplanes followed me. One biplane fell and the tip of its wing bounced off several brightly colored Chinese lanterns, which turned into a volcano and then swallowed the plane. Then I woke up with my heart pounding.

The patient had no real desire to work with the dream and interpret it. What he really wanted and needed was reassurance. He had never dreamed so vividly in the past.

He feared that the dream might be a bad omen, or that he was losing his mind and in danger of hallucinating. When he learned the role of tranquilizer withdrawal in producing his dreams, he could understand that the situation was temporary and not serious.

One widower had the following dream which expressed one of his fears.

> I was walking down the street. When I got underneath the elevated tracks, I saw a language book for learning German. The dialogues had bulldog cartoon characters dressed up in modern, sexy clothes. They had sex and one bulldog was angry because he got VD.

This man had been widowed for several months and had just resumed sexual relations. He reflected that he had always been true to his wife while she lived, except for one time when he was stationed in Germany. Although he denied any guilt feelings about having sex now, it was clear that he had not reintegrated such activity into his total life-style. He conceded this point, but said that he was not really bothered by it, although he was grateful for the insight.

Sometimes dreams can demonstrate to the dreamer that his life-style involves a way of coping that is ineffective or frustrating to his true goals. A 60-year-old, hard-driving, self-made man had the following dream.

> There was a contest outside of this old European church. Maybe it was a cathedral. Everything looked like Shakespeare's English homeland. I had a stick or club in my hand and tried to fight my way through objects and people who tried to prevent me from going any further. The children gave me the most trouble, but I wiped them out with my club. Finally, I came to the statue or skeleton underneath the church. I knew that it represented the man who could not be conquered. I clubbed at him and knocked off a part of his hand. The crowd cheered me, but I began to wonder if it was

good to be down there below the church instead of up
above.

Although the dreamer was a renowned philanthropist,
he interpreted his own dream as indicating that he had
neglected human needs and the teachings of the church in
his blind quest for success, and that his quest had ultimately
destroyed his true spirit. He expressed a desire to retire
and devote more of his time to good causes.

The last chapter pointed out that insight does not always, by itself, lead to changed thought or behavior. Training is a much more efficient therapy, and dreams can be
used to facilitate the training process. Training takes place
when the therapist and patient work through a series of
dreams, one at a time, and the therapist provides suggestions which are recycled into the patient's later dreams.
This allows a patient to experience a dream in which he
ceases to become a victim, but is transformed into the vic-
tor or star. This elevates self-concept and has an effect on
his waking life (Faraday, 1972, 1974; Garfield, 1975; Corriere & Hart, 1977). The dream functions as a training
period in which the patient rehearses positive thinking and
doing.

One of the most common problems that interferes
with geriatric coping is a pervasive sense of helplessness.
This is portrayed in many dreams, and can be modified by
interpretation and recycling. A 61-year-old woman reported the following dream.

> I saw two little girls attacked by a black man who wanted to
> rape them. The older one was being raped. The man laid
> down, face up, and put her on top of him. The younger girl
> watched and screamed for help. I wanted to help, but felt
> immobile, due to fear I guess. Later I felt really bad, like I
> should have done something.

The dreamer was instructed to record her dreams
upon awakening, and to spend an extra two minutes before

arising to contemplate how she would have changed her dream if she could. She was told that in dreams, anything is possible. She could give herself superhuman powers and attack an army of husky rapists. The important thing that she had to do was act the way she really wanted to act.

A few weeks later she reported that although she had been skeptical of the method, she had given it a try, and noticed a gradual improvement in dream content, especially concerning her own role in the dreams. At this time she reported the following dream.

> I was at a party and saw my teenage granddaughter. She was obviously distressed, and then started to cry and take off her clothes. She exposed both breasts. I came and took a table cloth, covered her up, and brought her in the next room to talk to her. She explained that she was very confused and had some problems with her friends. I told her to be less concerned about her friends and more about her father, who loved her very much. Then both my granddaughter and I felt very good.

The dreamer enjoyed this dream very much, especially the feeling of being so close to her granddaughter. No real embarrassment was experienced by the dreamer in the first part of the dream. Her effective actions to deal with the problem precluded the development of nervousness, worry, or distressing emotions. Furthermore, the dreamer said that she had been able to carry that good feeling in the dream all throughout the day. She also felt that she could deepen her relationship with her family.

A 67-year-old man reported the following dream.

> I was walking home along the El Camino Real. I knew I had just passed Menlo Park and was now in Atherton. On the east side of the highway there were these rock houses, like ruins I saw in Egypt and Mexico. I wanted to go in one and look for treasure, but I was afraid some tough slum kids from East Palo Alto might be in there just waiting to jump me.

The dreamer's fear had made him helpless and afraid to explore and seek treasure. American elders, because of their fear of crime, are often afraid to get out and explore the good things that life still has to offer. To make life more meaningful for them, it is necessary to build up their confidence so that they will not be afraid to keep on living somewhat adventurously. This dreamer was told to record his dreams, contemplate them, and reflect on how he would change them to make life more satisfying. A month later he reported the following dream.

> My wife and I were walking to New York City by way of an underground tunnel under the Hudson River. Two men ran up from behind and stole my wallet and then ran away. We went to a large, old hotel in the city. It had been very elegant in its day, and we were somewhat disappointed to see it so run-down. Then I noticed the robbers and their wives living in the hotel. Then I went to a lecture about art given by Nasser. He was very short and stocky in the dream. Then he hugged all of his students, including me. My wife and I wanted to return to California, but just as we were about to check out of the hotel, we saw the robbers and their wives leaving, and decided to wait for another bus. Then we returned to a spacious mansion in California where my paintings hung. There was one special painting that I had there, one with different boxes with different symbols inside of it. One of the boxes was blank. I had both the original painting and a copy. Some robbers came and stole the copy, but I knew where they took it, so I went and stole it back. They came back for the original, and cut through the window. I shotgunned them both.

The dreamer had recently taken up art as a hobby. His real home was lavish and decorated with some of his work, but the dream had a grandiose mansion with numerous paintings. The dreamer is Jewish and had always despised Nasser. He interpreted that segment of the dream as indicating that sometimes we can learn something even from the people that we dislike. Furthermore, the dreamer did not flinch or get nervous when he was hugged by Nasser. I interpreted the painting with the boxes containing symbols to be his life, which had been very rich with the dreamer having done many things and served in different roles. The one blank box signified that the life was not yet over, and that more rich experiences could be created. The dreamer's experience with the robbers indicated that he was still a bit cautious under some circumstances, and also unwilling to react when his loss was only monetary, but he acted directly and effectively over what was most important. His dream symbolizes his determination to prevent anyone or anything from stealing his opportunity to make his life interesting and meaningful.

Dreams can also be used to help diagnose and resolve anxiety or other fears about growing old. The following dream was reported by a 51-year-old man. He was suffering from cancer and his chances for living more than a couple of years seemed to be pretty slim.

> I was in Peru and heard of a half-mile high tidal wave coming. Then I saw a terracotta picture of an ancient Inca man who was running from a tidal wave.

The dreamer reported that his main emotion during the dream was not fear, but fascination with the picture. I interpreted this dream to mean that the portent of death did not paralyze him with fear. In fact, the dreamer was coming to see that his situation was not unique in history. Other people have been in similar positions. This interpretation seemed most consoling to the dreamer.

A 40-year-old terminally ill cancer patient, a woman, told me this dream two weeks before she died.

> I was with Gloria (the therapist's wife) and we were rototilling and hoeing the garden at your new home. We wanted to plant some seeds, but some man came and said that it was not the right time yet. We were very disappointed.

The dreamer had never had children. When she left, her parting words to me were, "I hope you and Gloria have a lot of nice babies." The dream symbolized her wish to live on vicariously through us. The seeds represent children, and her disappointment that in two years of marriage my wife and I had not produced any offspring.

Another childless woman experienced these anxiety dreams, although she was not stricken with a terminal illness.

> I was watching an elderly couple. Both of them were very wrinkled. The lady was wearing some beautiful pearls. Then she got out a small jar of water and put it on her face, as if it were some sort of makeup.

The meaning of this dream was made more clear by another dream she had a week later.

> I was a young girl again. I was back in Omaha. I crawled over a fence in hopes of stealing some honey from a hive. Then I heard someone say, "Now it's Ruth's turn." (Ruth is my younger sister with five children.) I secretly delighted upon hearing this because I hoped she would get stung. Then I could see her go after the honey, and wince as she was being stung. Then a man on a large horse rode up. I was right under the horse's head so the man could not see me. Then someone said, "Why don't you get her? Because she's Jewish?"

Children are symbolized by the pearls (which are the result of a grain of sand gestating in an oyster), and also by the honey in the second dream. The dreamer envied the other older couples who always talked about their children, and also her sister. But the dreamer was consoled by the fact that her sister's life with the kids has had its painful moments as well. The dreamer interpreted the man on horseback as her ex-husband, whom she described as a man more interested in other things than in her, and a man who never wanted kids. The dreamer was encouraged to become more active in intellectual affairs, and attended several slide and lecture shows at a local community college. Several of these were on local history and archaeology. A month later she reported the following dream.

> I was walking around the mountains and could see San Francisco ahead, and the bay on one side and the ocean on the other. The mountains were treeless in the dream. They were like dried mud mounds. I saw steam coming out of one of the mounds, and thought that it might be related to volcanic or earthquake activities. I dug into the mound and saw potatoes and other things growing, nourished by the steam. Then I saw an old Indian temple which had been converted into a gold-rush era store. Then I saw people of various ethnic groups who had emigrated to California in the last century.

The dream was interpreted to mean that the dreamer was really very happy in California, and although she had been transplanted there, she had become part of California history and had contributed to it through her career activities. This seemed to be a most satisfactory interpretation for the dreamer.

Another woman, perhaps experiencing some crisis related to the bio-psycho-social events of middle age, reported the following recurring dream.

> I was walking around a train accident, collecting parts of bodies. Then someone came and asked for the flesh to make soap. I let them have it. Then someone asked me for the bones to make soup, and I became very upset.

This dream occurred on the eve of the thirty-third aniversary of the day that the dreamer's family was taken away on a train to a concentration camp. The dreamer could never see the purpose in the deaths of her parents. I reminded the dreamer that we should not ask about the purpose of death, but of life. The dreamer's parents had always lived very purposive lives, and they had given birth to a daughter (the dreamer) who had raised five children, all of whom seemed to be on their way to successful lives. The next week, the dreamer reported the following.

> All my family was gathered together at a large picnic. There were distant relatives I had not seen since childhood. We went to the lake and swam. Then I wanted to take a picture, and there were about 200 people that I wanted to get in. They decided to climb a tree and pose. First they sat on the boughs. Then they stood, but there was a fear of falling, so they sat down again.

The dreamer really enjoyed this dream, and awakened with a great sense of relief. The dream was interpreted to mean that her family life had been a very rich experience in the past and present, and would continue to be so in the future.

The dreams of elders are also useful in determining what anxiety is associated with entering a nursing home or residential care facility. A 76-year-old man had this dream.

> My wife and had just purchased a new home. I began to water some of the plants in the yard, and then realized that I was not on my own property. I felt very bad, because of the water rationing. We went into our home and noticed that it was much more elegant than we had remembered. There was a gigantic party inside. In the living room there was a sunken bath with Oriental people. My wife and I started to speak Italian so that they would not be able to understand us.

The dreamer and his wife had been contemplating moving into an apartment complex for senior citizens. The dreamer admitted having serious reservations about abandoning his garden, which had proved such a meaningful activity for him, and also about the great number of minority workers (particularly Orientals) who worked at the complex. He feared that they would not be able to understand him.

This dream was reported by an 81-year-old man, recently paralyzed on one side by a stroke.

> I was at the pool and tennis club in San Francisco. I was sunbathing, lying down on my stomach wearing only my underpants. It seemed like a reunion of the people that I had worked with on an engineering project in Mexico during the 1930s. Then I saw Jackie, the bratty teenage daughter of a Mexican family I knew. She ran up and pulled my underwear down and shouted, "Cacas!" I was greatly embarrassed and awoke, believing that I had defecated in my sleep. I woke up my wife and asked for assistance, but then we found nothing.

The dreamer had spent some time in a nursing home after his stroke, and recalled that he greatly objected to the way some of the teenage aides treated him like a baby, and to the way they handled his penis to help him urinate.

Therapists should also analyze their own dreams to help identify countertransference patterns that may not be therapeutic. One therapist who had just started working with elders related the following pair of dreams which he had had in the same week.

> I was with a slender blond woman of 64 who complained that she had been a widow for 11 years and misses sex. Then she undressed and came over to be with me.

> I was having sex with an older woman whom I had dated before meeting my present wife. We were having sex right in the middle of the road by my home. Then we walked hand in hand down to my house, about a hundred feet away. I told her that I really should get sterilized. She said, "Are you going to cut your peeper off?" I explained the process of vasectomy to her. She urged that we resume our relationship on a permanent basis. She stopped walking when I entered my yard. I ignored her and just kept on walking to my front door. My wife opened it, and came out to greet me. We

hugged and embraced. She then showed me the boxes of patterns for old ladies' dresses. She hugged me again.

This therapist was able to admit that he had always considered older women attractive, and was somewhat fearful of how he would handle the situation if one of them actually made a pass at him. A very good solution is offered by the second dream. The therapist can turn away (or cut off) his past sexual experiences and attachments to older woman and embrace his wife. Furthermore, he can compartmentalize, or box, his relations with elders.

Another male therapist reported the following dreams.

I went to downtown Palo Alto to rent an apartment. I found the building on the corner. It looked like a one-story house, but actually it had three apartments in it. I talked to the old lady who ran the apartments. We spoke of my education and work. Then she noticed that one of her stockings was down. She raised her dress slightly to take the stocking all the way off, and finally I could see her furry grey patch of hair between her legs. I got very excited and wondered if she would want to have sex with me right there. But I noticed a black woman cleaning up in the kitchen. I felt very relieved because then I knew that she would not want to have sex with me.

I went down to the radio station where I worked five years ago. It was 6:00 AM and time to begin broadcasting. An older woman chased me around the building, wanting to touch "that cute announcer." I finally got inside without her getting in. I worried because it was late, and all the equipment was in disarray. I struggled frantically to put it back together. My coworkers came in and helped me get everything ready. It was almost 7:00 AM and the situation was really getting to me. I was so worried about getting on the air an hour late. I asked for the logs, and was told that everything was now written on magic slates which were erasable by lifting the sheet off the back. I began to scribble a few words, and then someone took the slate and wrote in big letters, "AUTHORITY."

This therapist-in-training was having problems with his first patient, a widow who tried to manipulate him. He thought that the idea of coming across as more of an authority figure would be the best approach, even though it was now a little late for that. The dream also pointed out that he felt himself to be relying on the other members of the team right now for guidance in the case.

SUMMARY

This chapter discusses the use of dream interpretation in geriatric psychotherapy. Dreams can be used as diagnostic, prognostic, and therapeutic tools. Patients with distressing dreams need to be calmed by an explanation of the dream mechanism. Dreams can also be used to furnish insight. A therapeutic tool that is most effective is using a series of dreams and recycling the dreamer's feelings and actions so that self-concept is raised and proper behavior is rehearsed. The live review process can be facilitated by dreams that affirm the richness of one's life, or one's link to the past or future. Dreams are especially useful in understanding and combating the kind of anxiety found in patients who are entering an institution or who are terminally ill. Therapists, especially at the beginning of their work in geriatrics, can benefit from studying their own dreams.

Chapter 11

GROUP THERAPY

Group therapy, in which one or two therapists treat several patients together, is a more efficient use of mental health personnel. This makes sense with elders, in whom the incidence of psychopathology is higher and economic resources are often limited. The outstanding pioneer studies in geriatric psychotherapy are those of Linden (1953) and Wolff (1957, 1962). Both reported high rates of improvement for institutionalized elders involved in group therapy. Among Linden's senile patients, discharge rates rose to 45%, which was several times higher than rates for comparably diagnosed untreated patients. For Wolff (1957), 80% of the patients improved, and 50% were significantly improved.

Wolff (1957) noted two drawbacks to group therapy: its inability to attend to the specific needs of the withdrawn patient, and the lack of insight because the conversation remains on a superficial level. However, those factors were more than offset by numerous advantages. According to Wolff (1957), group therapy for elders

1. takes most institutionalized patients out of their withdrawn state;
2. awakens their interest in others;
3. provides opportunities for new friendships;
4. is not as alarming as a private office visit with a therapist;
5. provides group control over excessive dependency and temper tantrums;
6. promotes self-confidence and esteem by having many listeners; and
7. reduces illusions of grandeur and paranoia through realistic mutual criticism.

Linden (1953) claimed a benefit even for quiet and undemonstrative group members. They too are able to profit from the group dynamics even without verbal participation. The only contraindications for this group therapy would be severe communication disorders (deafness or speech impediments) or pronounced hostility due to paranoia or schizophrenia (Wolff, 1957).

CBS is *not* a contraindication. All of Linden's patients were classified as "senile." Wolff (1957, 1962), who dealt with patients with different diagnoses, claimed that he achieved his best results with CBS patients. Other favorable experiences with group psychotherapy were reported by Rustin and Wolk (1963), Shere (1964), Feil (1967), Yalom and Terrazas (1968), Manaster (1972), and Saul and Saul (1974). Burnside (1970) reviewed the literature up to that point.

What should be the focus of group therapy? To a large extent this must depend on the nature of the group. Is it a group of grieving widows? disenchanted retirees? poorly acculturated Latinos? long-term institutionalized mental patients? CVA victims? Each group has specific problems common to its members. Since the purpose of geriatric psychotherapy, with individuals or groups, is to solve problems, the different types of problems encountered by different groups require different foci. Nevertheless, there are certain common themes that can be applied to most, if not all, geriatric psychotherapy groups.

First, the patients can benefit just by being in each other's presence and trying to communicate. Interaction is a significant benefit, especially for the socially withdrawn patient. It seems too obvious to mention that group therapy facilitates social interaction, but all too often, this is taken for granted. This is a mistake. Interaction among elders is sometimes difficult to facilitate. Many times I have observed long-term patients in nursing homes and residential care facilities who refer to each other as "hey, you" and "that man." While such behavior can be caused by failing memories, it can also be due to the fact that these different residents were never really brought into successful interaction.

Beyond this, there is the danger that some activities of group psychotherapy can jeopardize interaction. Many elders, especially those with psychopathologies, are not going to respond well to therapists who stress confrontation, insight, or abreaction, and they usually tend to assume a defensive posture in such groups. When group therapy fosters interactions and safeguards them by avoiding activities for which the members are not prepared, the benefits of interaction can be realized. When interaction does take place, it can lead to the formation of individual friendships, increased sociability outside of the group, and in some cases, group cohesiveness (Wolff, 1962; Yalom & Terrazas, 1968; Manaster, 1972). The benefits are the desirable extensions of the initial interactions, but the therapists should not feel that they are requisite for the group project to be a success. Too high an expectation on the therapist's part can lead to his own disillusionment, which is all too readily transmitted to the patients. One more point needs mention. To stimulate interaction, frequent brief sessions are preferable to hour-long or marathon sessions. Manaster (1972) started with 15 minutes and worked up to 40.

Second, group therapy with elders should focus on reality. While this sounds obvious to those working with elders, it is not obvious to those who have done group work with younger adults. Much group work, especially on the West Coast, emphasizes fantasy. Such an approach may be useful with certain types of patients. In general, it should not become the focus of group work with elders. Limited use of guided fantasies may be employed for specific purposes, when the therapist knows full well what reality-based goals will be served by such experiences. Some of the reality factors that should receive emphasis are specific goals related to present life situations and to the strengths and limitations of the patients (Yalom & Terrazas, 1968).

Third, group work can assist the life review process. Group exposure gives each patient the chance to hear how others lived their lives. It also gives him the opportunity to talk about his own life and to have others react to it. The ninth chapter mentioned life review and pointed out that it could be used to foster effective present coping, but that it could also lead to brooding and a sense of despair. The same is true of group therapy and its relation to the life review. The group must be structured so that the patient will receive positive reinforcement for recounts of effective coping, and nonreinforcement (but supportive encouragement) for ineffective coping.

Fourth, group therapy should include some form of remotivation. For geriatric populations remotivation therapy is superior to conventional group therapy without motivation (Birkett & Boltuch, 1973). This remotivation ties in nicely with the focus on reality and the life review.

The former defines the elders' tasks and the means at their disposal; the latter demonstrates that they have coped successfully in the past. The purpose of the group is to motivate them to use their own present resources to cope with their own present problems. Such motivation is made possible by proper leadership, structure, and language.

MODELS FOR GERIATRIC GROUP THERAPY

One excellent approach to group therapy, which integrates leadership, structure, and language, is that of Low (1950). Low was an old-time neurologist and psychiatrist from the Vienna Adlerian circle. After moving to Chicago, he elaborated on his own theory of mental illness. He preserved some of Adler's basic theories, specifically that the neurotic is perfectionistic and becomes dejected because his own self-imposed standards are often unrealistically high. Furthermore, Low believed that the proper treatment for psychopathology was medical management plus training the patient to act, think, and relate to others in a nonpathological way. Guided by these simple beliefs, Low set up Recovery in 1937. Recovery is a type of peer therapy similar to Alcoholics Anonymous. Members are taught a specific terminology which they are to use at group meetings and in their everyday lives. The words and slogans are referred to as the Recovery language.

One slogan that the members repeat over and over again is that "feelings are not reality." This means that the type of judgments we make and the kind of emotions we experience under mental disorder do not portray reality accurately. and that we must stop thinking and acting as if they did. If a member feels physically exhausted and on the verge of a "nervous breakdown," he is told by the group that such feelings do not necessarily reflect the true state of his body. Likewise, if a member complains that fear paralyzes his actions, the group reminds him that there is nothing wrong with his nervous system, and that such paralysis is only a delusion. The group will empathize with a member, but only to the point of concurring that such symptoms are distressing. The group may do this by testimonials, in which they individually recount how bad their own symptoms were, but how they brought them under control by recognizing that they were not to be regarded as dangerous, only distressing. Members are prohibited from making any kind of diagnosis of themselves. "Only doctors can diagnose." This preserves the physicians' authority and prevents the patients from construing normal or minor problems as major ones.

Along with physical symptoms, members are trained to avoid overinterpreting everyday frustrations and disappointments. The Recovery term for these is "triviality." The senior members of the group recount what they did during the week, how they coped with trivialities, and how the same kinds of provocations would have undone them before Recovery training. For the first few times, the new members do not speak; they only listen to these testimonials and to selected readings from Low's works.

When the new member finally reports on his own behavior, reports of success are positively reinforced by the group. Reports of fear or anger in confronting trivialities are not castigated. The member is told that he is still new, and that he needs more Recovery training, and that in time he will be able to succeed. He is reminded that anger is his own worst enemy, that it is still uncontrolled, but that it is not uncontrollable. Although the failing member is accepted, his attempts to give an excuse are not. The group refuses to consider his heredity (for example, a "nervous constitution") or environmental factors. Failure to control one's own emotions is attributed to insufficient training and to no other cause.

Essentially, the Recovery group's success is the result of an alteration of self-concept and training in healthy coping skills. Attempts at insight and getting in touch with feelings are precluded. Specifically, the members are trained in the following skills and attitudes.

First, they are trained to "spot" the beginning of a vicious cycle in which they allow fear or anger full sway and magnify minor physical symptoms or trivialities into major anxiety, depression, or blowups. This is a type of self-monitoring similar to those discussed in the chapter on behavioral modification.

Second, Recovery members are taught that they can and should control their muscles. The feeling of being paralyzed, or of being in a blind rage, is just that—a feeling, and not a reality. The motor nerves still hook up the brain with the muscle, and the patient can always command his muscles to move.

Third, he is taught to "endorse" himself. In other words, when he succeeds in spotting the vicious cycle and manages to stifle it by controlling his thoughts and muscles, the patient is supposed to tell himself "well done." This has a dual function. It raises self-concept, as if one were saying, "I have mastered my own thoughts and actions, and I really appreciate myself for it." Furthermore, this endorsement process serves as a kind of positive reinforcement and conditions the individual to cope effectively in the future.

Fourth, and finally, the Recovery member is taught to be group-centered rather than self-centered. The self-centered individual runs the risk of developing perfectionistic standards and thereby of regarding his less-than-perfect behavior as dangerously abnormal. The group discussion of past experiences provides realistic, objective standards of what is normal, and indicates that distressing symptoms and frustrations are common, but manageable. Of course, above and beyond these goals, Recovery succeeds in building interaction, and even deep caring and responsibility for the other members.

It is difficult to judge objectively the effectiveness of the Recovery program. The case studies and testimonials of individual members are impressive. Statistical evaluation would be impossible, for several reasons. First, Recovery members are frequently patients who have been discharged from mental hospitals, and thus they probably over-represent the highly motivated patients who have the best prospects for cure. Second, many of the Recovery members receive other forms of treatment concurrently with their participation in the Recovery group. Some patients are receiving medication and others are getting individual psychotherapy. Since there are no dues or fees, attendance at Recovery meetings tends to be somewhat haphazard, and the dropout rate is high.

Nevertheless, anyone who has been to a Recovery meeting and has had a chance to know some long-term members is deeply impressed. I am convinced that Recovery offers one of the best models for what group therapy can do to promote mental health. Recovery has won widespread acceptance among physicians and psychiatrists, perhaps because of its abiding respect for medical authority. Many Recovery members are encouraged to go by their physicians. Unfortunately, Recovery is not well known outside of medical circles, and many psychologists who dogmatically adhere to insight, abreaction, or feelings are most unsympathetic with Revovery's aims.

Recovery represents an impressive harmony of authority, structure, and language. In many group therapies, one or more of these elements are lacking; usually the results are unfortunate, and only rarely disastrous. The lack of clear-cut leadership, a real stumbling block in a geriatric group, can take two forms: the lack of any leadership, or competing claims for leadership. The former frequently occurs when the patients are merely thrown together and it is presumed that the group will somehow generate its own energy, and that this energy will magically motivate the group members and guide them through therapeutic activity. To be sure, the group does generate certain dynamics, which can be systematically studied, understood, and controlled, but this only points to the need for someone or something to control the group dynamics. When there is no leader, it becomes difficult to keep the group's activity within the proper structure or even directed toward the proper goals.

The problem of competing leadership is especially relevant to geriatric groups. On one occasion I had a role in setting up a group therapy project for aged Latinos for the county mental health department. A priest and I organized a meeting for some of the older members of the Latino community. He explained the psychotherapeutic nature of the group being proposed, and the idea was generally well received. At the same meeting there was a community worker who also spoke to the people present. She explained her hopes that the Latino elders could organize themselves into an effective political force to safeguard themselves and assure themselves of further government services.

The leadership of the group had been assigned to two psychiatric social workers from the mental health department. To their dismay, the meetings were also attended by community workers and self-styled activists and representatives of various causes. These interlopers attempted to use the assembled Latino elders for their own political designs. At one meeting, the entire time allotted for the group was taken up by these nonauthorized personnel. This left the group members very confused about what the purpose of the group really was. The designated co-therapists turned to the priest and me for help. Since we were there at the group's inception, and the natural authority figures for the Latino elders, we reaffirmed the psychotherapeutic purpose of the group and proscribed further visits from uninvited, unauthorized personnel.

The group seemed to go along quite well after then, and I attribute this success solely to the abilities of the co-therapists and the motivation of the group members. In retrospect, the issue of leadership when the group started was probably as confusing as could be. Just who the leader was had never been made clear. Was it I? the priest? the co-therapists? The best way of avoiding these types of problems is to have the group formed and managed by the same person. It is also helpful if the group members are somewhat familiar with the therapist before the group is formed. This can be accomplished by individual therapy. Such prior establishment of a person as a leader makes the group leadership more clear-cut from the beginning.

Even though Recovery groups are lay (peer) led, the leadership is very clear-cut. Leaders go through a long period of training and apprenticeship. Such leadership is also facilitated by the structure of the Recovery meeting. The first part of the meeting centers around Low's writings. Then the discussion takes place, and the experienced members are allowed to speak. This type of structure guides the group toward the realization of its goals. Structure also eases a lot of initial tension on the part of first-time members, especially if the structure is explained to them and is comprehended. Structure, enforced by a strong leader, also resolves such uncertainties as, "Have we started yet?"

Psychotherapy alleviates psychopathological behavior only inasmuch as it succeeds in training patients to think and behave in nonpathological ways. Therefore we can think in terms of re-educating the patient in mental health. As in any type of educational process, group therapy has its "teaching moments"—moments when something concrete can be learned. This is obvious when the therapy focuses on insight, abreaction, or feelings. There are times when

the patients come very close to achieving something curative. But there is also the danger that the group action or
conversation will shift to something else, and that this
teaching moment will be lost. The risk can be minimized by
strong leadership or by a structure that makes sure that the
group gets as much as it can out of each participant's responses.

In Recovery, each person who shares his experience
with the group follows a written list of steps, which are read
to the group at the beginning of the meeting. This keeps
the speaker brief and to the point when describing his
experience, and makes sure that he does not get side-
tracked by discussing his feelings. He completes his point
by describing how he used (or failed to use) Recovery techniques, and what it was like for him before he had mastered
them. The next unwritten step is for the group to respond,
either by praising the member's success or by reassuring
him that he will succeed after he has had more training and
practice. In this way, the structure of Recovery makes the
most of each teaching moment and marks a clear conclusion to each member's contribution. The absence of such
a structure puts the burden on the leader, who must frequently cut in and make sure that each of the speakers and
the group in general gets out of each segment of the
group's activity the maximum possible gain.

There are some excellent therapists who can operate
this way, in the absence of a rigid structure. They succeed
only when the group accepts their leadership. One argument against structure is that it inhibits the expression of
the patient's feelings. It certainly does. In the absence of
clear-cut leadership and structure, training and insight are
most difficult to attain. The more unstructured the group
becomes, the more it becomes a free-for-all competition for
attention, and whoever expresses the most anxiety, anger,
love, joy, or emotion in general wins. The group's structure
can be internalized by each patient so that he develops

comparably ordered and healthy thought and action. Another argument against structure is that the therapeutic outcome depends more on the personality of the leader than on structure. This is a moot point. What is important is that structure is not inimical to the beneficial effect of the leader's personality. Furthermore, it is easier to internalize the structure of the group than the personality of its leader.

Each human culture has its own language, without which they would not be able to communicate. The same is true of each therapy group. It needs a common set of terms. One of the greatest advantages of Recovery groups is that they have a special language. Members are not permitted to use any other language. If they use their private terms, they are accused of using neurotic logic. The use of a common language precludes the patient's use of the language of his individual therapy—Freudian, Rogerian, or whatever. The common language also helps to maintain structure. The lack of a common language, or the use of private languages or languages external to the group, tends to retard the efficiency of the group process. I observed one young adult group that included one woman who was a devotee of EST. She spoke about being "centered" and having her "body space." She was truly vivacious and entertained the group, even though her language succeeded only in obfuscating the transmission of her own experience to the rest of the group. The same group also contained some followers of popularized Oriental religions. They talked about karma and Tao and were similarly more entertaining than helpful. In my opinion, the only person who contributed something of value to that group was one blue-collar worker who used plain English, unadulterated by pop theories or embellishments from literary metaphor, to talk about his problems the way he tried to deal with them.

Another real risk with allowing loosely defined terms or unstructured conversation within the group is that someone will take offense even when there is no intent to offend. Two examples spring to my mind. In one group there was little formal structure, and frequently when the group was large, it would break down into several small groups. One time one of the small groups heard an old joke of rural Mexican origin told by the oldest member of the group. For some strange reason, another women in another group overheard bits and pieces of the conversation and became incensed, because she thought that the joke had been directed against her. She verbally expressed her anger, and drove the innocent joke-teller to tears. When the group rallied and comforted their eldest member, the indignant member walked out and did not return.

In another example from a different group of women of varied age, the problem arose when one woman talked about her experiences with her grandchild. She said the boy was about five and was just learning to distinguish between right and wrong. She quoted the boy as saying, "There are two parts to everybody's brain. One part is good and the other is bad. I can hear both, but I know that I should only listen to the good." The group conversation continued as other members talked about their grandchildren, and about how kids need a certain degree of independence in order to try things and learn things by trial and error. Then the therapist called on the youngest group member, an attractive divorcee of 43 who had been silent up to this point. "Well," she said, "I am really embarrassed to say how I feel today, and bring it out in the open, especially with our guest [indicating my presence] here today, but I am really upset with X [the patient who had initiated the conversation about grandchildren]." X responded at this point, and indicated that she did not know what she had done to anger anyone, and this had certainly not been her intention. The young patient continued, "You offended me very much right here in this group, in front of everyone, including Dr. Brink. You said that half of my brain was bad." X was very apologetic and explained that the words had been those of her grandson, and that in repeating them in front of the group, she had not desired to cast any aspersions on the state of any member's brain.

At this point the male therapist joined in and said that he had not interpreted X's words as an insult to anyone. He then attempted to get a group concensus on this point. However, the young divorcee resumed her attack on X. "I do not have to listen to you when you say my brain is bad. You are the one who was in the mental hospital, and I never went." Now most of the group members began to chatter, saying that it was no sin to go to a mental hospital. Several members who were formerly hospitalized talked about how their treatments had been. Interestingly enough, none of these patients showed any real anger at the young divorcee for her implication that people who had gone to a mental hospital were bad in some way. X at first responded with full composure and stated that she had not been in a mental hospital. The divorcee pursued her attack, "But just last week you said you were in the mental hospital for several months." X explained that it was hospitalization for a heart attack, and re-emphasized that she had never been in a mental hospital. X endured the situation about a minute longer and then packed her things and announced she was leaving. The co-therapists and another group member tried to encourage her to stay, but X said that she would not sit there and listen to such lies and insults. She left the room and slammed the door with great force.

X had been very active in various committees around the community, and it was certain that I would see her again, and the fact that her reputation had been tarnished in my presence had made the situation especially difficult for her to bear. At this time the female therapist tried to explain to the divorcee that she had not responded fairly to X. At first, the divorcee seemed quite proud of herself, reflecting that the basic problem was that she had been unable to confront her tormentors in the past (for example, her husband) and had let them walk all over her. "Now I am learning how to fight and defend myself." The female therapist tried to explain the difference between fighting fairly and unfairly. After a few minutes, the divorcee claimed the ability to understand the difference between the two, and said that she would attempt to behave more fairly in the future, but I doubted her sincerity.

I consider both of the co-therapists to be truly excellent. I believed that they handled the situation as well as could be expected. They had utilized a great deal of strong leadership in the group, and the group itself had evolved a structure over several years of ongoing activity. I attribute the above difficulty solely to a language problem. First of all, none of the members or either of the co-therapists had said anything when X quoted her grandson's remarks about the brain. I was very tempted at that point to clarify that the boy's statements were symbolic and in no way reflected the true nature of the brain's differentiation as it has been scientifically determined. However, I had resolved to maintain my role as a silent observer. The co-therapists told me after the group session that they had both assumed that no one would take the five-year-old's model of the psyche seriously. But there is always the danger of misunderstanding in a group. When the group uses a standardized language, and the therapist circumscribes any other type of language or models, misunderstanding can be controlled.

A second language problem arose about the precise meaning of "fighting" and defending oneself against frustrators. The divorcee had previously explained her expectation that group therapy would help her be able to fight and defend herself. For her these words meant trading insult for insult, and rigidly adhering to a position until the enemy was driven off. The co-therapists assumed too readily that the divorcee was talking in terms of assertiveness. Assertiveness training is an excellent idea for women and elders, but assertiveness needs to be redefined as effective communication of one's desires and effective resistance to unjust manipulation by others. If such language is not clear from the beginning, assertiveness may become equated with aggressiveness.

AGERS ANONYMOUS

When I was in Guadalajara, I worked with several of my graduate students at ITESO to prepare a structure and language that would be appropriate for elders living in the community or in institutions. We felt that the major emphasis should be on helping to motivate elders to make use of their existing talents despite recent heavy losses. We adhered to Adlerian personality theory and therefore felt it best to stimulate social interest in the form of taking responsibility for others. Furthermore, we wanted a guiding philosophy that would be consistent with and mutually reinforcing of basic Judeo-Christian doctrine. Finally, we decided that the Recovery structure and language was the best for group work, and that we should attempt to follow it as much as possible, changing the language to relate specifically to the problems of aging rather than to those of former mental patients. The resulting outline of the group's philosophy is presented below.

Responsibility

1. Responsibility is the ability and desire to respond to other persons.
   a. Passive responsibility is responding to contact initiated by others.
   b. Active responsibility is taking the initiative in making human contacts. All the world's great religions emphasize the necessity of active responsibility.

2. Each person has responsibility for himself on three levels. On each level, one must maintain responsibility with a high level of activity.
   a. Physical: keep the body strong, flexible, and healthy.
   b. Mental: maintain problem-solving ability.
   c. Spiritual: maintain worship, prayer, and fellowship.

Aging

1. In the course of life there are changes in the way we assume responsibility.
   a. There are changes in the persons for whom we are responsible.
   b. There are changes in the manner of our being responsible for them.
   c. But always we are responsible for someone other than ourselves in some way.
2. There are changes in our capacity to assume responsibility.
   a. We have little control over our ability to respond.
      1) Being human is being limited. Only God has infinite capacity to respond.
      2) The process of aging is a process of encountering more limitations.
   b. When we cannot overcome our limitations, we must accept them.

Psychopathology

1. Symptoms of pathological aging:
   a. Lack of satisfaction with life.
   b. Lack of contact with reality.
2. Dynamics that produce these symptoms:
   a. The person who cannot accept his limitations and their implications for his responsibility.
      1) Retirement: liberation from responsibility of maintaining a career; obligation and responsibil-

        ity and opportunity to use these talents in new forms.

  2) Widowhood: liberation from responsibility of loving a spouse; obligation and opportunity to love new persons in new ways.

  3) Chronic physical diseases: these are limitations, never liberations.

 b. The person who tries to use various methods for evading responsibility.

  1) Excess disability: exaggeration of legitimate organic limitations.

  2) Ignoring the demands of the environment to the point where all contact with reality is lost.

  3) Looking for pity from others, instead of looking for ways to serve them.

  4) Shifting blame onto others, instead of accepting the blame.

  5) Developing a pseudo-responsibility which tries to usurp the autonomy of others, and thereby places them in a dependent relationship.

Therapy

1. We form a group to help each other combat the psychopathology of aging that we encounter day to day in our own lives.

2. We do not accept excuses for evading responsibility.

 a. Avoiding responsibility is being less than human.

  1) Avoiding responsibility for others is being like an animal.

  2) Avoiding responsibility for ourself is being like a vegetable.

 b. We do not blame the person who evades responsibility.

3. We offer training in assuming responsibility.

 a. The will is trained.

  1) We learn to recognize when we are evading responsibility.

2)   We confront and conquer fears about assuming responsibility.

3)   We reinforce ourselves emotionally for assuming responsibility.

b.   There is training for increasing the capacity of responding at each level.

1)   Physical: we train our muscles to be directed by the will.

2)   Mental: we stimulate our problem-solving capacities by discussing the problems we face in our lives.

3)   Spiritual: we provide an atmosphere of acceptance and fellowship.

A group of *ancianos anonimos* was started in an asylum for indigents operated by the social security administration of the state of Jalisco. When the principles of Agers Anonymous were published in the local English language newspaper, their office was inundated with calls from the American community requesting information on how they might be able to join or start such a group. Some typical comments made during a session of Agers Anonymous follow:

> *Joe:*   I am only 63 and still in good health, but since I retired from the Air Force and moved down here I think I have really needed something that I could be active in or take care of, especially since my wife died. I used to spend a lot of time at the American Legion hall, and there are a lot of nice guys down there, but it is just too easy to go there and sit and drink. I like coming to Agers Anonymous because it has opened up a new and wider circle of friends for me—Mexican and American. It has also reminded me that I cannot be wholly healthy and happy as a human being if I don't take responsibility for others. I learned that I couldn't sit back and hope that someone would come up to me and say, "Hey, I need you." It's my duty to go and look for some human need and to try to relieve it. Since I started my meetings here, I've been active in an administrative capacity, although a minor one, at a large orphanage. I also helped a group of young Mexicans who have a crop-dusting

company develop a new system for repairing their planes. I really loved using some of my old skills.

Pete (leader): I'm 77 and a retired engineer. When I first retired, I really let myself slip. I became uninterested in things and people. I guess I decided to move here because the vision of the *manana* life-style appealed to my apathy. I put on weight and grew weak physically. At first I blamed the Mexican food for my weight and the high altitude for my physical inactivity, but I know now that this attempt at giving excuses is unacceptable. I would have gotten just as fat and lazy back in Chicago, and I would have blamed Polish sausage and the rotten weather. I finally just got so sick of myself. I had been athletic in college and very active in my working years. I somehow managed to muster enough of that old will power to go on a diet and start some daily exercise. I got my physician's advice, and really stuck to it. Not only did I begin to look better and feel better, but I felt proud of myself. The big decision came about four years ago. Now I hike, sail, ride, and jog. I keep my weight at 175, which is not bad for 6'2". I am glad that I got involved with Agers Anonymous. It helps me keep on doing what I should be doing, and it also gives me a chance to help others.

Alice: I'm 69, and lost my husband two years ago. I think it was hard on me because my kids were in the states, and I had left so much of the responsibility up to Edgar. He handled all the finances and did all of the driving. I had always been afraid to drive here, and I hadn't learned that much of the language. It's been very difficult trying to learn how to assume responsibility. I was very tempted to move back to the states and live with the kids, but they have their own lives, and I shouldn't usurp their responsibilities. I've been learning how to assume responsibility for myself. I've gotten enough confidence to drive downtown. My Spanish has improved, although I'm still a little shaky when confronting a petty bureaucrat. I think that it's really good for me to come here. You people remind me that success is possible. You reinforce me when I report the smallest increment of success. And when I fail to perform as I should, you give me encouragement to keep on trying.

John: This is only the second time I've been here, and the first time I've spoken. I think it's really great that Pete can jog and Joe can fix planes, but I have this @*#" arthritis, and I'm lucky even to get down here.

Pete: Well, John, your arthritis certainly can be a crippler, and as such, it's one of the limitations in our capacity for assuming responsibility. But such limitations can never be allowed to become excuses. We must always try to make the most of what we have and try to salvage what we can from what's been lost. What has your doctor prescribed?

John: Well, I haven't seen him for about two years. I've been pretty healthy otherwise, and everybody knows that arthritis is incurable.

Alice: John, you may very well have an incurable arthritis, or the symptoms may be treatable. Perhaps the symptoms are not due to arthritis at all. I don't know and neither do you. We're not physicians. We all have a responsibility to refrain from self-diagnoses and to seek medical help for physical limitations. Will you see your doctor?

John: Well, all right. It may do some good.

Margaret: You live only a few blocks from my apartment. If you feel you can't do something around the house, just give me a call and I'll come over and help you.

John: I'd be much obliged and all, you being a retired nurse. But you'd have to let me pay you.

Margaret: Let me tell you what I'd prefer. My eyesight isn't very good, and I really enjoy reading. How are your eyes?

John: Fine, but sometimes I have trouble turning pages.

Margaret: I could do that for you. Could you read to me out loud? I do enjoy a good novel.

John: Me too! Especially mysteries. I sure get bored with the local TV stations. Would you like to come over Tuesday afternoon?

Margaret: That sounds OK. I'll go down to the American bookstore and pick out a good new mystery. I'll be over at three. I can take responsibility for you, helping you overcome your arthritic limitations, and you can take responsibility for helping me overcome my eyesight limitation. That's how Agers Anonymous works.

DREAM GROUPS

Dreams have been used effectively in group work (Klein-Lipschult, 1953; Fielding, 1967; Zimmerman, 1967). Another rationale for a group of elders would be to study their dreams. Such a group has the advantages of interaction and socialization, and even intellectual stimulation. However, there are more dangers with such a group. First of all, for those elders not well grounded in coping with reality, there is the danger of overemphasizing fantasy at the expense of contact with reality. Second, to maximize the training in coping yielded by the dream study, and to minimize the dangers of insights and feelings that certain individuals are not able to handle, a structure and an interpretive language must be adhered to. The Corriere and Hart (1977) approach is probably the most easy to understand and the least harmful. It avoids interpretation and stresses the importance of getting good dreams through training. When the members are well educated and can handle Jung's ideas, his approach to dream interpretation may be employed. A psychoanalytic format is generally contraindicated, especially when leadership and structure are lacking, because of the probability that unpleasant insights will be generated.

SUMMARY

Group therapy is a very efficient way to restore or maintain geriatric mental health. While severe communication disorders or pronounced hostility are contraindications for group work, CBS patients receive significant benefits. Group therapy is helpful in four ways. It facilitates interaction, focuses on reality, assists the life review process, and remotivates patients. A good model for geriatric group therapy is Recovery training, which emphasizes clear-cut leadership, structure, and language. The lack of any of these means that there is a danger that the purposes of the group will not be met and that tense and counterproductive interactions may take place. Dreams can be used in group work, but only according to certain guidelines.

Chapter 12

FAMILY THERAPY

Three-quarters of all American elders live with some other family member: a spouse, sibling, or adult offspring. The bio-psycho-social crises experienced by elders do not affect only them. Through physical proximity and emotional bonds, those persons close to elders are affected by these crises. Many times, the most significant aspect of the elder's crisis is the stagnant or pathological emotional system of a family (Hall, 1976).

On the other hand, the family's emotional system could have been quite healthy until a recent crisis was experienced by the elder. Such a crisis can upset the emotional system of a family either directly or indirectly. Real privations and distortions in the family's life-style can be directly caused by the biological or social crises suffered by the patient. For example, a CVA patient is going to require a more intense level of care from other members of the family, and will inconvenience them, and perhaps also change the emotional climate of the family. The effect can also be indirect. Even if the other members of the family are not directly affected, many times the loss will cause the elder to change the way he relates to other persons, by being more dependent, depressed, or hostile. These attitudinal and behavioral changes on the part of the elder change the emotional climate of the family, and the entire household is affected.

Even when there is no obvious pathology in the emotional system of the family, a family approach to therapy may be indicated. This is especially true when the elder is extremely dependent—physically, economically, or emotionally—on other family members, because their cooperation is essential in the formulation and implementation of a solution (even if they are not now part of the problem). Therefore the geriatric counselor should consider bringing the other family members in on the counseling process. Another wise move is to consider doing the counseling at the patient's residence. Not only is it more convenient for many patients (and their families), but it gives the counselor a chance to examine the patient's environment first hand.

APPLICATIONS OF FAMILY THERAPY

Family therapy, like individual and group psychotherapy, had several major pioneers who developed theoretical views and practical techniques for their endeavor. Growing out of marriage counseling and treatment for problem children and adolescents, family therapy focuses on trying to secure changes in the family system. Especially at the beginning of therapy, the parties may define a particular family member (an alcoholic parent, an autistic child, or a delinquent adolescent) as "the problem." Family therapists view this finger pointing as an attempt to scapegoat a member in order to deny more serious problems in the way that the family system functions. Therapists view the family's designation of "the problem" as but a symptom, an admission ticket for therapy. Because family therapy focuses on changing the family system, it frequently uses conjoint treatment in which all important members in a family are present. Less common techniques are concomitant therapy, in which the same therapist treats the family members individually, and collaborative therapy, in which different therapists treat different family members, and consult about their progress.

Nathan Ackerman (1970) outlined several important tasks of the family therapist for improving the family system. First, he should try to help the family clarify the content of its conflict and counteract inappropriate displacements of conflict (scapegoating). Second, he should attempt to rescue those family members who are overly victimized by the conflict. Third, he should strive to improve the ability of the family to resolve conflict in an atmosphere of emotional supportiveness and rational discourse. To accomplish these tasks, the therapist must frequently act as a facilitator or even offer direct advice or training. There are various points at which the therapist may intervene in the dysfunctional family's cycle of conflict. The important thing is to intervene when it will appear most fruitful, to stop the conflict, and not to assign blame for it.

Zuk (1971) believes that the basic problem in most dysfunctional family systems is the overuse of silencing strategies. The majority of a family, seeking to punish the deviance of a member, attempts to isolate him via noncommunication. If the deviant member refuses to reform, the silent treatment can lead to other pathologies in him. Some of these isolated deviants respond through absurd speech and action, and this only convinces the majority of the family that he must be isolated even more. Unfortunately, the members of a dysfunctional family fail to realize the impact of their behavior on the others. When intervening in such a family, the therapist encounters a central paradox. The majority says that it wants to solve the problem and demands that the expert (the therapist) tell them what to do, but they are extremely reluctant to change the status quo. However, because of their desire to prove to the therapist that nothing is really wrong with them, the therapist can get them to improve the way that they participate within the family system.

An interesting approach suggests that there are typologies of family participation (Satir, Stachowiak & Taschman, 1975). The healthy type is the *congruent* type who considers self, other, and context in his interactions with the other family members. He is able to communicate and even to assert his interests without driving the other family members into some type of pathology. The *placating* type neglects self, but manages to serve the needs of other and context. The *blaming* type is the exact opposite, neglecting both other and the context so that he can preserve self-esteem. The *super-reasonable* type attends only to the context as if people (self and other) did not matter. The *irrelevant* type disregards everything—self, other, and context—and behaves in an inappropriate fashion designed to distract people.

Satir demonstrates how most dysfunctional families are composed of configurations of several complementary unhealthy types. Although Satir devised her typologies from work with marriage counseling and treating families with disturbed children and adolescents, they are relevant to geriatrics. Many dependent elders or their adult offspring relate to each other by placating, blaming, super-rationality, or irrelevance, thereby making it more difficult for the other party to relate in a truly congruent fashion.

Chapman (1968) also identified typologies of dysfunctional participation within family systems. He referred to each type as a strategem which a particular family member employed at the expense of the family system. There are four turvey-top strategems frequently employed by elders who move into homes of adult offspring: "I'm going to help you rear your children," "I'm going to support you," "I'm going to redeem you," "I'm going to reform you." Silverstone and Hyman (1976) produced a list of strategems including withdrawal, oversolicitousness, domination, fault finding, denial, outmoded role playing, protracted rebellion, and blind overinvolvement. These strategems represent ways in which the elder tries to compensate for his own losses by attempting to usurp the roles and responsibilities of other family members. These strategems can produce the most difficult situations, placing the other family members in the bind of feeling incompetent if they play along and guilty and disrespectful toward the elder if they do not.

In addition to typologies of dysfunctional family participation, family therapy can contribute some specific techniques to geriatrics. This is especially true of Multiple Impact Therapy (MacGregor, Ritchie, Serrano & Shuster, 1964), which was designed for intervention into families with disturbed children or adolescents. The distinguishing features of Multiple Impact Therapy are the team approach and the extended initial interview. The entire team (psychologists, psychiatrists, physicians, social workers, clergy, and anyone else who takes a major role in the treatment of the family or its members) is assembled for the initial interview, which may last two and a half days. A challenging statement by one of the more authoritative members of the team instigates the family's response, in which they demonstrate, individually and collectively, their perception of the problem and their communication system for handling it. Then the team splits up to give each family member a chance to discuss his side of the situation on a one-to-one basis with a team member. Then the team reassembles, and in the presence of the family, discusses the course of treatment. Such an approach to treatment is highly appropriate to geriatrics, where the understanding of the problems and formulation of the solutions demand the expertise of a multidisciplinary team and the cooperation of the elder patient's family.

Some family therapy techniques, especially those derived from marriage counseling, may not be appropriate to geriatrics. For example, attempts at intergenerational role playing may become opportunities for cruel parodies. They are definitely contraindicated with confused, paranoid, or hypochondriacal patients. Another inappropriate technique is metacommunication, in which everyone goes around saying "I hear you saying . . ." A frequent geriatric response to this is "Then you're not listening very well because I said . . ." Metacommunication is particularly futile with a rigid or confused patient. Behavioral modification is much more effective in translating the family's desires into changes in conduct and attitude.

PRACTICAL CONSIDERATIONS

When family therapy is indicated, whether it is because of a marital problem, an adolescent problem, or a geriatric problem, it is frequently hard to get all of the family to agree to counseling. The reluctant parties may be responding to several different kinds of motives or fears. They may have a deep fear that the counselor may want to probe too deeply and uncover some underlying conflicts that have been repressed. (Interestingly enough, it is usually these same people who really unfold their problems in the counseling process, and are frequently the very ones who get the most out of it.) Another fear of the reluctant party is that the other parties will form a secret alliance with the counselor and move against him. This is especially true if the complaining party has already seen the counselor on an individual basis (and had an opportunity to present his side) and now is trying to get the reluctant party to go. The latter fears that the complainer has already prejudiced the counselor so that he will not be able to receive a fair hearing. A final factor in reluctance in that some individuals seek to maintain self-esteem by telling themselves that the problem is not their fault, but entirely the fault of the other party. For example, one husband responded to his wife's request that they get marriage counseling by saying, "Why do we need to see a marriage counselor? You need to go to a mental hospital!" Frequently, parents of delinquent adolescents are reluctant to participate in family counseling, telling themselves that the kid is just plain bad, or that he has associated with bad company, and that they have already tried their best. In many of these cases, the emotional system of the family never was healthy, and the son or daughter's trouble with the law is just a surface symptom.

In general, the best way to get everyone to cooperate is to redefine the nature of the counseling. If counseling is defined as the quest for a solution, the reluctant members can usually be encouraged to participate, unless their real desire is to wash their hands of the entire matter. Securing everyone's cooperation is much easier in geriatric cases, compared with other forms of family therapy, because in marriage and adolescent counseling, the other parties have a greater reason to fear that they will be blamed for the problem. This fear arises only rarely in geriatric cases. Most adult offspring, siblings, and even spouses are most willing to come, perhaps out of a sense of confidence that the counselor will view them as a helper rather than as the agent responsible for the patient's problems. There might be a slightly greater resistance with spouses, and usually such a resistance is a fairly reliable indicator either of a marital problem that preceded the patient's most recent crisis, or of one spouse's current desire to disengage from the relationship.

The initial interview for family therapy should pretty much follow the format for individual therapy. The therapist must assure the family that his goal is for brief therapy that will strive to enable the patient and his family to cope with the total problem, and that his goal is not to psychoanalyze any of them or restructure their personalities. (This emphasis tends to lower much of the initial resistance and actually facilitates a certain degree of personal growth in the family members.) The opening remarks themselves must set a realistic and objective tone and elicit the cooperation of all parties.

Now in most cases of geriatric counseling, the procedure was not initiated by the elder patient. The most frequent pattern is that he is there because of a bio-psycho-social crisis that put him in touch with an acute-care hospital, social welfare agency, or the long arm of the law, and counseling is just an aftereffect. The second most likely situation is that the crisis itself led indirectly to the counseling by placing a burden on the elder's family, and they sought to find a way out of an increasingly difficult situation. In both cases, and particularly in the latter, the elder is likely to be the reluctant party, and there is a danger that he will view the counseling process as something beyond his control, designed to legitimatize the others' decisions about his fate.

To avoid this trap, the counselor must focus on the elder, much the same way that individual therapy would. The questions should be directed to the patient—the elder —and not to the other family members. This approach will reassure the elder that the counselor is there to help *him.* The therapist should have faith that if there is some inaccuracy in the patient's answers, the other family members will be sure to contribute. The kinds of questions asked are similar to those in individual therapy, except that more elaboration on the current family scene is appropriate, with feedback from the other family members.

A full family session is usually the best way to begin the therapy. After one or two sessions like this, the therapist may want a private session with the patient, the family, or both. The final session should be of a debriefing, again with the whole family, clarifying each person's role in the total plan for managing the bio-psycho-social crisis. The degree to which the therapist will want to use the intervening sessions for individual therapy or family therapy should depend on the patient's choice and what the therapist feels would be most fruitful.

After a thorough history has been taken, and if the therapist has decided to handle the case within the context of family therapy, it must be decided if the problems that have surfaced are the "real problems" of the family. There is one insight of Multiple Impact Therapy that is extremely useful in geriatric cases: collusion. In many cases the underlying dynamics of the family's problem are known by the family members, but they choose, consciously or unconsciously, to ignore them, and even try to steer the therapist away from them. The success of the therapist is directly related to the degree of success in dealing with these very matters (MacGregor, Ritchie, Serrano & Shuster, 1964).

One example of collusion comes from the case of Dona A (Brink, 1977). This widow had recently experienced an epileptic attack and suicidal fantasies associated with depression. The first session was with Dona A and her 34-year-old daughter, who lived with her. The next two sessions were with Dona A alone. Neither the first nor the second session contained any mention of the daughter's forthcoming marriage and her plans to move to another city. There was an unconscious collusion between mother and daughter to avoid mentioning this topic. The daughter did not want to think (or have me think) that she was abandoning her ailing mother. The mother did not want to think (or have me think) that she was standing in the way of her daughter's happiness. In this case, I got around the collusion quite by accident: A third party mentioned the upcoming marriage to me. I then introduced the topic into the third session and found that it tied right into the patient's physical problems and mental anxieties. If I had not found out about the marriage, my ability to focus on realistic solutions would have been greatly impaired.

DIAGNOSTIC UTILITY OF DREAMS

In many ways, collusion in family therapy is like the problem of repression in individual therapy. The problem cannot be attacked directly because unconscious forces prevent clients from addressing themselves to it. Freud's technique for getting around repression was to have the patient tell the analyst recent dreams. Then the analyst would isolate different dream symbols and encourage free-association with each symbol. Freud found this to be an excellent way to circumvent the mechanisms of repression, and concluded that dream analysis was the royal road to the unconscious.

Dream analysis has been used successfully in family therapy (Whitlock, 1961; Rutledge, 1961; Fielding, 1966; Brink & Brink, 1976). Its primary use is to open up clogged channels of communication and to permit a deeper understanding of each party by the therapist, the other parties, and the dreamer himself. In addition, dreams can be used as training sessions, as described in previous chapters. For all these reasons, the use of dreams in family-based geriatric therapy is an excellent diagnostic technique. Training in depth psychology (Freud, Adler, and Jung) may be helpful for the therapist seeking to use dreams, but it is not essential (Rutledge, 1961). A more important prerequisite is for the therapist to establish the trust of the family members so that they do not feel anxious about the project. One case study is a good illustration of the diagnostic value of dreams in patients who wish to keep something from the therapist.

Mrs. A, age 73, was referred by her gynecologist. Her current medical problem was fairly insignificant, but her brooding and anxiety were quite intense. A more important item in her medical history was a radical mastectomy some 18 months earlier. Mrs. A had lost her husband of 39 years some 6 years earlier. He had had a long bout with diabetes and other diseases, and died only after spending several months in the hospital. Mrs. A's account of the experience left no doubt that she felt a great deal of anguish over his sufferings, which she had identified very closely with. She had dutifully cared for him to the very end, and part of her anxiety seemed to be directed toward pondering the frightening prospect of who would take care of her when she got sick. Although Mrs. A had been a relatively young-looking, alert, and active woman, she seemed to develop a great interest, even an overconcern, with her own health after the death of her husband. (This is common in the first six months of widowhood.) The only thing mentioned about interpersonal relations in the first session was that she felt as though she were becoming somewhat alienated from her daughter.

The second session began with a discussion of Mrs. A's daily schedule. By comparison with most elders in therapy, she was living an interesting life, spending quite a bit of time at the library and with a social circle, and not missing a single performance of the Chicago Symphony Orchestra. However, she said that she felt she should use her talents more, especially in helping the disadvantaged. Through her own social contacts she knew of several opportunities for volunteer work. With only minor encouragement from the therapist, she agreed to talk with her friends about the possibility of doing some charitable work. The case at this point seemed very strange. It was not at all clear what in the patient's environment or physiology could be producing the anxiety, which showed no signs of diminution. The patient was encouraged to bring in a dream, and at the next session, she opened with the following dream.

> I was at work, at the office where I was employed until my late husband passed away. My husband was there, dressed elegantly as always. I think it was about quitting time and it was very hot. Three young women came and asked me if I would like to go swimming with them. I told them I could not go, because I had to spend some more time on the books. Then they looked at my husband and said, "But you can go." He said yes and left with them without saying anything at all to me. I felt angry and sad, but didn't say anything in the presence of the others.

The first question about this dream was if it had corresponded to reality. Her previous discussion of her late husband had indicated no hostility whatsoever. Some bereaved widows do develop the fantasy that the husband's death was actually a rejection of the wife's love, and this fantasy can result in a retrospective hostility toward the deceased. This interpretation was shared with the patient. Her response was totally unexpected. She remarked that her husband in the dream was not her late husband, but her *present* husband. This took the therapist by surprise, because in the initial session Mrs. A had answered a question about marital status by saying that she was a widow. Now Mrs. A admitted that she had married again about a year and a half after being widowed. Her real name was now Mrs. B. Mr. B had been a salesman at the office where she had worked for 12 years. He had always been a flashy dressing, big-talking womanizer who had been through two divorces before marrying the patient. But all this was inconsequential, said the patient, because she had married him on impulse, and the marriage had never really worked out, and just last month Mr. B said that he wanted to get a divorce.

Even when the marriage is a lackluster one, divorce

and widowhood are not easy. Not only is there a great change in the life-style, as well as the loss of a sparring partner. There is also a shock to one's self-esteem, especially in the case of a divorce in which the rejection is overt. It was hypothesized at this point that the anxiety-producing aspect of the patient's environment was her current marital situation, either the discord or the feeling of rejection due to the impending divorce. This hypothesis was confirmed when marriage counseling was initiated and proved successful in resolving the patient's anxiety.

Dreams as Therapeutic and Prognostic

The value of the dream in family therapy does not stop with diagnosis. Working through dreams can increase the levels of insight and communication between family members, whether they be husband and wife or parent and adult offspring.

Mrs. C, age 59, was also referred to therapy by her gynecologist. She had always been a very sickly person and was currently seeing two physicians, in addition to a chiropractor and a specialist in acupuncture. She was the type of patient who would call a physician in the middle of the night and talk for an hour. The initial interview covered the long and detailed medical history and ended with an interesting quip from the patient. She said that one physician had told her that all she really needed was to get her marriage taken care of, and everything would be OK. She was encouraged to have her husband attend the second session. He willingly obliged.

Mr. C was a healthy, handsome 62-year-old and clearly the dominant party in the marriage. Mrs. C did not drive and was afraid to use public transportation. Mr. C spoke about his job and how much he hated it, but of how he would try to hold on for a few more years in the hope of getting his pension. His job was chief controller of the subway trains, and there was always pressure due to mechanical failure or labor problems. He really enjoyed getting out of the city and going fishing in the Yucatan or Acapulco. Mrs. C said that she enjoyed going with him, but now she could not stand the heat. It was disclosed that although their sex life had been good in the past, Mrs. C had denied her husband for the past two years because she "could not stand to be touched." (But remember, she was going to a gynecologist, chiropractor, and acupuncturist.) Both parties were encouraged to bring a dream to discuss at the next session. Mr. C opened with this one.

> I was riding in front of one of the Metro [Mexico City subway] trains. I was riding on a mechanic's creeper, or something like that. My duty in the dream was to keep the trains on the track. A mechanic came by and told me to check the tires on the airplanes. I did, and put in 175 pounds of pressure. The airplane tire changed to my wife's mouth. The mechanic came by and told me that the pressure was too high.

The associations in the dream were fairly direct. The dreamer was contemplating his responsibilities at work, keeping the trains going. Mr. C felt that if the least little thing went wrong, he had to go in and straighten it out himself. He weighed 175 pounds, so that pressure indicates his full force. Mr. C's desire to have everything under control extended to his marriage, and he preferred to keep his wife in tow. When he would come home from work, he would unload his bad day on her. She had to listen to all of his pressures, but he had no interest in hearing about her problems.

Mrs. C brought this dream.

> I was mad at my husband. He was out with two women and had spent a thousand pesos on them. I complained that

when he takes me out, he won't spend a hundred. If I spend
20 pesos on myself, he gets mad. I told him I was going to
spend a lot of money now. He told me to be quiet. I said I
would not be quiet, and I broke a pottery dish. He told me
I shouldn't have done that, because the dish had been my
mother's favorite. I then felt very sorry, and went to pick up
the pieces.

This dream demonstrated that Mrs. C did have a pattern for dealing with her husband. She felt powerless to
confront him directly, so she had to displace her anger,
even onto things she did not want to destroy. She herself
seemed receptive to the idea that her marital situation was
exacerbating her physical illness. The therapist empathized
with her, saying that perhaps having to put up with all the
pressures brought home by her husband would make anyone ill. The dream was then interpreted so that the pottery
dish, Mrs. C's favorite, symbolized Mrs. C's body, and that
she took out her frustrations through physical illness or an
unconscious revulsion toward sex. Mr. C also concurred
with this interpretation, but he viewed this as the fault of
his job rather than the marital relationship.

At the next session, Mr. C reported the following
dream.

I was not in the dream. I was watching something akin to the
high-society movies of the 1930s. The husband and wife
argued over whether or not to attend the theater. The husband despised the theater and called the directors and actors
and writers "dogs." Then there was a comic interlude of
dogs dressed in these roles. The couple went to a café, the
wife conceding that they would not go to the theater and see
a new play. Finally, the husband acquiesced, and agreed to
go.

Mr. C reported that he had enjoyed the dream, and felt
that the ending was a happy one. The therapist asked Mr.
C if he felt that the man in the dream was less of a man

because he had finally agreed to his wife's demands. Mr. C reported that he was just as much of a man. Mr. C was reassured by the therapist and his wife that they both regarded him as very much of a man, and that he should not have to feel so much in control, at work or at home, in order to feel that he would be regarded as a man.

Mrs. C also reported this dream.

> My husband and I were in bed together, and I was fondling his penis. Then he ejaculated. I was disappointed because then I wouldn't be able to enjoy sex with him.

This dream was most strange, because Mrs. C had spoken of a revulsion to sex earlier. So the dream was viewed as an indication of growth and a good prognosis. She was apparently getting back to respect her body and its desires. She agreed that she could now contemplate the idea of sex. Mrs. C was advised to see a sex therapist, but was never able to make contact with one. Nevertheless, she was able to get over her anxieties and assume normal relations with her husband. Mr. C was advised to engage in recreational activities, especially with his wife, and was sent to a relaxation specialist.

Dreams can also be a valuable tool in family therapy involving adult offspring. Mr. D, age 74, was the image of a self-made man. When his wife had died 10 years ago, he chased every skirt in town and ate and drank himself to a stroke after eight years. He did remarkably well in physical and speech therapy, a fact that he credited primarily to his extraordinary strength of will. But he suffered another CVA on the opposite side two months before coming to therapy. At his request, his sole heir, his son, moved into his large suburban home. The son brought his wife. But this living arrangement soon became a strain on the son and his marriage. Fortunately, they were able to get some sympathy from one of his father's physicians, and counseling was recommended.

At first Mr. D was quite resistant, but when he was told that it was marriage counseling, he seemed almost pleased, perhaps in the hope that he could use the sessions to meddle in his son's marriage. The first two sessions got through nothing profound. It became obvious that Mr. D's rigidity and perfectionism were traits that ran deep in his personality. However, he was willing to bring a dream in the third session.

> I was back in Buffalo. I was accused of some sort of land swindle or horse theft. I was being hanged, but I grabbed the rope and was able to prevent myself from choking. Then a doctor dressed in Hindu garb, with a turban and everything, came over and was going to pronounce me dead. I grabbed him and put his beard in the rope, and this saved me.

Mr. D was in no way embarrassed by this dream. He seemed quite proud of it and mentioned that he had been in many jams in his day, but that his wits and will power had never failed him, and that he would recover from his latest stroke. The only association he could make with the Hindu was that he was currently doing a lot of reading about Eastern religions.

The junior Mr. D told this dream.

> I was back in my youth, living at the house of my parents (not the present residence). My father and I went downstairs because we heard a prowler. My father took a steel cable with a heavy weight on one end as a weapon, and gave it to me and told me that he wanted me to use it. Then my father grabbed the prowler and told me to hit him. I tried, but missed, and finally grabbed him around the neck and began to strangle him. Then I noticed that I was strangling my wife. Then we heard a very loud noise outside. It was my uncle next door with his chain saw. My cousin was there, and he

> was a boy too in the dream. Then I wanted to know where
> my old 1937 Plymouth (my first car) was. My father told me
> it was in the church parking lot down the street. Then I saw
> a woman try to get a locksmith and break into it.

In his associations with the dream, the son indicated that he was very confused about his present relationship with his father. He sometimes felt like a little boy again, and always tried to be a dutiful son, trying to live up to his father's great expectations. Even now he was the manager of a department in a large store in the city, but he could not compete with the record of his wheeler-dealer father. The daughter-in-law reported this dream.

> My husband and I were visiting my father-in-law's house.
> The doorbell rang and a large group of people entered. I
> was worried because I know that my father-in-law does not
> like a large group of people at his house. The people said
> that they were part of a club, and that they were celebrating
> at his house that week. Then there was a great, wild party
> going on inside. One woman tried to have sex with me. I
> looked for my husband and finally found him. I expressed
> my desire to escape. He got on my back and we started to
> fly around the room, but we were still too close to the peo-
> ple. I blew harder and slowly we rose. Then I awoke.

She also admitted that she felt very bad in the present living arrangement. She openly expressed her desire to move out, and had tried to convince her husband, but to no avail. She had thought about moving out on her own, leaving him with his father, and was keeping that option open.

When the counselor later reflected on these dreams, she concluded that they demonstrated two forces compet-ing for the son's loyalties: his father and his wife. Notice that both the father and the son had dreams about choking someone else. The father was doing it to survive, and felt no guilt about it. Perhaps the Hindu doctor he had in his dream symbolized his daughter-in-law, who was working on her doctorate in oriental art. The son was choking his wife at his father's command. The dream also had quite a bit of rich affect, tying the son to his father. The first car may have symbolized what the father had done for his son in the past, and the woman with the locksmith was seen as a threat to that relationship. The daughter-in-law's dream directly reflected her uneasy situation. She could make up her mind to escape, but it was apparent that she had to help her husband to escape from his father's clutches, for he was unable to fly away on his own.

The physical therapist reported to the counselor that the patient, Mr. D, was progressing, although not as rapidly as he had after his first CVA. The counselor concluded that the main target should not be reconstructing the patient's attitudes, but helping the son decide whether he was going to safeguard his marriage or perpetuate his dependent relationship with his father. Interestingly enough, Mr. D had requested a private session with the counselor, during which he reported the following dream.

> I was walking on this beach with an oriental girl I met in the 1930s when I visited Shanghai. Then a bluebird perched on my shoulder. The girl tried to take the bird, but the bird said that he had a message for me, and would speak for himself. The bird told me that I should be more *yang* with my son.

Mr. D had been reading about the Taoist religion and knew that *yang* referred to the masculine energy principle. He had always considered his son to be a ne'er-do-well, and always felt that it was his duty to model success for his son. Mr. D also reflected that he had always been intensely attracted to this oriental girl, and mused that he wished he could have married her, and that she could have borne his son. "The Chinese have will power and respect for their elders." The therapist suggested that perhaps Mr. D could never have been satisfied with his son, because he was not born from the woman he really loved. This prompted Mr. D to relate another dream he had had years before as a recurring dream.

> I was talking with someone and described an old brick house like the one we lived in when we first got married. The other person, who was like a shadow, commented that it would be a good place to commit a murder. I was shocked and offended that the other person would suggest such an idea.

Mr. D confessed that he had often contemplated murdering his wife, but never got around to it. This might explain the self-destructive behavior he engaged in after his wife died of natural causes: self-punishment. Mr. D seemed somewhat relieved after telling these dreams and past desires. Perhaps it in some way facilitated the release of his son from the dependency. Mr. D realized, the counselor later speculated, that he was trying to punish his daughter-in-law for supposedly holding his son back, because of his negative feelings about his own wife. Mr. D finally said that it was all right for his son to purchase a home of his own and live away from him. This was accomplished, however, only after the son completed some rather intensive, psychoanalytically oriented individual therapy.

Another problem that occurs in some families is the crisis surrounding institutionalization. Brody and Spark (1966) reported five case studies in which the decision to put the elder into an institution precipitated a family crisis. I would like to provide another with its referent dreams.

Mrs. E, age 57, came to see me about her octagenarian parents. Her mother had just died suddenly. Mrs. E was extremely attached and had not yet resolved her grief. But there was another, more pressing problem. The father was quite confused and physically dependent. In fact, the mother had been caring for him until she died suddenly of a massive CVA. Mrs. E wanted advice on nursing homes and their alternatives. Throughout the course of my contact with Mrs. E, various alternatives were tried and found to be inexpedient. Finally, placement in an extended care facility became necessary. I was able to convince Mrs. E that she had not finished working through her grief, and suggested some dream analysis for her. She offered a dream right on the spot.

> My mother had just died and the corpse was waiting in a room. I walked in and saw three coffins, the first being my mother's. I was shocked and could not believe it.

Mrs. E spoke of this as a recurring dream, which was quite disturbing. The dreamer's associations with death were worked through. She objected most to the cold finality of it, the rotting in the grave. However, she admitted being a religious woman, so I advised her to speak with her priest. She returned next week with the following two dreams.

> My husband and I were apparently in the secret service. Our job was to follow the presidential limousine and protect it. My first thought was, "What an elegant car! It is even more elegant than the Negroes have." The limousine stopped and the party got out. I could see President Ford and his assistants walk into a building. When my husband and I next noticed, the limousine was gone. We figured that they had come back and gone off while we were not looking. We raced on and tried to find the presidential limousine. We got very worried, and so began to pray.

> I was at the old Utah farmhouse where I was raised. My brother was looking for a spot to urinate. I looked in a tree and saw a rooster and a hen together, and the hen was about to lay an egg. Then I could see my mother. I got near her and wanted to kiss her, but she told me not to. She was like a spirit, not a real person.

The first dream indicated that the dreamer felt responsible for her confused old father, symbolized by the president. She felt that she was not doing a very good job, and the responsibility was weighing heavily on her and her husband. But fortunately, even in the dream, she had the good sense to seek spiritual counsel in times of stress. The second dream showed that she had started to conceive of her mother as a spirit, and not as a body rotting in a casket. The fond remembrances of the past, and its rich associations with life, also seemed to perk up the patient.

In the next week, Mrs. E brought in these two dreams.

I was back at my childhood home. I saw that it had been converted into a school. I told my companion, "This is the house that my father built."

I was trying to find my mother. I went to my aunt's house. I asked my cousin. She told me that my mother had gone elsewhere. I felt real disgust in talking with my cousin. Then my aunt came. She brought a ball in a paper bag. Then someone came and took it away from her, claiming that she had stolen it. I went on talking to my aunt, and then I saw a snake, and told my aunt. She said that it was normal there. I decided to leave. I walked through some very high mountains. I found myself descending on a circular path into a valley. It was so beautiful, and had many trees. I found myself in a cemetery. For the first time, it dawned on me that my mother might be dead. I was afraid to look around. Finally, I did, and saw some beautiful flowers, and all was clear, and calm, and I felt that I had found true peace.

The first dream showed that Mrs. E had strong affection for her father, but hopefully could retain pleasant memories of the past without dwelling on her inability to help him in the present. The second dream demonstrated a resolution of grief. Mrs. E could think about her mother in the grave, and have that be compensated for by the spiritual and life forces.

GROUPS FOR FAMILIES

In the past two decades, special groups have sprung up to meet the needs of parents of children who were autistic, retarded, delinquent, or terminally ill. There are groups for children of parents who are alcoholic, incarcerated, or undergoing psychiatric treatment or divorce. These groups can help in two ways: by providing emotional support for family members, and by sharing new resources and techniques.

There is a practical need for groups for families of dependent elders. Having a dependent elder is something most families are not prepared to cope with, economically or emotionally. Such groups can help train the other family members in how to cope with the elder patient by pointing out simple techniques which the family members can use as well as community resources. It is rare indeed that anyone not in the field can comprehend the labyrinth of programs, projects, and agencies with their divers eligibility requirements.

A further need is for emotional support. Caring for a dependent elder at home or away from home is a strain on the other family members, particularly the one designated as the primary service provider, usually a daughter or daughter-in-law. Individuals who are charged with the direct care of dependent family members must deny themselves some freedom and pleasure and even compromise the services they provide for other family members. Unfortunately, this may make the other family members contemptuous of the situation, rather than supportive of the service provider. The group fills in here as a surrogate support system and tells the provider that he is a good offspring, spouse, or parent, building up a self-concept which may have suffered severe criticism from several quarters.

On the other hand, service providers need assertiveness training. Specifically, they have to learn *when* and *how* to defend their own needs and to resist the demands of other family members in such a way that the family system does not become dysfunctional. The other family members, as their relative privation increases, may become more manipulative of the service provider, using strategems like, "If you were a better son (daughter/father/mother/husband/wife), you would provide more services to *me.*" It is not unusual that a service provider will receive such messages simultaneously from his dependent aged parent, his spouse, and his children, and it is utterly unrealistic to assume that he could or should attempt to meet such needs. Here, training in assertive diplomacy is called for, since purely assertive techniques may alienate their targets, and this is not an acceptable solution within the confines of a family system. Of course, the best overall solution is to get the entire family remotivated, with each member concerned about how to meet his own needs, and those of others, rather than about how to manipulate others to meet his own needs.

Families of deteriorating elders must also learn to cope with loss and guilt. Fond memories of the elder in his prime offer a bitter contrast with the harsh realities of the present. The grieving process does not always begin at the death of the elder; it may even have been completed by the time he dies, especially in cases of severe and long-term deterioration. The grieving process commences when the family realizes that deterioration is significant and probably irreversible. Groups for widows and widowers, spouses of deteriorated elders, and children of deceased or deteriorated elders are useful in circumscribing the degree and duration of the grieving process.

In addition, there are guilt complexes, even when the dependent elder does not use a strategem to induce them. Consciences will continue to nag families who institutionalized their elders: "Was it really necessary?" "Did we choose the right facility?" Whether or not the elder is in an institution, the conscience may bring up questions like, "Am I visiting enough?" Is there something else that I could or should be doing?" Group discussion can help families temper overly conscientious thinking with realistic perspectives based on experience.

CONCLUSION

Since most elders live with other family members, and the bio-psycho-social crises of aging become family problems, family therapy is frequently the best approach for geriatric psychotherapy. Many of the typologies and techniques derived from other areas of family therapy are appropriate for use in geriatrics, but some are not. There are several practical considerations for the therapist. A major problem is collusion of family members to avoid getting down to the real problems. Dream therapy is a very useful tool for diagnosing real problems behind the facade of collusion, and also for prognosis and therapy for family communication. Groups for the families of dependent elders are useful in providing information, valuable skills, and emotional support.

Chapter 13

INSTITUTIONALIZATION

The nursing home or convalescent hospital becomes the final residence for many elders. A more precise term for these institutions would be Long-Term Care facilities (LTCs). LTCs include extended care facilities, intermediate care facilities, and skilled nursing facilities. These different types of LTCs are distinguished by the degree of care, usually measured by the amount of time that a registered nurse is present. All of these types of LTCs have custodial care—aides and orderlies—around the clock. I would not include residential "board and care" facilities in my definition of LTC. Most residential care facilities are small and lack the services of an RN, though the quality of supervision is, in many cases, excellent.

For all practical purposes, state mental hospitals have served as geriatric LTCs, especially during the 1950s. Although elders constitute only about 11% of the American population, and 2% of the psychiatric outpatients, they accounted for 30% of the mental hospital admissions in

1971. Before this decade, the rate was higher. These changing figures do not, unfortunately, indicate a great improvement in geriatric mental health. The prior admission rates were grossly overinflated because many elders had nowhere to go but the state mental hospital to receive the kind of medical or custodial care they needed. Clever social workers devised ways of certifying their clients for mental hospitals. The annual per patient cost for American mental hospitals was only $1100 in 1955. By 1974 it had increased tenfold.

In response to the financial burdens, states such as California began reducing the patient population of the state mental hospitals in the 1960s. It was cheaper to send elder patients to proprietary nursing homes, especially after federal medicare monies became available. So new geriatric patients were only rarely admitted to the mental hospitals, and many geriatric wards were emptied. Many of the transferred patients were elders who had been institutionalized for socioeconomic reasons, but some were schizophrenics who had been admitted early in life and had grown old in the institution.

Private LTCs have increased their populations markedly in the past 15 years. Part of this increase is due to the transfers from state mental hospitals, but this is not the only or even the major factor accounting for the growth spurt. The number of American elders has increased dramatically throughout the century, and so has the percentage of elders in LTCs: 2½% in 1940, 4% in 1960, 5% today. After age 85, the percentage is closer to 14%. Now there are more LTC beds (1.2 million) in the U.S. than general and surgical hospital beds. In 1972, for the first time, medicare payments to LTCs exceeded those to acute-care hospitals. Between 1960 and 1970, nursing homes increased by 140%, and beds by 232%. The number of patients trebled, the number of employees quintupled, and the costs went up 465%.

Most LTCs have earned a healthy return on their investments during the last decade, but now they are hurt by overbedding which has raised the vacancy rate past 13% nationally. (It is somewhat higher in California.) In 1975 the price range in a private LTC was $200 to $1200 a month. The median price was about $600, but rising at a rate higher than the national inflation rate. The LTC that charges more has more money to provide the services that comprise quality care. If a high-priced LTC did not offer first-class care, it could not attract enough residents in the overbedded state of the industry. However, there is no straight relationship between price and quality. At any price level, some LTCs do a better job than others, and this difference is most pronounced in the smaller facilities, where coordination and individual initiative have a major effect on quality.

How do elders in LTCs differ from their counterparts in the community? Their socioeconomic and educational levels are generally lower, but the greatest single difference is illness—physical and mental. Most LTC residents suffer three chronic conditions, and 39% suffer from four or more. Almost two-thirds of the LTC population are widowed, and only 10% are married. Almost half do not have a viable relationship with any close relative. The median stay for current residents has been about two years, and most of them will die there or be readmitted to an acute-care facility. Less than half are ambulatory, one-third suffer urinary or fecal incontinence, or both, and 11% need help in eating. The rate of mental impairment has been estimated between 50 and 80%. Polypharmacology is another problem: The average patient receives about seven different drugs a week.

Physicians, psychologists, social workers, and clergy often find themselves in the position of having to recommend or decide whether or not to institutionalize an elder. This presents three basic issues for the professional making this decision. First, is this institutionalization really necessary? Second, which LTC should be selected? Third, what are the continuing responsibilities of the professional after placement has been made? The purpose of this chapter is to attempt to answer these questions.

ALTERNATIVES

In deciding whether institutionalization is necessary, it should be kept in mind that a competent judgment can be made only when there is a thorough knowledge of the alternatives to LTCs. The traditional alternative has been for a dependent elder to reside in the home of adult offspring, with the family taking over the functions of the nursing home staff: personal care, feeding, and the administration of medication if necessary. For every dependent elder in a nursing home, two others are being maintained in private residences. Most families try this solution first and consider an LTC only when it becomes too much of a burden or they fear that their level of care is inadequate.

Home health care is a new concept that is sweeping the nation. It may reverse the growth of LTCs by making it easier for families to take care of the medical needs of elders in private residences. A number of governmental, charitable, and proprietary agencies offer such care, but the efforts to date are a fragmented patchwork with gaps and duplications of effort. There are almost 300 home care agencies in the U.S., and 85% of them are certified for medicare coverage. Most of them offer nursing services (from RNs down to aides), and some also provide physical therapy, speech therapy, occupational therapy, social work, and even counseling on legal, financial, or psychological problems. Some agencies also work closely with physicians and pharmacists to provide coordinated care.

In fact, whatever services are provided in an LTC can

be provided in a private residence. (However, in some cases sophisticated equipment may be prohibitively expensive, but most LTCs lack such equipment as well. Some states prohibit home oxygen units.) The chief service provided by the LTC is labor. Only 7% of LTC employees are RNs, and most of their time is spent in charting medication and supervising other personnel, rather than in hands-on care. The vast majority of LTC employees are unskilled, poorly educated housekeepers, cooks, aides, orderlies, and laundry workers, many of whom are recent immigrants who are not fluent in English. Such personnel provide almost all the hands-on care: bathing, dressing, turning, changing, and feeding the patients. These services can be duplicated in the private residence.

In most southwestern states (and also in Chicago) it is possible to get illegal aliens to live in and take care of bedfast elders. The point of contact is usually a friendly priest down at the local Catholic church. Salaries usually start at about $100 a month plus room and board for a teenage girl with no references, experience, or knowledge of English. An illegal alien with references, experience, and some fluency in English can get over $500 a month plus room and board. Finding a good worker and keeping her are extremely difficult because of the intense competition from other American families who may be looking for a baby-sitter, cook, or maid. American workers, on the other hand, demand more money and more time off, and it is very difficult to get one of them to live in.

Home health care has many advantages over putting the patient in an LTC. The most obvious is that the patient remains in an environment that is familiar, and usually more supportive and stimulating than that found in an institution. Patients recuperate faster and with less confusion. Furthermore, they feel more in charge of the situation, as the employer or client, and not like an inmate who must conform to institutional regimentation. Home health care is also cheaper than an LTC, especially when the patient requires only intermittent skilled nursing care (Rossman, 1973). Think of it this way: Most of the services cost the same in an LTC or a private home (the workers will get about the same wage), but an LTC has to charge more to provide the patient with a room and meals.

Unfortunately, home health care has not received priority over LTCs. In 1975 the federal government spent over $9 billion for geriatric LTCs, but only $400 million on home health care. This differs markedly from the situation in other countries, where home care is the rule, and institutionalization is rare and usually only temporary. In Sweden almost 1% of the population receives such help, but in the U.S. it is only 15 per 100,000. The chief culprit in this trend is the federal government, which indirectly (through medicare and medicaid payments) foots the bills of the LTCs but is reluctant to reimburse individuals for the cost of home care. The resulting situation is that elders and their families often opt for institutionalization even though it may be medically and psychologically less desirable (for the patient) and financially less desirable (for the nation), simply because the government will pay for institutional care and the family must pay for home care. Fortunately, medicare is becoming more open to reimbursement for home care, but the red tape and guidelines are still there. There are two ways to qualify for up to 100 visits. The first way involves the following five conditions.

1. The patient must have been hospitalized for at least three consecutive days.
2. The continuing care he needs must include part time skilled nursing or physical or speech therapy.
3. The patient must be confined to his home.
4. A physician must determine that home care is needed and must establish a plan within 14 days

after the patient is discharged from a hospital or LTC.

5. The home health care must be for the further treatment of a condition for which the patient received treatment in the acute-care hospital or LTC.

The other way of getting home-care financing is to meet the following conditions.

1. The medicare beneficiary must need part-time skilled nursing care or physical or speech therapy.
2. He must be confined to his home.
3. A physician must determine that the patient needs home health care.
4. The physician must set up and periodically review the home health care plan.
5. The home health care agency must participate in the medicare program.

Another alternative to an LTC is a senior day care center. These centers care for ambulatory elders and those who are sufficiently mobile in wheelchairs. One of the greatest difficulties is getting the elder to the center and home again, especially when the patient is confused or chairfast. The best day care programs have arts, crafts, hobbies, exercises, group discussions, and a noon meal specifically tailored to individual dietary restrictions and nutritional needs. Screening for certain diseases (glaucoma, hypertension, and cancer) is also a welcome adjunct. Day care centers differ greatly in their ability to care for elders who are confused or incontinent. This alternative is not going to meet the needs of every patient, but it is very helpful in providing some modicum of structure and supervison in the life of an elder living alone, or some temporary relief of the burdens of care imposed on those living with a dependent elder.

Unfortunately, the alternatives to LTCs are inadequately considered. As a result, too many elders are inappropriately placed in LTCs. In Rochester an evaluation and placement unit was set up to review all referrals to LTCs. In the first 2½ years, the unit examined 332 patients and sent the majority back to their own homes or into a residential care facility, and sent only one-third of the total to LTCs (Williams, Hill, Fairbank & Knox, 1973). A study by the University of Michigan involved 40 LTCs around Detroit. This study concluded that only wealthy, married elders had used the LTCs for their intended purposes (rehabilitation or terminal care), holding off on admission until absolutely necessary. Many of the residents were there for relatively minor physical problems coupled with insufficient socioeconomic resources to maintain them in the community. The report concluded that about 40% of the LTC residents were able to carry on their activities without assistance and only needed a place to stay, while only one-quarter were completely helpless (Aging, 1974). Whereas the U.S. commits 5% of its elders to LTCs, few other modern nations are over 1%. This difference reflects the comparatively greater provision of home and community services in the other nations.

THE DECISION

After becoming fully acquainted with the community and family resources, the professional can help make the decision about institutionalization. The patient's level of physical and mental functioning are important, though not overriding considerations. Ultimately, socioeconomic factors must predominate. Ten questions must be asked.

1. How is the patient's orientation in space and time?
2. Can he feed himself, and prepare his own food if necessary?
3. Can he communicate effectively, and use a telephone if necessary?
4. Can he use money to purchase necessary items?
5. Can he use the bathroom by himself?
6. Can he groom himself?
7. Can he clean his quarters?
8. Can he get around his home?
9. Can he get around his neighborhood?
10. Is he a danger to himself or others?

When there are deficiencies in the patient's functioning, he will need assistance, either from the family or the community. When all functional deficits can be taken care of in the home and community, there is no need for institutionalization, regardless of the degree of physical or mental deterioration. However, deficits in performance place a strain on the patient's socioeconomic environment. It is when that environment can no longer support that strain that institutionalization becomes the unavoidable decision.

Once that decision has been made, the question becomes "which LTC?" There are a dozen tip-offs indicating quality care. These factors, plus the individual needs of the patient and his family, should be given thorough consideration.

1. Low Staff Turnover. In the average LTC, three out of four employees will be gone in less than a year. Most likely, the positions will be filled by new, untrained personnel. These high turnover rates reflect the low pay and depressing working conditions of the industry. A fairly low turnover rate is much more likely to indicate a facility with a well-trained and dedicated staff. Furthermore, if the workers

stay on, the home must be a nice place with good administrators and rewarding relations between patients and staff.
2. *Volunteers.* The additional labor of volunteers costs the
facility nothing, yet frees its staff to devote more time to
patient care. Also consider this: Poorly run facilities do not
want outsiders coming in and seeing the deplorable conditions. If the administrator encourages volunteers, that
means he has nothing to hide. Finally, volunteers, like staff,
tend to stay at LTCs with pleasant atmospheres. For all
these reasons, the presence of volunteers is a good sign of
quality.
3. *Sprinklers.* There were several thousand nursing home
fires last year. In 1975 31 patients died in different Chicago
fires less than a month apart. The fire department was on
the scene less than four minutes after receiving the automatic alarm. These tragic fires prove that, even with such
a prompt response, the evacuation of bedridden patients is
a slow and dangerous process. The best fire protection is
a complete sprinkler system that can put out a fire any-
where in the building. Only a few LTCs have them now.
4. *Individualized Diets.* Most patients have dietary restrictions due to disease or previous surgery. Unfortunately,
most nursing homes prepare two or three types of meals
rather than gearing each patient's nutrition to his particular
requirements and preferences.
5. *Reality Orientation.* The dull routine of regimented institutional life causes many geriatric patients to become
bored. As a result, they tune out sensory input and retreat
more and more to a fantasy world. They become more
confused about where they are, when it is, and with whom
they are speaking. Too many nursing home staffs try to
humor confused patients, but this only reinforces the confusion. Reality orientation, a program developed in Veterans Administration hospitals, is a systematic attempt to give
the patient correct information about his environment. Pa-

tients receive daily classes in which they are told the time of day, date, month, year, and information about the location of things and the persons around the facility.

6. *Rehabilitation.*   If the patient is entering the LTC primarily because of a physical injury, such as a fractured hip or CVA, a comprehensive rehabilitiation program is essential. Adequate physical and speech therapy can restore many patients' functioning to normal. In addition to licensed therapists, make sure that the LTC has the necessary equipment.

7. *Bowel and Bladder Training.*   One-third of all LTC residents are incontinent. They require frequent and immediate attention. If they do not get it, they acquire painful bed sores. The best solution is to control the problem at its source with bowel and bladder training. When such a program is not developed or adhered to, all patients suffer because the staff has to spend most of its time caring for the incontinent patients.

8. *Exercise.*   All human bodies require daily exercise to keep them working well. Patients confined to wheelchairs or beds should not be exempt. They are the ones who most need supervised exercise. The other patients should be ambulating as much as possible. An LTC with a high percentage of patients up and about is doing a good job.

9. *Social Activities.*   Everyone needs interpersonal contact. There should be regular activities to provide meaningful interaction between patients. Having a TV room or weekly bingo is not enough. Organized musical activities and discussion groups are helpful. Perhaps the best activity is a project that requires the use of cooperative and creative skills.

10. *Patient Councils and Committees.*   When the patients are organized and have a direct channel to the administrator, problems are resolved more quickly. Also, everyone needs a feeling of importance, and the assurance that he can influence his environment. Giving patients the opportunity

to form an effective decision-making body makes them alert and gives them a sense of dignity.

11. Religious Services. Most older people look to religion as a source of solace and inspiration. Often it becomes an essential part of their lives. A good facility makes arrangements for religious services and regular contact between patients and clergy.

12. Personal Freedom. Life in any institution cramps individuality. Patients should be allowed to furnish their rooms with their own cherished possessions. Patients' clothing should be distinctive and selected by the patients. They should be allowed to set their own schedules, within reason. There should be no censorship of mail or restrictions on visitors or telephones. Privacy must be preserved. Most important, the patient must retain as much decision-making power as possible.

In addition to these dozen characteristics of a good nursing home, it is also important to find one that meets the specific needs of the patient.

THE ENDURING RESPONSIBILITY

After the patient has been placed in an LTC, there is yet another responsibility in safeguarding his interests: monitoring the quality of care. Most federal and state regulations cover such things as safety, sanitation, and auditing. There are few enforced guidelines directly relating to patient care. Do not hesitate to report any deficiencies in care to the director of the facility, Social Security Administration, or appropriate state and local agencies. Many patients and their families are afraid to complain for fear of retaliation by the LTC staff. The physician and social worker have better bargaining positions. With the overbedding of LTCs, administrators cannot afford to offend someone who might send them future patients. If such complaints do not bring action, consider relocation of the patient. Relocation in itself may prove traumatic for certain patients, and this measure should be taken only when the deficiencies or disadvantages of care vastly outweigh the probable difficulties of relocation.

CONCLUSION

Neither elders nor their families can be counted on to make informed and rational decisions about institutionalization. Trained professionals—physicians, psychologists, social workers, therapists, nurses, and clergy—must counsel and assist those considering institutionalization. Such counseling can avoid unnecessary and intolerable institutionalization. Two of the best alternatives to consider are day care and home health care. If an LTC becomes necessary, the geriatric counselor can help make a wise selection and then continue to monitor the quality of the care and protect the patient's interests.

Chapter 14

MILIEU THERAPY

With Cynthia Decker, M.A.

When a patient has been institutionalized, it does not signal the end of the therapist's responsibilities, nor of the need for psychotherapeutic intervention. Indeed, institutional life places additional stresses on the aging psyche and should be considered one of later life's psychosocial crises which can exacerbate existing, or generate new pathology. The purpose of this chapter is to examine such pathology and to recommend prophylactic or therapeutic measures appropriate to the institutional context.

PATHOLOGIES OF INSTITUTIONALIZATION

Lieberman and Tobin (1976) surveyed the psychological effects of institutionalization at its various phases. It is difficult to determine the degree to which mortality or further deterioration of institutionalized patients is due to any one of the following factors: the change in residence and loss

of old supports, the fact that the patient was institutionalized because of a worsening condition, and the actual milieu of the long-term care facility (LTC). Our present focus
is on the last of these.

One of the more fundamental changes in psychoanalytic personality theory took place when R. W.
White (1963) formally introduced the concept of independent ego energies. White contended that human and animal behavior is motivated not only by erotic and aggressive
instincts, but also by a drive to interact with and successfully master one's environment. This drive sometimes assists the other instincts by reshaping the organism's
environment in order to facilitate their gratification. Nevertheless, the drive for mastery has a definite degree of functional autonomy, so that instinctually satiated organisms
often persist in manipulating their environments. In humans these independent ego drives could explain such
phenomena as playful and artistic activity.

Elders are not exceptions here. Even before White
formulated his theories, Goldfarb (1955) applied similar
notions to institutionalized elders. The bedridden OBS patient is still an organism with an environment, and has an
innate drive to interact with, manipulate, and master that
environment. Whatever behavior is effective in this is automatically reinforced by the intrinsic satisfaction derived
from the sense of competence. If psychopathological behavior is effective in manipulating the institutional environment, such behavior becomes ingrained.

Complicating all of this is the psychosocial role of patient. In most Western cultures, a person gains status to the
degree that he has managed to demonstrate mastery over
his environment. However, an entirely different set of rules
operates when a person is physically ill or incapacitated.
The sick role may be viewed anthropologically as a liminal
state (Cole, 1976). In it, there is a removal of all stigma for
the failure to cope with external (and even internal) neces-

sity. A patient is "not to blame" for his condition. The responsibility for his custodial care and rehabilitation now falls on his physician, on the staff at the LTC, or on both.

At one time or another, all of us are subjected to this liminal role of patient. However, we usually view it as a temporary relaxation of our normal duties. After a few days, we are very eager to shed the role of patient so that we can return to roles that foster a sense of mastery. The situation is somewhat different for the elder. In the final third of life, there is a progressive disengagement from many of the key positions of responsibility. Offspring acquire their physical and economic independence. Spouses and friends pass away. Elders retire from their careers. All of these factors accumulate to give the elder patient less motive to relinquish the special status of patient.

Granted, older persons do suffer from a greater number of chronic conditions, but the pampered role of patient can produce an excess or exaggerated disability (Filer & O'Connell, 1964). One characteristic of institutional neurosis is that the patient loses his will to live a normal life in the outside world (Isaacs, 1965; Stuart, 1970; Lieberman, 1969). He becomes meek and obedient, lacking the initiative to master the tasks necessary for independence, and perhaps even for an interest in his surroundings.

Most of the behavior commonly referred to as senility can be produced by usurping the problem-solving activities of an LTC patient (Meacher, 1972). Physicians, nurses, aides, and orderlies are preoccupied with the physical needs of the patient—so much so that they may not take into account emotional needs (Field, 1968; Whitehead, 1970). Physical restraint is sometimes imposed to prevent the patient from falling or otherwise harming himself. For a patient in an LTC, there is just too little that he has to be responsible for. His life is too often a featureless routine in which he is told when to get up, eat, bathe, and sleep. Should he fail to perform any of these tasks for himself, he may be rewarded by receiving more staff care and attention. These conditions foster a progressively dependent relationship in which some patients' excess disabilities increase to the point where they require hand feeding and are completely incontinent (Rudd, 1954).

The philosophy of assembly-line care in LTCs has a certain persuasive logic: The faster that the staff can meet the physical needs of the patients, the more health care is delivered per employee hour (and hence per unit cost). It seems more efficient to give meals and showers according to a tight schedule. It is also quicker to do things for the patient than to have him try to help. This is the rationale by which the staff takes over the personal tasks of the patient in an LTC. A logical corollary is that the more immobile and inactive the patients are, the easier it is for the staff to stick to a schedule. Therefore the staff gives patients consistent reinforcement for being inactive, whereas the patient's spontaneous activity disrupts the precision of scheduled staff time (Cautela, 1966). By precluding self-help and reinforcing immobility, assembly-line care defeats its own purpose by creating a greater need for the staff's time. Thus this philosophy of how to operate an LTC is both psychotherapeutically and economically counterproductive.

The theoretical perspective of Adler (1956, 1964) is useful in comprehending the psychodynamics of institutional neuroses. For Adler, the pivotal issue is inferiority feeling and how the individual responds to it. Adler's insights on the pampered child are most relevant to our consideration of the LTC patient. The prolongation of that role amounts to the prolongation of feelings of dependency and inferiority. On the other hand, the staff that does not truly respect the human potential of a patient, and subjects him to inadequate or assembly-line care, is also guilty of neglect or harsh treatment which can also exacerbate feelings of inferiority.

Adler noted that individuals subjected to pampering, neglect, or harsh treatment are more prone to use pathological behavior to attain their goals of feeling superior and mastering the environment. To a certain extent, these techniques are similar to those of children who also find themselves in a state of prolonged dependency. One pathological method is "organ dialect," which may be entirely unconscious. Organ dialect is the way that a person manifests his neurotic attempts to gain superiority (that is, the way he "speaks") through organic disability. As a physician in general office practice, Adler fully appreciated the physical origin of organic disease. However, he also recognized a tendency, especially among pampered children, to overexaggerate their symptoms to get more special attention. For geriatric LTC patients, the real physical conditions are abundant, and a pampering or otherwise inappropriate environment provides the requisite motivation for excess disability. Having physical limitations assures more contact with the staff. Incontinence is to a certain extent the product of the patient's desire to communicate with a staff that shows attention only when the sheets get wet (Schwartz & Stanton, 1950).

Another neurotic response to inferiority is masculine protest, which is manifested by combative and sexually assertive patients. Both try to compensate for a loss of status in their present patient role by clinging to the vestiges of masculinity. The combative patient follows a private logic which actively resists dependency and all of its symbols, even when his actions are counterproductive because they may lead to restraint or loss of privilege. He pursues a short, though ineffective path to mastering the environment by pure force. Ineffective aggression is a major reaction pattern of poor adjustment to institutionalization (Rodstein, Savitsky & Starkman, 1976). The sexually assertive patient may have real sexual needs and capabilities, but inappropriate license taken with the staff or other patients more directly reflects a private logic which says "If I'm still a *man* (sexual object), then I'm still superior."

Masculine protest is not limited to males or to combativeness. Any form of overassertiveness could qualify. Patients who shout at someone close by or who use insults also fit in this category. Even those patients who badger the staff with unnecessary questions are seeking attention and status. However, not all patients can assert themselves verbally, and these are precisely the patients most likely to utilize physical combativeness and resistance. For example, combativeness is especially common among those patients with poor verbal skills, especially CVA aphasics. Perhaps this could also explain the higher rates of combativeness common when either the patient or the staff is not fluent in English. Verbal channels break down and patients use other means to express themselves.

Of course, combativeness is not always a purposive tactic in the service of a superiority-seeking private logic. A great deal of it occurs at night when patients may be more confused because of fatigue, poor sensory discrimination, or a dreamlike state. Nevertheless, no pathological behavior is ever completely free from the dynamics inherent in the role of patient.

Yet another neurotic response to inferiority feelings is to become overly self-conscious and shun social participation. Patients who enjoy music and games may withdraw from exercise and bingo sessions because of the presence of so many other people. Indeed, these patients may develop phobias or physical symptoms as an excuse for their nonparticipation. Agoraphobia (fear of open spaces) is sometimes so extreme that the patient feels secure only in his room. Some patients will stay in bed all day because this is where they feel most secure. Frequently, this fear is associated with incontinence. The patient is afraid of what will happen if he has to urinate or defecate and he is in a crowd of wheelchairs unable to get to a bathroom in time.

PROPHYLAXIS AND TREATMENT

The Adlerian perspective is also useful in helping an LTC avoid excess disability, combativeness, and sexual assertiveness in its patients. Adler and his followers have occupied themselves with child-rearing formulae. The best way to raise a child is to help him and encourage him to do things for himself. In this way he becomes capable of meeting his own needs and gains a sense of mastery and achievement which counteracts feelings of inferiority. When a child fails to master a task, it is best to refrain from punishment, severe criticism, or any comment or action (such as completely taking over the task) that will exacerbate his inferiority feelings. A proper response includes praising the attempt, calm and constructive criticism directed at the behavior and not the person, and encouragement to try again. Performing the child's task for him is useful only to the degree that it enables him to do it for himself in the future.

One of the factors truly essential to whatever approach is taken is that the entire staff charged with the patient's care can be coordinated. Indeed, psychotherapeutic intervention in an institutional context cannot hope to achieve very much under the traditional "one therapist, one hour a week" approach. The therapeutic training given by the best psychotherapist can be too easily undone and reversed by the unknowning workings of the staff in daily interactions with the patient. Of course, private sessions are yet possible in an LTC. However, such individual sessions have enduring results only when the staff consolidates these efforts (Aronson, 1956). The psychotherapist in an LTC can be most effective if he adopts a milieu approach to therapy. The interdisciplinary team approach discussed in Chapter 8 is appropriate and necessary for any work done in an LTC. Ideally, the entire staff should function as an extension of the psychotherapist. In practice, the psychotherapist may be an outsider to the LTC staff, in which case he may not be able to do more than make suggestions and defend the patient's rights. He may have to alter both his goals and techniques to secure what is both desirable and possible under the confines of the institutional context.

Korbrynski (1973) and Birjandi and Sclafani (1973) have reported impressive results with well-coordinated teams. Many LTCs now have a weekly therapeutic community meeting in which the staff assembles to discuss some cases. Input comes from the departments of patient care, dietetics, physical therapy, and sometimes even from maintenance or the front office. These sessions must be more than community gossip. They must serve the goals of formulating specific courses of action and coordinating the different departments.

If there is one key word in milieu therapy it is *activity*. The most deleterious effect of aging in general and institutionalization in particular is inactivity due to a loss of roles and the necessity for providing for oneself and others. The first and foremost kind of activity to encourage in an LTC is physical. Patients should be encouraged to walk as much as possible. There should be a comprehensive daily exercise program for all patients, including those who are chairfast and bedridden. Obviously, no one program could be expected simultaneously to suit the limitations of the more debilitated patients and to be stimulating to the more able-bodied. The important point is to exercise whatever can be safely moved. The emphasis should be on getting the patients to be more limber and confident in their physical potential. Therefore range of motion exercises are the most appropriate.

An exercise program also has dividends in social, cognitive, and attitudinal realms (Powell, 1972). Indeed, an organized exercise program has diagnostic, therapeutic, and prognostic dimensions. The staff can observe how well the patients follow simple instructions, accept self-responsibility, and interact. Of course, even the best run exercise program is no substitute for individualized physical therapy under the supervision of a qualified physical therapist.

Organized programs for mental exercise are also helpful. These can take the form of quizzes and games requiring various mental and intellectual abilities. Such games can be combined with manual dexterity tasks in crafts and communal projects. Mental activity can also be stimulated by educational courses. Many localities have adult education or community college extension programs that go into LTCs and teach the patients without cost to the LTC.

Patient activity also depends on the staff's expectations about patients' ability to help themselves. When the staff expects the patients to be utterly incapable of meeting their own basic needs, and treats them accordingly, it is not too long before the patients come to rely on the staff to do everything for them. One patient recuperating from a CVA liked to wear his pants, which happened to have buttons in the fly. Unfortunately, he needed some help unbuttoning and rebuttoning whenever he wanted to urinate. One orderly complained about this bother and encouraged the patient to wear a hospital gown. The patient ambulated less because he felt improperly attired in public. And he became increasingly incontinent when he learned that the staff did not expect him to be able to handle voiding by himself.

The other side of the coin is also true. When the staff lets the patients know that they are expected to play a larger role in self-care, and the staff furnishes the requisite opportunity, encouragement, training, and assistance, functional levels rise (Filer & O'Connell, 1964). Threats and coercion must be avoided, but demands can be made in a warm and reassuring atmosphere (Ginzberg, 1955). Indeed, a psychotherapeutic milieu must inevitably make a number of demands in self-management (grooming, cleaning quarters, preparing food) as well as in meaningful social roles

(Coons, Gottesman & Donahue, 1969). To facilitate self-help, patients should have special mechanical devices to help them compensate for real physical limitations: large-type reading material, hearing aids, magnifying glasses, button hooks, long-handled shoe horns, special eating and drinking utensils, and so on.

There is much to be said in favor of a work therapy project which assigns responsibility for various tasks around the institution: greeting visitors, delivering mail, folding laundry, and similar tasks. Especially with those patients who are alert and better educated, these tasks can stimulate problem-solving ability and prevent old skills from atrophying. All of these types of assignments have the advantage of giving patients a feeling of achievement, and also a sense that the LTC is a hospitable environment with which they may interact. These tasks also contribute to social interest by giving participants a feeling of contributing to the whole, a sense of belonging, and an experience of cooperation. Of course, there is the possibility that the resulting social interactions will lead to bickering and criticism. Here is the real task for the staff and the psychotherapist: to provide the requisite supervision to prevent hostility and hurt feelings (Cosin, Mort, Post, Westropp & Williams, 1958).

Another way of promoting patient responsibility and activity is by some form of self-governing body, whether councils or committees. Such governmental processes involve both social interaction and problem-solving skills. Self-government gives the participants feelings of being competent and of contributing to the whole (Bourestom, 1958). There are additional benefits for the LTC. One is that by informing the patients of their rights, and by giving them a voice, a channel is established for bringing grievances to the attention of the administrator. Another is that the patient government can serve as an extension of the administrator in order to explain to patients why things are run as they are, or to secure enforcement of the facility's regulations without having to involve the staff. Social pressure from fellow patients is frequently more effective in curbing deviant behavior than pressure that comes directly from the administration or staff.

In addition to increasing the patient's level of activity and responsibility, milieu therapy promotes restoration. One of the most important things to restore is the patient's orientation to reality. Probably the best article on this topic is by Folsom (1968), although there are numerous reports of successful applications (Taulbee & Folsom, 1966; Browne & Ritter, 1972; Citrin & Dixon, 1977). Reality orientation requires the following principles: a calm environment; a set routine; clear directions, questions, and answers; prohibition of confused speech or action; and firmness and sincerity. Reality orientation specifically seeks to reorient the patient to the here and now by daily classes and audiovisual cues that remind him of the correct time, date, month, year, day of the week, name of the institution, location, and names of people. Reality orientation has resulted in improved confidence, sociability, activity, eating habits, staff morale, mutual respect between patients and staff, and responsibility for dressing and grooming.

A useful adjunct to reality orientation is sensory retraining, in which patients are put into small groups and asked to use their senses to identify objects. This can increase the alertness and coordination of patients and also make their environments more interesting to them. Another approach is to use color and architecture to compensate for diminished sensory acuity. This gives patients a sense of territory and direction. Furniture and steps that contrast with the floor are easier to navigate. A stripe painted on the floor about a foot from the walls helps the wheelchair patients and those in walkers judge distances. All of this encourages ambulation and makes the patients less dependent on the staff.

Another aspect of restoration is remotivating the patient. Perhaps the biggest stumbling block to change is the attitudes of the patients and their families. Especially if they are paying for services, they expect to be served very well. They are upset if the patient has to tend to his own needs, or worse yet, if he has to help the other patients. Yet this is precisely what geriatric LTCs need if they are to regain a sense of usefulness, accomplishment, and importance. Attitudes can be changed, but inasmuch as attitudes are internalizations of socially constructed reality, attitudinal change is best effected through a group process. Group psychotherapy has proved effective with LTC patients. The group philosophy of "Agers Anonymous" discussed in Chapter 11 is one way of getting institutionalized elders to stop thinking of themselves as patients and start thinking of themselves as residents with responsibilities.

One useful adjunct in remotivating patients is to resocialize them in interpersonal roles that foster interaction and mutual responsibility taking. One policy that impedes this type of interaction is segregating patients of different levels of impairment, for example, putting the incontinent and confused patients on a separate ward. If a patient is transferred to this ward as soon as he shows any signs of disorientation, there may be little hope of rehabilitation. Life on such a ward lacks the quality of reality-based interpersonal relations. The only people a patient has to talk with are other confused patients and a staff which treats his confusion with a mixture of scorn and humoring.

The opposite approach is to design an integrated ward in which different kinds of patients interact. One solution employed by a Mexican LTC was to join with an orphanage. The elders had the time to bottle-feed infants or talk to the older children. This plan met two sets of needs: the need of the elders to feel useful and the need of the infants to be held while fed. However, such infant-elder integration has only a limited utility. Both children and elders become bored if they have only each other's company. Both prefer to spend most of the time with peers. In several state mental hospitals, administrators have tried to integrate old and young adults and to foster a buddy system in which the stronger and more active younger patient would assume the responsibility of helping an elder on a regular basis. This gave the elders the necessary assistance, while relieving the staff and giving the younger patients interpersonal contact and a feeling of usefulness (McNiel & Voerwoerdt, 1972).

Most American nursing homes cannot accomplish such an age integration, and the best that can be done is to put patients of different levels of impairment together. The advantage for the more alert and able-bodied patient is that he is taking responsibility for someone else, stops thinking about his own comparatively minor problems, and gains a feeling of importance and status around the facility. The poor patient receives a dual benefit also. First, he has someone to help him in his basic needs. Second, by interacting with less impaired patients, he is exposed to another elder who is stimulating and also a role model for more effective coping and responsibility taking (Atkinson, Fjeld & Freeman, 1955).

However, introducing disoriented or incontinent patients into a ward where they have been previously excluded must be done with the utmost tact and care. There is the danger that the more normal patients will view the deteriorated patients as harbingers of their own future state. A further danger is that the healthier patients will view the others as a drain on the staff time, reducing their own level of care (Richmond, 1964). Such integration should be initiated by degrees, and only after some responsibility-oriented group therapy has begun to change the attitudes of the normals; otherwise they may ostracize the confused and incontinent patients, making everyone more prone to paranoia and combativeness.

Another aspect of restoration in an LTC is the maintenance or re-establishment of attitudes and skills necessary for effective living on the outside. For example, most elders living in the community maintain a healthy degree of individuality and autonomy. They can make their own decisions about what to wear, how to decorate their rooms, or when to schedule daily activities. The institutionalized routine first usurps decision-making opportunity, and then decision-making ability atrophies, converting the patient into someone who only has to breathe, swallow, and excrete. The more opportunity for autonomy and individuality that patients are given, the more alert and active they remain. Allow and even encourage them to dress up, fix their hair, decorate their rooms, and plan their time.

Along with preserving attitudes and skills, LTCs must seek to retrain their patients when disuse has resulted in the loss of a skill. This is especially important in rehabilitating patients for release. The demands placed on the patients should become progressively more complex. They should relearn in paced steps: how to take medication, use the bus, go shopping, and so on (Coons, Gottesman & Donahue, 1969.) Especially with CBS patients, who will inevitably rely on the assistance of family members, a major aspect of planning release is training their families to accept and care for them (Clow, 1940).

Behavioral modification, which was discussed in Chapter 6, is central to many systems of milieu therapy. Indeed, behavioral modification takes place in every institutional environment, whether the staff knows it or not. The nature of staff interaction with patients constitutes a schedule of reinforcement capable of conditioning desired or undesired behavior. For example, the practice of humoring confused patients reinforces confusion via the positive reward of a smile or attention. Cautela (1966) argued that the low behavioral output of aged residents of LTCs was largely due to the fact that the staff had systematically and positively reinforced passivity, while punishing or ignoring active patients. Some patients spend all day saying "nurse, nurse" because it has brought rewards. The response is more difficult to extinguish because it has been conditioned on a variable ratio schedule.

When the staff gets together and systematically reinforces activity, helpfulness, responsibility, self-care, socialization, and other desirable behaviors, the patients adopt these traits (Ullman & Krasner, 1966; Birjandi & Sclafani, 1973.) Ayllon and Azrin (1965) conducted six experiments on institutionalized psychotics. Token economies were developed, and payment was given for positive behavior. Tokens were redeemable for small luxuries and privileges: a personal chair, privacy, or leave. The desirable behavior increased and reached a plateau under reinforcement, and it fell to near zero when reinforcement was removed or offered to patients who did not manifest the desired behavior. The effectiveness of the experiments was found even with patients who were quite old and also with those with some degree of OBS. Atthowe and Krasner (1968) implemented a token economy in a Veterans Administration psychiatric ward. Tokens were given for desired behavior and were redeemable for passes, movies, and well-located beds, in addition to some small material items. This project was successful in motivating 90% of the patients.

Senile behavior and institutional passivity lend themselves well to positive reinforcement. Rickard, Dignam, and Horner (1960) used verbal reinforcement (a smile, nod, word of conversation, praise, encouragement) for rational speech, and looked away or otherwise ignored the patient when the speech became confused or delusional. After a while, these researchers found that they could turn the delusional stream on or off by this type of manipulation. They also found that the conditioned response—rational speech—was very susceptible to extinction when the rate of reinforcement was reduced. In other words, to keep the patient lucid, it was necessary to interact with him on a very intense basis. Positive reinforcement can also be used with combative patients (Aronson, 1956).

Incontinence is another condition that responds well to behavioral modification. Most of the research has been done with child and adolescent enuresis. The patient is awakened by an alarm as soon as the urine begins to flow. This conditions the stimulus of urination to the response of getting up. Gradually, the patient is conditioned to awaken before the alarm goes off, and even before micturition begins. A supplemental operant approach is to reward the patient for dry nights, and gradually to increase the number of consecutive nights necessary for the reward.

The specific techniques of milieu therapy are divers and ingenious, but the basic approaches are standard: rehabilitate, remotivate, resocialize, reorient to reality and responsibility. A comprehensive, multidisciplinary, coordinated approach can be highly successful. Atkinson, Fjeld, and Freeman (1955) reported on a Minnesota state hospital project which combined ECT (even on CBS patients), work therapy, and staff retraining. Discharges went up 337% in the first six months (perhaps exhausting the best candidates), but remained high for the next six months. A University of Michigan milieu therapy project was able to discharge half of LTC patients in a year, compared with only a fourth of an untreated control group.

Such therapy can also dramatically improve the behavior of CBS patients. In 1971 Karl Menninger reported to the Senate Committee on Aging that after a year's treatment of 88 badly deteriorated patients, only six were still incontinent. Almost one-fourth had been released to life in the community. Brody, Kleban, Lawton and Silverman (1971) reported a statistically significant (p $<$ 0.01) result in the treatment of excess disabilities. Snyder and Harris (1976) presented recent case studies demonstrating how milieu therapy improved CBS patients to a baseline level of functioning.

CONCLUSION

Throughout this book I have emphasized the appropriateness of Alfred Adler's ideas in geriatrics, and the necessity for elders to feel important and useful. Nowhere is this truer than in LTCs. The big danger is that institutional life and the role of the patient will result in an institutional neurosis comprising apathy, dependency, and disorientation. Too many patients who go into LTCs for purely physical reasons develop mental problems. The only solution is for the staff to provide an uncompromising orientation to reality together with insistence on each patient's responsibility for helping himself and others. The psychotherapeutic milieu trains patients how to care for themselves and others, not how to be cared for.

REFERENCES

Abraham, K. *Selected papers of Karl Abraham.* New York: Basic Books, 1927.

Ackerman, N. W. *Family process.* New York: Basic Books, 1970.

Adler, A. *The individual psychology of Alfred Adler.* H. L. Ansbacher & R. R. Ansbacher (Eds.). New York: Harper & Row, 1956.

Adler, A. *Superiority and social interest.* H. L. Ansbacher & R. R. Ansbacher (Eds.). New York: Viking, 1964.

Aging. March–April *233,* 14, 1974.

Albrecht, R. The social roles of older persons. *Journal of Gerontology,* 1951, *6,* 138–145.

Alexander, F. G. The indications for psychoanalytic therapy. *Bulletin of the New York Academy of Medicine,* 1944, *20,* 319–334.

Altschuler, K. Z., Barad, M., & Goldfarb, A. I. A survey of dreams in the aged. II. Non-institutionalized subjects. *Archives of General Psychiatry,* 1963, *8,* 33–37.

Alvarez, R. R. Comparison of depressive and brain injured subjects on the trail making test. *Perceptual and Motor Skills,* 1962, *14,* 91–96.

Ames, L. B., Learned, J., Mextraux, R., & Walker, R. N. *Rorschach responses in old age.* New York: Hoeber-Harper, 1954.

Angel, R. W. Understanding and treating senile dementia. *Geriatrics,* 1977, *32,* 47–49.

Ankus, M., & Quarrington, B. Operant behavior in the memory-disordered. *Journal of Gerontology,* 1972, *27,* 500–510.

Aronson, M. Psychiatric management of disturbed behavior in a home for the aged. *Geriatrics,* 1956, *11,* 39–43.

Ashcraft, C., & Fitts, W. H. Self-concept change in psychotherapy. *Psychotherapy: Theory, Research, Practice,* 1964, *1,* 115–118.

Atkinson, S., Fjeld, S. P., & Freeman, J. G. An intensive treatment program for state hospital geriatric patients. *Geriatrics,* 1955, *10,* 111–117.

Atthowe, J. M., & Krasner, L. Preliminary Report on the application of contingent reinforcement procedures (token economy) on a chronic psychiatric ward. *Journal of Abnormal Psychology,* 1968, *73,* 37–43.

Ayllon, T., & Azrin, N. H. The measurement and reinforcement of behavior of psychotics. *Journal of the Experimental Analysis of Behavior,* 1965, *8,* 357–383.

Banaka, W. H. *Training in depth interviewing.* New York: Harper & Row, 1971.

Barad, M., Altschuler, K. Z., & Goldfarb, A. I. A survey of dreams in aged persons. *Archives of General Psychiatry,* 1961, *4,* 419–424.

Batchelor, I. R. C., & Napier, M. B. Attempted suicide in old age. *British Medical Journal,* 1953, *2,* 1186–1190.

Bellin, S. S., & Hardt, R. H. Marital status and mental disorders of the aged. *American Sociological Review,* 1958, *23,* 155–162.

Biran, S. Die Hypochondire und der Sammelbegriff des eingebildeten Krankseins. *Acta Psychoterapeutica und Psychosomatica,* 1963, *11,* 343–369.

Birjandi, P. F., & Sclafani, M. J. An interdisciplinary team approach to geriatric patient care. *Hospital and Community Psychiatry,* 1973, *24,* 777–778.

Birkett, D. P., & Boltuch, B. Remotivation therapy. *Journal of the American Geriatrics Society,* 1973, *21,* 368–371.

Blau, D., & Berezin, M. A. Neurosis in character disorder. In J. G. Howells (Ed.), *Modern perspectives in the psychiatry of old age.* London: Churchill & Livingston, 1975.

Blessed, G., Tomlinson, B. E., & Roth, M. The association between quantitative measures of dementia and dementia change in the cerebral grey matter of elderly subjects. *British Journal of Psychiatry,* 1968, *114,* 797–811.

Bonime, W. *The clinical use of dreams.* New York: Basic Books, 1962.

Bonime, W. The use of dreams in the therapeutic engagement of patients. *Contemporary Psychoanalysis,* 1969, *61,* 13–30.

Botwinick, J. *Aging and behavior.* New York: Springer, 1973.

Botwinick, J., & Thompson, L. W. Depressive affect, speed of response, and age. *Journal of Consulting Psychology,* 1967, *31,* 106.

Bourestom, N. C. Self-government for patients on a geriatric service. *Journal of the American Geriatrics Society,* 1958, *6,* 667–671.

Braceland, F. J. The art of psychotherapy. In J. H. Masserman (Ed.), *Handbook of psychiatry therapies.* New York: Grune & Stratton, 1966, 597–603.

Brena, S. F. *Pain and religion.* Springfield: Charles C Thomas, 1972.

Brenman, M., & Knight, R. P. Hypnotherapy for mental illness in the aged. *Bulletin of the Menninger Clinic,* 1943, *7,* 188–198.

Briganti, F. J. Side effects of drugs used by the elderly. In *Drugs and the elderly.* Los Angeles: University of Southern California Press, 1975, pp. 25–32.

Brink, T. L. Family counseling with the aged. *Family Therapy,* 1976a, *3,* 163–169.

Brink, T. L. Psychotherapy after forty. *MH,* 1976b, *60,* 22–25.

Brink, T. L. Brief psychotherapy: A case study illustrating its potential effectiveness. *Journal of the American Geriatrics Society,* 1977, *25,* 273–276.

Brink, T. L., & Brink, G. S. Can your dreams save your marriage? *Pageant,* 1976, *31,* 54–60.

Brocklehurst, J. C. Treatment of urinary incontinence in the elderly. *Postgraduate Medicine,* 1972, *51,* 184–187.

Brody, E. M., Kleban, M. H., Lawton, M. P., & Silverman, H. A. Excess disability of mentally impaired aged: Impact of individualized treatment. *Gerontologist,* 1971, *11,* 124–133.

Brody, E. M., & Spark, G. M. Institutionalization of the aged: A family crisis. *Family Process,* 1966, *5,* 76–90.

Browne, L. J., & Ritter, J. I. Reality therapy for geriatric patients. *Perspectives in Psychiatric Care,* 1972, *10,* 135–139.

Burgess, A. C. W. Depressive and aggressive behavior: Intervention techniques used in resolving adolescent conflicts. Boston University School of Nursing dissertation, 1967.

Burnside, I. M. Group work with the aged: Selected literature. *Gerontologist,* 1970, *10,* 241–246.

Burnside, I. M. *Sexuality and aging.* Los Angeles: University of Southern California Press, 1975.

Busse, E. Hypochondriasis in the elderly. *Journal of the American Geriatrics Society,* 1976, *24,* 145–149.

Busse, E., Barnes, R. H., Silverman, A. J., Shy, G. M., Thaler, M., & Frost, L. L. Studies on the process of aging: Factors that influence the psyche of elderly persons. *American Journal of Psychiatry,* 1954, *110,* 897–903.

Busse, E., & Pfeiffer, E. *Mental disorders in later life.* Washington, D.C.: American Psychiatric Association, 1973.

Butler, J. M., & Haight, G. V. Change in the relation between self-concept and ideal concepts consequent upon client-centered counseling. In C. R. Rogers & R. F. Dymond (Eds.), *Psychotherapy and personality change.* Chicago: University of Chicago Press, 1954, pp. 55–75.

Butler, R. N. Intensive psychotherapy for the hospitalized patient. *Geriatrics,* 1960, *15,* 644–653.

Butler, R. N. Life review. In R. J. Kastenbaum (Ed.), *New thoughts on old age.* New York: Springer, 1964, pp. 265–280.

Butler, R. N. *Why survive?* New York: Harper & Row, 1975.

Butler, R. N. *Sex after sixty.* New York: Harper & Row, 1976.

Caird, F. I., & Judge, T. G. *Assessment of the elderly patient.* Oxford: Allen & Mowbray, 1974.

Cameron, N. A study of thinking in senile deterioration and schizophrenic disorganization. *American Journal of Psychology,* 1936, *51,* 650–664.

Cameron, N. Deterioration and regression in schizophrenic thinking. *Journal of Abnormal and Social Psychology,* 1939, *34,* 265–270.

Cautela, J. Behavior therapy and geriatrics. *Journal of Genetic Psychology,* 1966, *108,* 9–17.

Cautela, J. A classical conditioning approach to the development and modification of behavior in the aged. *Gerontologist,* 1969, *9,* 109–113.

Chance, P. Behavioral sciences. *Encyclopedia Britannica Book of the Year,* 1977, p. 169.

Chapman, A. H. *Put-offs and come-ons: Psychological maneuvers and strategems.* New York. G. P. Putnam's Sons, 1968.

Chessick, R. D. Empathy and love in psychotherapy. *American Journal of Psychotherapy,* 1965, *19,* 205–219.

Chrzanowski, G. Neurasthenia and hypochondriasis. In S. Arieti (Ed.), *American handbook of psychiatry* (2nd ed.). New York: Basic Books, 1974, pp. 141–154.

Citrin, R. S., & Dixon, D. N. Reality orientation: A milieu therapy used in an institution for the aged. *Gerontologist,* 1977, *17,* 39–43.

Clow, H. E. A study of 100 patients suffering from psychosis with cerebral arteriosclerosis. *American Journal of Psychiatry,* 1940, *97,* 16–26.

Clow, H. E., & Allen, E. B. A study of depressive states of aging. *Geriatrics,* 1949, *4,* 11–17.

Clow, H. E., & Allen, E. B. Manifestations of psychoneuroses occurring in later life. *Geriatrics,* 1951, *6,* 31-38.

Cole, J. O., & Stotsky, B. Improving psychiatric drug therapy: A matter of dosage and choice. *Geriatrics,* 1974, *29,* 74-78.

Cole, M. G., & Mueller, H. F. Sleep deprivation used for depressed elderly. *Journal of the American Geriatrics Society,* 1976, *24,* 308-313.

Cole, S. A. Liminality and the sick role. *Man and Medicine,* 1976, *2,* 41-53.

Coleman, L. L. The modification of rigidity in geriatric patients through operant conditioning. Louisiana State University dissertation, 1963.

Coons, D. H., Gottesman, L. E., & Donahue, W. *A milieu therapy for geriatric patients.* Ann Arbor: University of Michigan Press, 1969.

Coons, W. H. The dynamics of change in psychotherapy. *Canadian Psychiatric Association Journal,* 1967, *12,* 239-245.

Corriere, R., & Hart, J. *The dream makers: Discovering your breakthrough dreams.* New York: Funk & Wagnalls, 1977.

Corsellis, J. A. N. *Mental illness and the aging brain: The distribution of pathological change in a mental hospital population.* London: Oxford University Press, 1962.

Cosin, L. Z., Mort, M., Post, F., Westropp, C., & Williams, M. Experimental treatment of persistent senile confusion. *International Journal of Social Psychiatry,* 1958, *4,* 24-42.

Cowdry, E. V. *Problems of aging.* Baltimore: Williams & Wilkins, 1939.

Cumming, E., & Henry, W. E. *Growing old: The process of disengagement.* New York: Basic Books, 1961.

DeAlarcon, R. Earlier diagnosis of the depressions of the aged. *Revista de Medicina de la Universidad de Navarra,* 1968, *12,* 193-207.

DeGroot, M. H. L. The clinical use of psychotropic drugs in the elderly. *Drugs,* 1974, *8,* 132-138.

Dement, W. C., & Fischer, C. The effect of dream deprivation and excess: An experimental demonstration of the necessity for dreaming. *Psychoanalytic Quarterly,* 1960, *29,* 607-608.

DeRopp, R. *The master game.* New York: Harper & Row, 1968.

DeVaul, R. A., & Zisook, S. Unresolved grief: Clinical considerations. *Postgraduate Medicine,* 1976, *59,* 267-271.

Dichter, M. Aggressive expression as a function of self-esteem level, insult and no insult, and ego involvement and task oriented directing set. Temple University dissertation, 1965.

Dorken, H. Normal senescent decline and senile dementia. *Medical Services Journal,* 1958, *14,* 18-23.

Dorken, H., & Kral, V. A. Psychological investigation of senile dementia. *Geriatrics,* 1951, *6,* 151-163.

Dymond, R. F. A preliminary investigation of the relation of insight and empathy. *Journal of Counseling Psychology*, 1948, *12*, 228–233.

Eisner, D. A. Can hyperbaric oxygenation improve cognitive functioning in the organically impaired elderly? *Journal of Geriatric Psychiatry*, 1975, *8*, 173–188.

Erikson, E. H. *Childhood and society.* New York: Norton, 1950.

Erikson, E. H. *Identity and the life cycle.* New York: International Universities Press, 1959.

Ernst, P., Badash, D., Beran, B., Kosovsky, R., & Kleinhauz, M. Incidence of mental illness in the aged: Unmasking the effects of a diagnosed CBS. *Journal of the American Geriatrics Society*, 1977, *25*, 371–375.

Estabrooks, G. H. *Hypnosis.* New York: Dutton, 1957.

Eysenck, H. J. *Uses and abuses of psychology.* Baltimore: Penguin, 1953.

Faraday, A. *Dream power.* New York: Coward, McCann & Geogahagen, 1972.

Faraday, A. *Dream game.* New York: Harper & Row, 1974.

Farhner, B. G. Perspectives on psychotherapy: Drive expressions and self-esteem as related to outcome. Michigan State University dissertation, 1970.

Feigenbaum, E. M. Ambulatory treatment of the elderly. In E. W. Busse & E. Pfeiffer (Eds.), *Mental illness in later life.* Washington, D.C.: American Psychiatric Association, 1973, 153–166.

Feil, N. W. Group therapy in a home for the aged. *Gerontologist*, 1967, *7*, 192–195.

Fenichel, O. *The psychoanalytic theory of neurosis.* New York: Norton, 1945.

Fenyon, F. E. Hypochondriasis: A clinical study. *British Journal of Psychiatry*, 1964, *110*, 478–488.

Fenyon, E. E. Hypochondriasis: A survey of some historical, clinical, and social aspects. *British Journal of Medical Psychology*, 1965, *38*, 117–133.

Ferreira, A. J. Empathy and the bridge function of the ego. *Journal of the American Psychoanalytic Association*, 1961, *9*, 91–105.

Ferris, S., Crook, T., Sathananthan, G., & Gershon, S. Reaction time as a diagnostic measure of senility. *Journal of the American Geriatrics Society*, 1976, *24*, 533.

Fierman, L. B. Myths in the practice of psychotherapy. *Archives of General Psychiatry*, 1965, *12*, 404–414.

Field, M. *Aging with honor and dignity.* Springfield, Charles C Thomas, 1968.

Fielding, B. B. The utilization of dreams in the treatment of couples. *Psychotherapy and Psychosomatics*, 1966, *14*, 81–89.

Fielding, B. B. Dreams in group psychotherapy. *Psychotherapy: Theory, research, and practice,* 1967, *4,* 74–77.

Filer, R. N., & O'Connell, D. D. Motivation of aging persons. *Journal of Gerontology,* 1964, *19,* 15–22.

Fink, M., Green, A., & Bender, M. B. Face-hand test as diagnostic sign of organic mental syndrome. *Neurology,* 1952, *2,* 46–58.

Fishback, D. B. Mental status questionnaire for organic brain syndrome: With a new visual counting test. *Journal of the American Geriatrics Society,* 1977, *25,* 167–170.

Folsom, J. C. Reality orientation for the elderly mental patient. *Journal of Geriatric Psychiatry,* 1968, *1,* 291–307.

Ford, J. M., & Roth, W. T. Do cognitive abilities decline with age? *Geriatrics,* 1977, *32,* 59–72.

Forrer, G. *Psychiatric self-help.* Rosslyn Heights, N.Y.: Libra, 1973.

Frank, J. D. Therapeutic factors in psychotherapy. *American Journal of Psychotherapy,* 1971, *25,* 350–361.

Frank, J. D. Psychotherapy: The restoration of morale. *American Journal of Psychiatry,* 1974, *131,* 271–274.

Freeman, E. M. H. Effects on aggressive expression after frustration of performance: A test of catharsis hypothesis. Stanford University dissertation, 1962.

Freud, S. *The standard edition of the complete psychological works of Sigmund Freud.* 24 volumes. London: Hogarth, 1966.

Friedman, A. S. Minimal effects of severe depression on cognitive function. *Journal of Abnormal and Social Psychology,* 1964, *69,* 237–243.

Galton, L. *Don't give up on an aging parent.* New York: Crown, 1975.

Gardner, E. A., Bahn, A. K., Mack, M. Suicide and psychiatric care in the aging. *Archives of General Psychiatry,* 1964, *10,* 547–553.

Garfield, P. *Creative dreaming.* New York: Simon & Schuster, 1975.

Garfield, S. L., & Bergin, A. E. Therapeutic conditions and outcomes. *Journal of Abnormal Psychology,* 1971, *77,* 108–114.

Garner, H. H., & Korzeniowski, S. N. The older patient: A confrontation problem-solving technic in treatment. *Postgraduate Medicine,* 1971, *49,* 202–208.

Gershberg, J. Dreams and reality testing. *Comprehensive Psychiatry,* 1969, *10,* 391–397.

Gershman, H. Dream power. *American Journal of Psychoanalysis,* 1973, *33,* 167–177.

Gibson, R. W. Medicare and the psychiatric patient. *Psychiatric Opinion,* 1970, *7,* 17–22.

Gilbert, J. G. *Understanding old age.* New York: Ronald Press, 1952.

Gilbert, M. M. Reactive depression as a model psychosomatic disease. *Psychosomatics*, 1970, *11*, 426–428.

Ginzberg, R. Attitude therapy in geriatric ward psychiatry. *Journal of the American Geriatrics Society*, 1955, *3*, 445–462.

Godbole, A., & Verinis, J. S. Brief psychotherapy in the treatment of emotional disorders in physically ill geriatric patients. *Gerontologist*, 1974, *14*, 143–148.

Goldfarb, A. I. Psychiatric problems of old age. *New York State Journal of Medicine*, 1955a, *55*, 494–500.

Goldfarb, A. I. Psychotherapy of aged persons. IV. One aspect of the psychodynamics of the therapeutic situation with aged patients. *Psychoanalytic Review*, 1955b, *42*, 180–187.

Goldfarb, A. I. The rationale for psychotherapy with older persons. *American Journal of the Medical Sciences*, 1956, *232*, 181–185.

Goldfarb, A. I. Patient-doctor relationship in treatment of aged persons. *Geriatrics*, 1964, *19*, 18–23.

Goldfarb, A. I. Geropsychiatry in the general hospital. *Mt. Sinai Journal of Medicine*, 1971, *37*, 40–57.

Goldfarb, A. I. & Sheps, J. Psychotherapy of the aged. *Psychosomatic Medicine*, 1954, *16*, 209–219.

Goldfarb, A. I., & Turner, H. Psychotherapy of aged persons: Utilization and effectiveness of brief therapy. *American Journal of Psychiatry*, 1953, *109*, 916–921.

Gonda, T. A. Coping with death and dying. *Geriatrics*, 1977, *32*, 71–73.

Gramlich, E. P. Recognition and management of grief in elderly patients. *Geriatrics*, 1968, *23*, 87–92.

Greenberg, R., Pillard, R., & Pearlman, C. Dream deprivation and adaptation to stress. *Psychophysiology*, 1968, *5*, 238.

Grof, P. Doxepin versus amitriptyline in depression. *Current Therapeutic Research*, 1974, *16*, 470–476.

Grotjahn, M. Psychoanalytic investigation of a 71-year-old man with senile dementia. *Psychoanalytic Quarterly*, 1940, *9*, 80–97.

Grotjahn, M. Some analytic observations about the process of growing old. In G. Roheim (Ed.), *Psychoanalysis and social science*. New York: International Universities Press, 1951, pp. 301–312.

Grotjahn, M. Analytic therapy with the elderly. *Psychoanalytic Review*, 1955, *42*, 419–427.

Grunewald, D., & Fromm, E. Hypnosis, simulation, and brain damage. *Journal of Abnormal Psychology*, 1967, *72*, 191–192.

Gubrium, J. F. *Time, roles, and self in old age*. New York: Human Sciences Press, 1976.

Guerney, B. G. *Psychotherapeutic agents: New roles for non-professionals.* New York: Harper & Row, 1969.

Haas, J. B., & Kuypers, S. A. *From thirty to seventy.* San Francisco: Jossey-Bass, 1975.

Hall, C. M. Aging and family processes. *Journal of Family Counseling,* 1976, *4,* 28–42.

Hall, C. S. *Meaning of dreams.* New York: McGraw-Hill, 1966.

Hammer, M. *The theory and practice of psychotherapy with specific disorders.* Springfield: Charles C Thomas, 1972.

Hart, J., Corriere, R., & Binder, J. *Going sane: An introduction to feeling therapy.* New York: Aronson, 1975.

Havighurst, R. Personal and social adjustment in old age. In W. Donahue & C. Tibbitts (Eds.), *New frontiers of aging.* Ann Arbor: University of Michigan Press, 1957, pp. 172–179.

Havinghurst, R., & Albrecht, R. *Older people.* New York: Longmans, Green, 1953.

Havinghurst, R., Neugarten, B. L., & Tobin, S. S. Disengagement and patterns of aging. In B. L. Neugarten (Ed.), *Middle age and aging.* Chicago: University of Chicago Press, 1968, pp. 161–172.

Hensi, L. K., Whitehead, A., & Post, F. Cognitive functioning and cerebral arousal in elderly depressives and dements. *Journal of Psychosomatic Medicine,* 1968, *12,* 145–156.

Herkimer, J. K., & Meerloo, J. A. M. Treatment of mental disorder in elderly women. *Social Casework,* 1951, *32,* 419–425.

Hiatt, H. Dynamic therapy of the aged. In J. Masserman (Ed.), *Handbook of psychiatric therapies.* New York: Grune & Stratton, 1966, pp. 329–333.

Hodkinson, H. M. *An outline of geriatrics.* New York: Academic Press, 1975.

Hoffman, A. *The daily needs of older persons.* Springfield: Charles C Thomas, 1970.

Hollister, L. Prescribing drugs for the elderly. *Geriatrics,* 1977, *32,* 71–73.

Huston, P. Treatment of depression. In J. Masserman (Ed.), *Handbook of psychiatric therapies.* New York: Grune & Stratton, 1966, pp. 229–236.

Isaacs, B. *An introduction to geriatrics.* Baltimore: Williams & Wilkins, 1965.

Janov, A. *The primal scream.* New York: Simon & Schuster, 1970.

Janov, A. *The anatomy of mental illness.* New York: Simon & Schuster, 1970.

Janov, A. *The primal revolution.* New York: Simon & Schuster, 1972.

Janov, A. *The feeling child.* New York: G. P. Putnam's Sons, 1973.

Janov, A. *The primal man.* New York: G. P. Putnam's Sons, 1976.

Jeffers, F. C., & Nichols, C. R. The relationship of activities and attitudes to physical well-being in older people. *Journal of Gerontology,* 1961, *16,* 67–73.

Jelliffee, S. E. The old age factor in psychoanalytic therapy. *Medical Journal Record,* 1925, *121,* 7–12.

Jung, C. G. *Collected Works.* 17 volumes. New York: Pantheon, Princeton: Princeton University Press, 1953–1976.

Kahn, E., & Fischer, C. Dream recall in the aged. *Psychophysiology,* 1968, *5,* 222.

Kahn, E., & Fischer, C. Sleep characteristics of normal aged males. *Journal of Nervous and Mental Disease,* 1969, *148,* 477–494.

Kahn, E., Fischer, C., & Lieberman, L. Dream recall in the aged. *Journal of the American Geriatrics Society,* 1969, *17,* 1121–1126.

Kahn, R. L., Pollack, M., & Goldfarb, A. I. Factors related to individual differences in mental status of institutionalized aged. In P. H. Hoch & J. Zubin (Eds.), *Psychopathology of aging.* New York: Grune & Stratton, 1961, pp. 104–113.

Kardener, S. H. EST and the MD. *Psychiatric Opinion,* 1970, N*31,* 110–115.

Kastenbaum, R. The mental life of dying geriatric patients. *Proceedings of the seventh international conference on gerontology,* 1966, pp. 153–159.

Kastenbaum, R., & Aisenberg, R. *Psychology of death.* New York: Springer, 1972.

Kaufman, M. R. Psychoanalysis in later life depressions. *Psychoanalytic Quarterly,* 1937, *6,* 308–335.

Kaufman, M. R. Old age and aging. *American Journal of Orthopsychiatry,* 1940, *10,* 73–84.

Kelman, H. A new approach to dream interpretation. *American Journal of Psychoanalysis,* 1944, *4,* 89–107.

Kelman, H. Techniques in dream interpretation. *American Journal of Psychoanalysis,* 1965, *25,* 3–20.

Kendrick, D. C., & Post, F. Differences in cognitive status between healthy, psychiatrically ill, and diffusely brain damaged elderly subjects. *British Journal of Psychiatry,* 1967, *113,* 75–81.

Kent, S. Classifying and treating organic brain syndrome. *Geriatrics,* 1977, *32,* 87–96.

Kinsbourne, M. Diagnosis of cognitive deficit in the aged. *Postgraduate Medicine,* 1971, *50,* 191–194.

Kiørbe, E. Suicide and attempted suicide among old people. *Journal of Gerontology,* 1951, *6,* 233–236.

Kleban, M. H., Brody, E. M., & Lawton, M. P. Personality traits in the mentally impaired aged and their relationship to improvements in current functioning. *Gerontologist,* 1971, *11,* 134–140.

Klein-Lipshult, E. Comparison of dreams in individual and group psychotherapy. *International Journal of Group Psychotherapy,* 1953, *3,* 143–149.

Knight, G. Intractable psychoneurosis in the elderly and infirm: Treatment by stereotactic tratotomy. *British Journal of Geriatric Practice,* 1966, *3,* 7.

Knopf, O. *Successful aging.* New York: Viking, 1975.

Kopell, B. S. Treating the suicidal patient. *Geriatrics,* 1977, *32,* 65–67.

Korbrynski, B. Innovations in programs of care of the elderly. *Gerontologist,* 1973, *13,* 50–53.

Kramer, M., Roth, T., & Trinder, J. Dreams and dementia. *International Journal of Aging and Human Development,* 1975, *6,* 169–178.

Kübler-Ross, E. *On death and dying.* New York: MacMillan, 1969.

Kurtz, R. A., & Grummon, D. L. Different approaches to the measurement of therapist empathy and their relationship to therapy outcomes. *Journal of Consulting and Clinical Psychology,* 1972, *39,* 106–115.

Laxer, R. M. Self-concept changes of depressive patients in general hospital treatment. *Journal of Consulting Psychology,* 1964, *28,* 214–219.

Lazarus, A. Notes on behavior therapy, the problem of relapse, and some tentative solutions. *Psychotherapy: Theory, Research, Practice,* 1971, *8,* 192–194.

Lazarus, A. & Fay, A. *I can if I want to.* New York: William Morrow, 1975.

Lepp, I. *Death and its mysteries.* New York: MacMillan, 1968.

Lesse, S. Patient's expectations in psychotherapy: Their effect on results. In J. Masserman (Ed.), *Handbook of psychiatric therapies.* New York: Grune & Stratton, 1966, pp. 604–610.

Lesse, S. Depression masked by acting-out behaviors. *American Journal of Psychotherapy,* 1974, *28,* 352–361.

Lesser, W. M. The relationship between counseling progress and emphatic understanding. *Journal of Counseling Psychology,* 1961, *8,* 330–336.

Levin, S. Depression in the aged: The importance of external factors. In R. Kastenbaum (Ed.), *New thoughts on old age.* New York: Springer, 1964, pp. 179–185.

Levitt, E. E., & Lubin, B. *Depression.* New York: Springer, 1975.

Levinson, T., & Sereny, G. An experimental evaluation of insight therapy for the chronic alcoholic. *Canadian Psychiatric Association Journal*, 1969, *14*, 143–146.

Lieberman, M. A. Institutionalization of the aged: Effects of behavior. *Journal of Gerontology*, 1969, *24*, 330–340.

Lieberman, M. A., & Tobin, S. *Last home for the aged.* San Francisco: Jossey-Bass, 1976.

Linden, M. E. Group psychotherapy with institutionalized senile women. *International Journal of Group Psychotherapy*, 1953, *3*, 150–170.

Lion, J. R. The role of depression in the treatment of aggressive personality disorders. *American Journal of Psychiatry*, 1972, *129*, 347–349.

Lipsett, D. R. Psychodynamic considerations of hypochondriasis. *Psychotherapy and Psychosomatics*, 1974, *23*, 132–139.

Livson, F., Reichard, S., & Peterson, P. G. *Aging and personality.* New York: Wiley, 1962.

Lofholm, P. Quoted by *National Enquirer*, November 9, 1976, p. 47.

Lopata, H. Z. *Widowhood in an American city.* Cambridge, Mass.: Schenckman, 1973.

Low, A. *Mental health through will-training.* Boston: Christopher, 1950.

Lowenthal, M. F., & Berkman, P. L. *Aging and mental disorder in San Francisco.* San Francisco: Jossey-Bass, 1967.

Lowenthal, M. F., & Haven, C. Interaction and adaptation: Itinerary as a critical variable. In B. L. Neugarten (Ed.), *Middle age and aging.* Chicago: University of Chicago Press, 1968, pp. 390–400.

Maas, H. S., & Kuypers, J. A. *From thirty to seventy.* San Francisco: Jossey-Bass, 1975.

McCranie, E. J. Depression, anxiety, hostility. *Psychiatric Quarterly*, 1971, *45*, 117–133.

MacGregor, R., Ritchie, A. M., Serrano, A. C., & Schuster, F. P. *Multiple impact therapy.* New York: McGraw-Hill, 1964.

McNiel, J. N., & Voerwoerdt, A. A group treatment program combined with a work project on the geriatric unit of a state hospital. *Journal of the American Geriatrics Society*, 1972, *20*, 259–264.

Mahrer, A. R. Personal life change through systematic use of dreams. *Psychotherapy: Theory, Research, Practice*, 1971, *8*, 328–332.

Malamud, N. A comparison of the neuropathological findings in senile psychoses and in normal senility. *Journal of the American Geriatrics Society*, 1965, *13*, 113–117.

Malek, Z. B. The effect of group experiences on the aged. University of Southern California dissertation, 1961.

Manaster, A. Therapy with the senile geriatric patient. *International Journal of Group Psychotherapy*, 1972, *22*, 250–258.

Martin, A. R. The dynamics of insight. *American Journal of Psychoanalysis,* 1952, *12,* 24–38.

Martin, L. J. *Handbook for old age counselors.* San Francisco: Geertz, 1944.

Martin, L. J., & DeGruchy, C. *Salvaging old age.* New York: MacMillan, 1930.

Martin, L. J., & DeGruchy, C. *Sweeping the cobwebs.* New York: MacMillan, 1933.

Masters, W. H., & Johnson, V. E. *Human sexual response.* Boston: Little, Brown, 1966.

Masterson, J. F. Psychotherapy for the adolescent: A comparison with adult psychotherapy. *Journal of Nervous and Mental Disease,* 1958, *127,* 511–517.

Meacher, M. *Taken for a ride.* London: Longmans, 1972.

Meares, A. *Relief without drugs.* Garden City, N.Y.: Doubleday, 1967.

Meerloo, J. A. M. Contribution of psychoanalysis to the problem of the aged. In M. Heiman (Ed.), *Psychoanalysis and social work.* New York: International Universities Press, 1953, pp. 321–337.

Meerloo, J. A. M. Psychotherapy with elderly people. *Geriatrics,* 1955a, *10,* 583–587.

Meerloo, J. A. M. Transference and resistance in geriatric psychotherapy. *Psychoanalytic Review,* 1955b, *42,* 72–82.

Merrill, S., & Cary, G. L. Dream analysis in brief psychotherapy. *American Journal of Psychotherapy,* 1974, *29,* 187–193.

Moberg, D. O. Church membership and personal adjustment in old age. *Journal of Gerontology,* 1953, *8,* 207–212.

Moberg, D. O., Religious activities and personal adjustment in old age. *Journal of Social Psychology,* 1956, *43,* 261–277.

Meberg, D. O. Christian beliefs and personal adjustment in old age. *Journal of the American Scientific Affiliation,* 1958, *10,* 8.

Muzio, M., Cicchetti, V., & Gabrielli, F. Sulpiride in the treatment of psychoneuroses. *Revista de Psichiatria,* 1973, *8,* 252–261.

Neugarten, B. L. *Middle age and aging.* Chicago: University of Chicago Press, 1968.

Neumarker, K. J. Iatrogene hypochondrische Neurosen und ihre Individualtherapie. *Psychiatrie, Neurologie und Medizinische Psichologie,* 1966, *18,* 182–189.

Nichols, W. C., Rutledge, A. L. Psychotherapy with teenagers. *Journal of Marriage and the Family,* 1965, *27,* 166–170.

Nies, A., Robinson, D. S., Davis, J. M., Ravaris, L. Changes in MAO with aging. In C. Eisdorfer & W. E. Fann (Eds.), *Psychopharmacology and aging.* New York: Plenum, 1973, pp. 41–54.

Nighswander, J. K., & Mayer, G. R. Catharsis: A means of reducing elementary school children's aggressive behavior. *Personnel and guidance journal,* 1969, *47,* 461–466.

Novaco, R. W. *Anger control: The development and evaluation of an experimental treatment.* Lexington, Mass.: Heath, 1975.

Nowlin, J. B. Physical changes in later life and their relationships to mental function. In E. W. Busse & E. Pfeiffer (Eds.), *Mental illness in later life.* Washington, D.C.: American Psychiatric Association, 1973, pp. 145–153.

Oberleder, M. Psychotherapy with the aging: An art of the possible. *Psychotherapy: Theory, Research, Practice,* 1966, *3,* 139–142.

O'Dea, J. D., & Zeran, F. R. Evaluating effects of counseling. *Personnel and Guidance Journal,* 1953, *31,* 241–244.

Orme, J. E. Intellectual and Rorschach test performances of a group of senile dementia patients and of a group of elderly depressives. *Journal of Mental Science,* 1955, *101,* 863–870.

Orme, J. E. Non-verbal and verbal performance in normal old age, senile dementia, and elderly depression. *Journal of Gerontology,* 1957, *12,* 408–413.

Pattison, E. M. The experience of dying. *American Journal of Psychotherapy,* 1967, *27,* 32–43.

Paul, G. L. *Insight versus desensitization in psychotherapy.* Stanford: Stanford University Press, 1966.

Paul, G. L. Insight versus desensitization in psychotherapy: Two years after termination. *Journal of Consulting Psychology,* 1967, *31,* 333–348.

Paykel, E. S. Life events and depression. *Archives of General Psychiatry,* 1969, *21,* 753–760.

Peterson, D. M., & Thomas, C. W. Acute drug reactions among the elderly. *Journal of Gerontology,* 1975, *30,* 552–556.

Pfeiffer, E. *Disordered behavior.* New York: Oxford University Press, 1968.

Pfeiffer, E. Psychotherapy with elder patients. *Postgraduate Medicine,* 1971, *50,* 254–258.

Pfeiffer, E. Use of drugs which influence behavior in the elderly. In *Drugs and the elderly.* Los Angeles: University of Southern California Press, 1975, pp. 33–51.

Pinkerton, P., & Kelly, J. An attempted correlation between clinical and psychometric findings in arteriosclerotic dementia. *Journal of Mental Science,* 1952, *98,* 244–255.

Plutchik, R., Conte, H., Lieberman, M., Bakur, M., Grossman, J., & Lerhman, N. Probability and validity of a scale for assessment of function of geriatric patients. *Journal of the American Geriatrics Society,* 1970, *18,* 491–500.

Plutchik, R., Conte, H., & Lieberman, M. Development of a scale (GEIS) for assessment of cognitive functioning of geriatric patients. *Journal of the American Geriatrics Society,* 1971, *19,* 614–623.

Poe, W. D. *The old person in your home.* New York: Scribner's, 1969.

Popper, K. R. *Conjecture and refutations: The growth of scientific knowledge.* New York: Harper & Row, 1965.

Post, F., Rees, W. L., & Schurr, P. H. An evaluation of bimedial leucotomy. *British Journal of Psychiatry,* 1968, *114,* 1223–1246.

Powell, R. R. Psychological effects of exercise therapy upon institutionalized geriatric mental patients. University of Southern California dissertation, 1972.

Prinz, P. N. Sleep patterns in the healthy aged: Relationship with intellectual function. *Journal of Gerontology,* 1977, *32,* 179–186.

Regan, P. F. Brief psychotherapy for depression. *American Journal of Psychiatry,* 1965, *122,* 132.

Reichard, S., Livson, F., & Peterson, P. G. *Aging and personality.* New York: Wiley, 1962.

Reid, J. R., & Finesinger, J. E. The role of insight in psychotherapy. *American Journal of Psychiatry,* 1952, *108,* 726–734.

Reisman, J. M. *Toward the integration of psychotherapy.* New York: Wiley, 1971.

Resnick, H. L. P., & Kantor, J. M. Suicide and aging. *Journal of the American Geriatrics Society,* 1970, *18,* 152–158.

Rhudick, P. J., & Dibner, A. S. Age, personality, and health correlates of death concerns in normal aged individuals. *Journal of Gerontology,* 1961, *16,* 44–49.

Richmond, M. B. Preventive psychiatry in a home. In M. Leeds & H. Shore (Eds.), *Geriatric institutional management.* New York: G. P. Putnam's Sons, 1964, pp. 150–166.

Rickard, H. C., Dignam, P. J., & Horner, R. F. Verbal manipulation in a psychotherapeutic relationship. *Journal of Clinical Psychology,* 1960, *16,* 364–367.

Riley, M. W., & Foner, A. *Aging and society: An inventory of research findings.* (Vol. 1). New York: Russell Sage Foundation, 1968.

Roback, H. W. An experimental comparison of outcomes in insight and non-insight oriented therapy groups. New York University dissertation, 1970.

Roback, H. W. The comparative influence of insight and non-insight psychotherapies on therapeutic outcome: A review of the experimental literature. *Psychotherapy: Theory, Research, Practice* 1971, *8,* 23–25.

Roberts, J. L., Kimsey, L. R., Logan, D. L., & Shaw, G. How aged in nursing homes view death and dying. *Journal of Gerontology,* 1970, *25,* 115–119.

Rodstein, M., Savitsky, E., & Starkman, R. Initial adjustment to long-term care institutions: Medical and behavioral aspects. *Journal of the American Geriatrics Society,* 1976, *24,* 65–71.

Rogers, C. R. *On becoming a person.* Boston: Houghton-Mifflin, 1961.

Rosenthal, H. Psychotherapy for the aging. *American Journal of Psychotherapy,* 1959, *13,* 55–65.

Rosenthal, S. Recognition of depression. *Geriatrics* 1968, *23,* 111–115.

Rossman, I. Home health care: An alternative to the nursing home. *Bulletin of the New York Academy of Medicine,* 1973, *49,* 1084–1092.

Rossmann, I. Why we shy away from geriatric medicine. *Geriatrics,* 1976, *31,* 36–37.

Rudd, T. N. *The nursing of the elderly sick.* Philadelphia: J. P. Lippincott, 1954.

Rustin, S. L., & Wolk, R. L. The use of specialized group psychotherapy in a home for the aged. *International Journal of Group Psychotherapy,* 1963, *16,* 25–29.

Rutledge, A. L. Discussion and reply. *Marriage and Family Living,* 1961, *23,* 260–263.

Safirstein, S. L. Institutional transference. *Psychiatric Quarterly,* 1967, *41,* 1–8.

Safirstein, S. L. Psychiatric aftercare in a general hospital. *Psychiatric Quarterly,* 1968, *42,* 1–10.

Safirstein, S. L. Psychotherapy for geriatric patients. *New York State Journal of Medicine,* 1972, *72,* 2743–2748.

Safirstein, S. L. Institutional transference: Theoretical and practical considerations. *Journal of the American Academy of Psychoanalysis,* 1973, *1,* 85–98.

Sager, C. J. Insight and interaction in combined therapy. *International Journal of Group Psychotherapy,* 1964, *14,* 403–412.

Satir, V., Stachowiak, J., & Taschman, H. A. *Helping families to change.* New York: Aronson, 1976.

Saul, S. R., & Saul, S. Group psychotherapy in a proprietary nursing home. *Gerontologist,* 1974, *14,* 446–450.

Schoenberg, B., Carr, A. C., Peretz, D., & Kutscher, A. H. *Loss and grief: Psychological management in medical practice.* New York: Columbia University Press, 1974.

Schofield, W. *Psychotherapy: Purchase of friendship.* Englewood Cliffs, N.J.: Prentice-Hall, 1974.

Schwartz, M. S. & Stanton, A. H. Psychological study of incontinence. *Psychiatry,* 1950, *13,* 399–416.

Scott, J., & Gaitz, C. M. Ethnic and age differences in mental health measurements. *Diseases of the Nervous System,* 1975, *36,* 389–393.

Seegal, D. Principles of geriatric care. *Journal of Chronic Diseases,* 1956, *3,* 100–103.

Seligman, M. E. P. Depression and learned helplessness. In R. J. Friedman & M. M. Katz (Eds.), *The psychology of depression.* Washington, D.C.: Winston, 1974, pp. 83–113.

Shader, R. I., & Harmatz, J. S. A new scale for clinical assessment in geriatric populations: Sandoz clinical assessment, geriatric (SCAG). *Journal of the American Geriatrics Society,* 1974, *22,* 107–113.

Shapiro, D. A. Empathy, warmth, and genuineness in psychotherapy. *British Journal of Social and Clinical Psychology,* 1969, *8,* 350–361.

Sheldon, W. H., & Stevens, S. S. *Varieties of temperament.* New York: Harper, 1942.

Sheps, J. Psychotherapy of the neurotic aged. *Journal of Chronic Diseases,* 1955, *2,* 282–286.

Shere, E. S. Group therapy with the very old. In R. Kastenbaum (Ed.), *New thoughts on old age.* New York: Springer, 1964, pp. 146–160.

Shires, E. B., Peters, J. J., & Krout, R. M. Hypnosis in neuromuscular reeducation. *U.S. Armed Forces Medical Journal,* 1954, *5,* 1519–1523.

Shrut, S. D. Attitudes toward old age and death. *MH,* 1958, *42,* 259–266.

Siegler, M., & Osmond, H. *Models of madness, models of medicine.* New York: MacMillan, 1974.

Siegler, P., Mapp, Y., Shulkin, M. W., Ducanes, A. D., Bodi, T., & Nodine, J. H. Depression in medical practice. *Postgraduate Medicine,* 1963, *42,* 159–164.

Silverstone, B., & Hyman, H. K. *You and your aging parent.* New York: Pantheon, 1976.

Simon, A., & Cahan, R. B. The acute brain syndrome in geriatric patients. In W. M. Mendel & L. J. Epstein (Eds.), *Acute psychotic disorder.* Washington, D.C.: American Psychiatric Association, 1966.

Skinner, B. F. *Walden II.* New York: MacMillan, 1947.

Snyder, B. D., & Harris, S. Treatable aspects of dementia syndrome. *Journal of the American Geriatrics Society,* 1976, *24,* 179–184.

Snyder, W. U., & Snyder, J. B. *The psychotherapy relationship.* New York: MacMillan, 1961.

Soulen, R. N. *Care for the dying.* Atlanta: Knox, 1975.

Spanijaard, J. Manifest dream content and its significance for the interpretation of dreams. *International Journal of Psychoanalysis*, 1969, *50*, 221–235.

Spiegel, R. Anger and acting-out: Masks of depression. *American Journal of Psychotherapy*, 1967, *21*, 597–606.

Spiegel, R. Anger, rage, and aggressiveness in a state of depression. *Revista de Psicologia, Psiquiatria, y Psicoanalysis*, 1968, *10*, 54–65.

Stamey, H. C. The mad at God syndrome. *American Journal of Psychotherapy*, 1971, *25*, 93–103.

Stenbäck, A. Research in geriatric psychiatry and the care of the aged. *Comprehensive Psychiatry*, 1973, *14*, 9–15.

Stern, K., & Metzger, D. The mechanism of reactivation in depression of the old age group. *Psychiatric Quarterly*, 1946, *20*, 56–73.

Stern, K., Smith, J., & Frank, M. Mechanisms of transference and countertransference in psychotherapeutic and social work with the aged. *Journal of Gerontology*, 1953, *8*, 328–332.

Stern, K., & Williams, G. M. Grief reactions in later life. *American Journal of Psychiatry*, 1957, *108*, 289–294.

Stone, M. H. Therapists' personalities and unexpected success with schizophrenic patients. *American Journal of Psychotherapy*, 1971, *25*, 543–552.

Stonecypher, D. D. *Growing older and staying younger*. New York: Norton, 1974.

Straker, M. Prognosis for psychiatric illness in the aged. *American Journal of Psychiatry*, 1963, *119*, 1069–1075.

Strupp, H. H., Fox, R. E., & Lessler, K. *Patients view their psychotherapy.* Baltimore: Johns Hopkins University Press, 1969.

Stuart, R. B. *Trick or treatment.* Champaign, Ill.: Research Press, 1970.

Sturges, S. G. Understanding grief. *Menninger Perspective*, 1970, *1*, 9–12.

Sullivan, H. S. *Studies in Psychiatry.* New York: Norton, 1940a.

Sullivan, H. S. *Conceptions of modern psychiatry.* New York: Norton, 1940b.

Sullivan, H. S. *The interpersonal theory of psychiatry.* New York: Norton, 1953.

Swab, J. J., Holzer, C. E., & Warheit, G. J. Depressive symptomology and age. *Psychosomatics*, 1973, *14*, 135–141.

Swanson, D. W., Bohnert, P. J., & Smith, J. A. *The paranoid.* Boston: Little, Brown, 1970.

Sweet, W. H. Treatment of medically intractable mental disease by limited prefrontal lobotomy: Justifiable? *New England Journal of Medicine*, 1973, *289*, 1117–1125.

Swenson, W. M. A study of death attitudes in the geriatric population and their relationship to certain physical and social characteristics. University of Minnesota dissertation, 1958.

Symonds, P. M. A comprehensive theory of psychotherapy. *American Journal of Orthopsychiatry,* 1954, *24,* 697–714.

Taulbee, L. R., & Folsom, J. C. Reality orientation for geriatric patients. *Hospital and Community Psychiatry,* 1966, *17,* 133–135.

Taylor, D. M. Changes in self-concept without psychotherapy. *Journal of Consulting Psychology,* 1955, *19,* 205–209.

Taylor, R. B. *Feeling alive after sixty-five.* New Rochelle, Arlington House, 1973.

Tharp, R. G., Watson, D., & Kaya, J. Self-modification of depression. *Journal of Consulting and Clinical Psychology,* 1974, *42,* 624.

Thompson, P. The experience of mastery principle. Paper presented at the 44th Annual Convention of the Kansas County Welfare Directors Association, Wichita, 1964.

Thornton, W. E. Dementia induced by methyldopa with haloperidol. *New England Journal of Medicine,* 1976, *294,* 1222.

Thorpe, F. T. An evaluation of prefrontal lobotomy in the affective disorders of old age: A follow-up study. *Journal of Mental Science,* 1958, *104,* 403–410.

Tobin, S., & Lieberman, M. A. *Last home for the aged.* San Francisco: Jossey-Bass, 1976.

Ullman, L. P., & Krasner, L. *Case studies in behavioral modification.* New York: Harper & Row, 1966.

Ullman, M. The dream process. *Psychotherapy,* 1955, *1,* 30–60.

Ullman, M. Dreams and arousal. *American Journal of Psychotherapy,* 1958a, *12,* 222–228.

Ullman, M. The dream process. *American Journal of Psychotherapy,* 1958b, *12,* 671–690.

Ullman, M. The adaptive significance of the dream. *Journal of Nervous and Mental Disease,* 1959, *129,* 144–169.

Ullman, M. *Behavioral changes in patients following strokes.* Springfield: Charles C Thomas, 1962.

Wahl, C. W. The differential diagnosis of normal and neurotic grief following bereavement. *Psychosomatics,* 1970, *11,* 104–106.

Walsh, A. C. Hypochondriasis associated with organic brain syndrome: A new approach to therapy. *Journal of the American Geriatrics Society,* 1976, *24,* 430–431.

Walsh, A. C., & Walsh, B. H. A regimen of psychotherapy and dicumarol. *Journal of the American Geriatrics Society,* 1972, *20,* 127–131.

Watson, G. *Nutrition and your mind.* New York: Harper & Row, 1972.

Wayne, G. Psychotherapy in senescence. *Annals of Western Medicine and Surgery,* 1952, *6,* 88–91.

Wayne, G. Modified psychoanalytic therapy in senescence. *Psychoanalytic Review*, 1953, *40*, 99–116.

Weinberg, J. Sexual expression in later life. *American Journal of Psychiatry*, 1969, *126*, 713–716.

Weisman, A. D. *On dying and denying: A psychiatric study of terminality.* New York: Behavioral Publications, 1972.

Whanger, A. D., & Busse, E. W. Geriatrics. In B. B. Wolman (Ed.), *The Therapist's Handbook.* New York: Van Nostrand & Reinhold, 1976, pp. 287–324.

White, R. W. *Ego and reality.* New York: International Universities Press, 1963.

Whitehead, A. *In the service of old age: The welfare of psychogeriatric patients.* Baltimore: Penguin, 1970.

Whitehorn, J. C., & Betts, B. J. A study of psychotherapeutic relations between physicians and schizophrenic patients. *American Journal of Psychiatry*, 1955, *111*, 321–327.

Whitlock, G. E. The use of dreams in premarital counseling. *Marriage and Family Living*, 1961, *23*, 258–260.

Wilkins, W. Client's expectancy of therapeutic gain: Evidence for the active role of the therapist. *Psychiatry*, 1973, *36*, 184–190.

Williams, R. H. Changing status, roles, relationships. In C. Tibbitts (Ed.), *Handbook of social gerontology.* Chicago: University of Chicago Press, 1960, pp. 261–297.

Williams, T. F., Hill, J. G., Fairbank, M. E., & Knox, K. G. Evaluation and placement of geriatric patients. *Journal of the American Medical Association*, 1973, *226*, 1332–1335.

Wilson, W. P., & Major, L. F. Electroshock and the aged patient. In C. Eisdorfer & W. Fann (Eds.), *Psychopharmacology and the Aging.* New York: Plenum, 1973, pp. 239–244.

Wolberg, L. R. Self-esteem in psychotherapy. *New York State Journal of Medicine*, 1943a, *43*, 1415–1419.

Wolberg, L. R. Resistance to cure in psychotherapy. *New York State Journal of Medicine*, 1943b, *43*, 1751–1754.

Wolberg, L. R. *Hypnosis.* New York: Harper & Row, 1972.

* Wolff, K. Group psychotherapy with geriatric patients in a mental hospital. *Journal of the American Geriatrics Society*, 1957, *5*, 13–19.

Wolff, K. Group psychotherapy with geriatric patients in a psychiatric hospital: A six-year study. *Journal of the American Geriatrics Society*, 1962, *10*, 1077–1180.

Wolff, K. Individual psychotherapy with geriatric patients. *Diseases of the Nervous System*, 1963, *24*, 688–691.

Wolff, K. *The emotional rehabilitation of the geriatric patient.* Springfield: Charles C Thomas, 1970.

Wolff, W. *The dream: Mirror of conscience.* New York: Grune & Stratton, 1952.

Wolpe, J. *The practice of behavior therapy.* New York: Pergammon, 1969.

Worden, F. G. Psychotherapeutic aspects of authority. *Psychiatry,* 1951, *14,* 9–17.

Yalom, I. D., & Terrazas, F. Group therapy for psychotic elderly patients. *American Journal of Nursing,* 1968, *68,* 1690–1694.

Zilboorg, G. The emotional problem and the therapeutic role of insight. *Psychoanalytic Quarterly,* 1952, *21,* 1–24.

Zimmerman, D. Some characteristics of dreams in group analytic psychotherapy. *International Journal of Group Psychotherapy,* 1967, *17,* 524–535.

Zinberg, N. E. Geriatric psychiatry: Needs and problems. *Gerontologist,* 1967, *4,* 130–135.

Zuk, G. H. *Family therapy: A triadic based approach.* New York: Behavioral Publications, 1971.

INDEX

Abreaction, 127–128, 139–142,
149, 161, 191–192, 213, 218,
220
Acetaminophen, 110
Adler, A., 69–72, 79, 143, 181,
184, 226, 242, 274–277, 287
Adolescence, 62, 64, 68, 73, 139,
148, 185, 190, 234, 236–238
Agers Anonymous, 226–231, 282
Aging
behavioral view, 117–121
bibliography on, 11–14
bio-psycho-social crises of,
15–34
defined, 8
and dreams, 195–196
Agism, 10, 30–31, 34, 78
Alcohol, 52, 107, 109, 110
Alcoholism, 43, 124–125,
163–165, 234, 255
Alzheimer's disease, 52
See also Organic brain

syndrome; Neurofibrillary
plaque
Ambulation, 121, 260, 278, 279,
281
Amitriptyline, 104
Amphetamines, 105
Analgesics, 102, 109, 110
Anger, 130, 141, 185, 189,
216–217, 221, 223, 224, 239
Anemia, 51
Anorexia, 45, 108, 130, 170–173
Antianxiety medication, 104,
106–107, 110
Anticholinergics, 59, 104–105,
107, 110
Anticoagulants, 108, 114
Anticonvulsants, 102
Antidepressants, 104–105, 112,
113, 114
See also Tricyclics; Monoamine
oxidase inhibitors
Antihistamines, 102

Antipsychotic medication,
107–108
Anxiety, 104, 106–107, 110, 118,
125–129, 152, 162, 204, 217,
221, 243–245
Aphasia, 58, 276
Appearance, 18, 45, 89–90
Arteriosclerosis, cerebral, 52–53,
55, 59, 168
Arthritis, 17, 88, 102, 106, 154,
164, 170, 230–231
Aspirin, 22, 110
Assertiveness, 126–128, 185,
192, 224–226, 255–256, 276
Assessment (see Psychometry)
Auditory disorders, 17, 89
Aversion therapy, 124–125, 129

Barbiturates, 106
Behavior modification, 116–131,
137, 145, 188–189, 238, 284,
287
Benzodiazepines, 106
Benzotropine, 107
Bereavement (see Widowhood;
Grief)
Bio-psycho-social crises, 15–34,
81, 149, 233, 240, 241, 257,
271
and theoretical explanation,
62, 65–71, 75, 76, 78, 79
Blindness (see Visual disorders)
Bromides, 106

Calcium, 91, 168
Cardiac disorders, 17, 19, 102,
104, 105, 107–108, 112,
170–173
Catecholamines, 107
Catharsis (see Abreaction)
CBS (see Organic brain
syndrome)

Cerebral vascular accident,
43–44, 59, 186, 187, 233,
248–252, 268, 276
Cerebral vascular insufficiency,
52–53, 102, 104, 105, 108,
114
Childishness, 49, 50
Chloral hydrate, 104, 110
Chlordiazepoxin, 106
Chlorpromazine, 107, 111
Cholinesterase, 105
Chronic brain syndrome (see
Organic brain syndrome)
Chronic diseases (see Disabilities)
Cinnarizine, 108
Cohort, 8–9, 37–38
Collusion, 231–232, 257
Combativeness, 276, 277, 283,
286
Conditioning, 116–123
Confidant relationship, 29–30,
151
See also Friendship
Constipation, 45, 59, 101, 104
Convulsion, 106, 107
Cortex, 52, 56, 118
Corticosteroids, 101
Countertransference, 158–159,
173, 183, 208–210
Crime, 23–25, 42–43, 93,
203
Creutzfeld-Jakob disease, 52
Cross-sectional studies, 20,
37–38
CVA (see Cerebral vascular
accident)
CVI (see Cerebral vascular
insufficiency)
Cyclandelate, 108

Day care, 264–265, 270
Deafness (see Auditory disorders)

Death, 12, 25, 34, 52, 67, 73, 75,
    82, 95
Dehydration, 51
Delusion, 41–42, 50, 54, 216,
    285
Depression, 45–46, 59, 217
    and anger, 191
    and antihypertensives, 101
    and behavior modification,
        129–130
    cases, 154, 162, 164
    and cerebral vascular
        insufficiency, 55
    and grief, 44
    and hypochondriasis, 47, 114
    and incontinence, 59
    and insight, 139, 179
    and medication, 104–105, 108,
        109, 112–114
    and monoamine oxidase, 105
    and organic brain syndrome,
        55–58
    and psychotherapy, 176, 178,
        179, 189
    and senility, 54–56, 58
    somatotherapies for, 111–113
    and suicide, 46, 113, 179, 180
    theories of,
        Erikson's, 66
        Lewin's, 68
        psychoanalytic, 135
Desensitization, systematic,
    125–126
Desipramine, 104
Developmental theory, 64–66,
    72–74, 78
Diagnosis (see Psychometry)
Diarrhea, 44, 51, 106
Diazepam, 106
    See also Tranquilizers, minor
Diet, 51, 91–92, 105, 167–168,
    170–173, 264, 267

Digitalis, 102
Digitoxin, 102, 171
Digoxin, 102
Dihydroergotoxine, 108, 114
Diphenhydramine, 107
Disabilities, excess, 161, 192,
    272–277, 286
    physical, 15–20, 46, 86–87, 98,
        228, 260
Disengagement theory, 31–33,
    72
Diuretics, 59, 102, 106, 171
Divorce, 244–245, 255
Dopamine, 102
Doxepin, 104, 114
Dreams, 74–75, 106, 107,
    194–210
    and therapy, 145, 194–210,
        231–232, 242–257
Drugs (see Medication)
Dying, 139, 162, 179, 204–205
Dyskinesia, 107–108

Echoencephalography, 55
ECT (see Electroconvulsive
    therapy)
Education, 37, 53, 94–95
EEG (see
    Electroencephalography)
Ego psychology, 66–67
Elder, 8, 16, 84
Electroconvulsive therapy,
    112–114, 137, 186
Electroencephalography, 55,
    105
Electrolytes, 102, 106
Emotional expression, 139–142,
    190–193
    See also Abreaction
Empathy, 175, 178, 179,
    182–185, 192, 193, 216
Enuresis (see Incontinence)

Environment
  modifying patient's, 68–69,
    132, 135–136, 143–146
  and senility, 53–54, 118
Erikson, E. H., 64–66, 78, 181
Ethchlorvynol, 106
Extrapyramidal effects, 107–108

Face-Hand Test, 57
Family (see Intergenerational
  relations)
Family therapy, 233–257, 261,
  269, 270
Fantasy, 30–31, 49, 50, 214, 232,
  267
Fecal impaction, 59
FHT (see Face-Hand Test)
Financial concerns of elders,
  22–23, 34, 85–86
Flooding, 128–129
Flurazepam, 106
Food, 22, 75, 91–92, 130
  See also Diet
Freud, 11, 62–64, 132, 134, 138,
  140, 149, 157, 182, 186, 194,
  242
  See also Psychoanalysis
Friendship, 28–29, 70–71,
  93–94
Fromm, E. 76–77, 79
Furosemide, 102

Geriatrics, 9–10
Gerontology, 9
  See also Aging
Glycol derivatives, 93
Government, patient, 268,
  280–281
Government programs, 83–97,
  263–264
Granuvacular changes, 52
Grief, 43–46, 54, 207, 252–257

Group therapy, 144, 163, 165,
  211–233, 255–257
Guanethidine, 102
Guilt, 44–46, 48, 167, 180, 200,
  252, 256

Hallucination, 54, 102, 104, 195
Haloperidol, 108, 111, 171–172
Hearing (see Auditory disorders)
Heart (see Cardiac)
Hemorrhage, 51, 101
Hepatic function, 101
Hobbies, 33
Home for Aged and Infirm
  Hebrews, 153, 160
Home care, 261–265, 270
Homeostasis, 99, 141
Hostility, 44, 48, 126–140, 191,
  280
Housing, 22–23, 91–93
Hydrocephalus, 54, 114
Hyperbaric oxygenation, 114
Hypertension, 87, 107, 164,
  170–173
Hypnosis, 54, 133, 186–187
Hypnotics, 107, 109–111
Hypochondriasis, 44, 46–48, 58,
  59, 70–71, 238
  treatment of, 113–114, 148
  See also Disability, excess
Hypokalemia, 101, 167
Hypotension, 51, 104, 106–108
Hypothermia, 53

Iatrogenic effects, 48
Imipramine, 59, 104
  See also Tricyclics
Immigrants, 53
Impaction, fecal, 59
Implosion therapy, 129
Incontinence, 58–59, 104, 186,
  260, 268, 276, 279, 282, 286
Indomethacin, 101

Infection, 51
Inferiority feeling, 41, 45, 49,
    67, 69–71, 76, 275–277
Inhibition
    proactive, 49
    reciprocal, 127, 129
Insight, 135, 138–139, 144, 161,
    178–179, 201, 210, 213, 216,
    218, 220, 221, 232, 245
Insomnia, 45, 105, 106, 110,
    111, 155
Institutionalization, 258–287
    alternatives to, 261–265
    and confusion, 51, 54, 260,
        271–287
    decision about, 265–269
    and dreams, 207–208, 210
    and family, 252–254, 256–257
    and incontinence, 256
    and lobotomy, 111
    and medication, 100, 103, 109,
        260
    and organic brain syndrome,
        51, 54
    and psychotherapy, 277–287
    and responsibilities of
        counselor, 269–271
    and suicide, 46
    See also Long-term care
Intelligence (see IQ)
Intergenerational relations,
    29–30, 65, 261, 269, 280
    See also Family therapy
Intracranial neoplasm, 51,
    112
Introspection, 139, 175
Introversion, 40–41
IQ, 37–38
Iscarboxid, 105
Isoxupine, 108

Jung, C. G., 39, 72–75, 78, 82,
    144, 186, 242

Laxatives, 101
Leucotomy, 113
Levodopa, 102
Lewin, K., 67–68, 79–80
Life expectancy, 15–16
Life review, 63, 66, 133, 135,
    180–182, 190, 193, 210, 214
Lithium, 107
Lobotomy, 111, 113, 137
Long-term care, 259–288
    and medication, 93, 94, 103,
        109, 260
    quality, signs of, 267–270
Longitudinal studies, 9, 37–38
Losses of elders (see
    Bio-psycho-social crises)
Low, A., 215
LTC (see Long-term care)

Mania, 45, 104, 107, 111
MAOI (see Monoamine oxidase
    inhibitors)
Maslow, A., 75–76, 79
Marital status, 46, 51, 258
    See also Widowhood
Martin, L. J., 132–134
Massed practice, 119, 125, 188
Mastery, sense of, 66–68, 89,
    144, 272
Medical care, 86–88
Medication, 17–18, 87, 88,
    93–115, 260
Memory, 44–49, 51, 53, 63, 104,
    112, 114–115
Menopause, 18
Mental disease (see
    Psychopathology)
Mental retardation, 49
Mental Status Questionnaire,
    55–56
Meperdrine, 102
Meprobamate, 105
Metacommunication, 238

Methaqualone, 106
Methyldopa, 102, 108
Methylphenidate, 105
Methyprylon, 106
Milieu therapy, 271–287
Modeling, 128, 129
Monoamine inhibitors, 105, 112
Monoamine oxidase, 105
Morphine, 102
Mourning (see Grief;
    Widowhood)
MSQ (see Mental Status
    Questionnaire)
Multiple impact therapy,
    237–239, 241
Muscle relaxation, 106–110, 115,
    119

Neumoencephalography, 55
Neurofibrillary plaque, 52–53,
    114
Norepinephrine, 102
Nortriptyline, 104
Nursing homes (see
    Institutionalization; Long-term
    care)
Nutrition, 91
    See also Diet; Vitamins

OBS (see Organic brain
    syndrome)
Obsessions, 111, 129, 142
Ombudsman, 97
Organic brain syndrome, 51–57
    and conditioning, 118–119,
        121
    and dreams, 195, 196
    and group therapy, 211–212,
        232
    and hypnosis, 186
    and hypochondriasis, 47
    and incontinence, 59

and institutionalization, 260,
    272, 285
and medication, 101–102,
    104–110, 114–116
and paranoia, 42
and psychotherapy, 147–148,
    184, 211–212, 232
treatment for, 114–116,
    147–148, 267, 286–287
Oxygen uptake, cerebral, 52
Oxygenation, hyperbaric, 114

Pain, 187
Pampering, 69–70, 273–275,
    279, 287
Papaverine, 108
Paradoxical intension, 129
Paraldehyde, 106
Paranoia, 41–42, 68, 104, 106,
    283
    treatment of, 110, 112, 160,
        212, 238
Paresis, syphilitic, 52
Parkinsonism, 102, 107–108
Patient
    government, 268, 280–281
    role of, 271–287
    segregation of, 282–283
Pavlov, I. V., 117–121
Pentylenetetrazol, 108
Personality, 36, 44, 60–81, 122
Pessimism, 38–40, 45–47
Pharmacology, 98–116
Phenelzine, 105
Phenothiazines, 107–109, 111
Phobia, 126, 127, 129, 185,
    215–217
Physicians as therapists, 151,
    152, 169
Physostigmine, 105, 108, 114
Pick's disease, 52
Placebo, 113, 161

Plaque, senile, 52–53, 114
Pneumonia, 51
Polypharmacology, 98–102, 260
Potassium, 102, 110, 167–168
Poverty, 90–91
    See also Financial concerns
Prayer, 81, 156
Prejudice against elders, 30–31,
    85
Prescriptions (*see* Medication)
Presenile dementias, 52
Primidone, 102
Proactive inhibition, 49
Problem-solving
    ability, 37–38, 49, 54
    and therapy, 133, 136,
        149–150, 152–156, 161, 173,
        175, 194, 213, 229, 239,
        268, 273, 280
Procaine, 108–109
Projective techniques, 40, 57–58
Propoxyphene, 102
Proptriptyline, 104
Psychiatry, 10
Psychoanalysis, 10, 62–67,
    76–77, 122, 133–137, 140,
    144, 148, 157–161, 188, 197,
    240, 252, 272
Psychodiagnosis (*see*
    Psychometry)
Psychology, 10
Psychometry, 45, 55–58, 133,
    194
Psychopathology, 34–59
    prophylaxis for, 80–97
Psychopharmacology, 98–115
Psychosomatic disorders, 44–45,
    47
Psychosurgery, 111, 113, 137
Psychotherapy
    and Adler, 71–72, 89
    authority in, 133, 159–161,

    185–186, 188, 190, 210,
        216, 218–221, 232, 237
    and behavior modification,
        117–119, 112, 113
    brief, 51, 133, 135, 136,
        149–150, 152–156, 160, 161,
        163, 173, 175, 178, 179,
        186, 194, 214, 240
    and cerebral vascular accident,
        90
    and countertransference,
        158–159, 173
    definition, 10, 151
    and depression, 111, 176, 178,
        179, 189
    and dreams (*see* Dream
        therapy)
    effectiveness, 138, 145–150,
        211
    and ego psychology, 67, 79
    and electroconvulsive therapy,
        123
    and Erikson, 65–66, 78
    failure, 170–173
    formal address in, 175, 185
    goals, 132–136, 149, 182, 214
    group (*see* Group therapy)
    history, 132–136
    and hypochondriasis, 113–114
    and institutionalization,
        277–287
    and Jung, 74–75, 78
    and Lewin, 68, 79
    milieu (*see* Milieu therapy)
    and organic brain syndrome,
        115, 147, 148, 184, 267,
        286–287
    and physicians, 151–152, 169
    probing past, 180–182
    psychoanalytic, 63–64, 78
        (*see also* Psychoanalysis)
    and psychotropics, 103, 112

pushing patient, 189–190, 193
questioning, 175–180, 184–185
and religion, 82–83
resistance to, 176, 185, 190,
    193, 239
and Rogers, 77–78, 132, 142,
    182, 183, 193
scheduling, 136, 179, 214
and schizophrenia, 50
short-term (see Psychotherapy,
    brief)
strategy of, 149–173
supportive, 135, 161–163, 179,
    214, 235
team approach, 163–173, 237,
    277–278, 286
techniques, 174–193
termination, 163
training for, 116, 149,
    174–175
transference (see Transference)
why it works, 137–145
Psychotropics, 103–115, 137
Punishment, 120, 121, 124–125,
    127, 272–273, 277–279

Rauwolfia derivatives, 102, 107
Reaction time, 37, 57
Reality orientation, 214, 215,
    232, 267, 281, 287
Reciprocal inhibition, 127, 129
Recovery, 215–223
Referrals, 168–169, 176
Regression, 49–51, 63
Reinforcement, 119–121, 125,
    129, 130, 184, 189, 192, 214,
    216, 217, 274, 284–286
Relaxation, 106, 110, 119, 125,
    186–187, 248
Religion, 38, 74–75, 81–83, 156,
    161, 184, 186, 187, 189, 198,
    200–201, 229, 269

Renal function, 102, 105, 106
Repression, 142, 238, 242
Reserpine, 107
Retirement, 20–22, 70, 71, 77,
    83–86, 227
Review, life, 63, 66, 133, 135,
    180–182, 190, 193, 210,
    214
Rigidity, 38–40, 72, 130, 134,
    153, 190, 238, 249
Rogers, C. R., 77–78, 132, 142,
    182, 183, 193
Role, of patient, 271–277
Role playing, 238
Rorschach test (see Projective
    techniques)

SAGE (see Senior Actualization
    and Growth Explorations)
Sandoz Clinical Assessment
    Geriatric, 56
San Francisco Old Age
    Counseling Center, 132–134
SCAG (see Sandoz Clinical
    Assessment Geriatric)
Schizophrenia, 49–50, 107, 111,
    112, 144, 148, 162, 183, 212,
    259
Screening, 87, 264
Sedatives, 106
Self-help, 187–189
Self-monitoring, 130, 217
Senility, 48–59, 63, 72, 77
    See also Organic brain
        syndrome
Senior Actualization and Growth
    Explorations, 94
Serotonin, 102
Sensory loss, 37, 38, 42
    deprivation, 49, 50, 54, 281
    See also Auditory disorders;
        Visual disorders

Sex, 12, 18–19, 43, 63, 124,
157–159, 185, 200, 208–209,
245–248
Sexually assaultive patient, 43,
275–276
Sight (*see* Visual disorders)
Skinner, B. F., 119, 124
Sleep disturbances, 45, 106,
109–111, 155
Socioeconomic status, 53
See also Financial concerns
Sodium, 92
Somatotypology, 60–62
Somnifacients, 106, 109–111
Staff ratings of patients, 56
Stereotypes of elders, 30–31, 38
See also Agism
Stroke (*see* Cerebral vascular
accident)
Suggestion, 133, 136, 186, 191
Suicide, 46, 59, 113, 155–156,
162, 179–180, 194, 241
Sulpiride, 114
Symptom removal, 185–193
Syphilitic paresis, 52
Systematic desensitization,
125–126

Tardive dyskinesia, 107–108
TAT (*see* Projective techniques)
Teeth, 17, 89, 92
Thematic Apperception Test (*see*
Projective techniques)
Theory
developmental, 64–66, 72–74,
78
personality, 62–81, 117
Thiazides, 102
Thioridazine, 107
Thought-stopping, 128, 129
Thyroid, 53, 101, 172–173
Tractotomy, 113

Tranquilizers
major, 107–109, 111
minor, 106–107, 109, 110,
199–200
Transactional analysis, 145
Transference, 156–161, 173,
182, 194, 197
Transportation, 22, 23, 93–94,
264
Tranylcypromine, 105
Treatment
delay of, 19, 36, 86–88,
168
effectiveness, 147
behavior modification, 123,
145–146
and depression, 111–113
electroconvulsive therapy,
112, 113, 145–146
group therapy, 211
and hypochondriasis,
113–114, 148
insight, 138
milieu therapy, 285–287
and organic brain syndrome,
114–115, 147, 211
and paranoia, 110–111
and psychoses, 110–111
psychosurgery, 113, 145
psychotherapy, 145–150,
211
psychotropics, 103, 109,
111, 146
vasodilators, 108
Tricyclics, 59, 104–105, 112,
114
Trihexyphenydyl, 107
Tumor, brain (*see* Intracranial
neoplasm)
Tyramine, 105

Uremia, 101

Vasodilators, 108–109, 114
Visual disorders, 17, 89, 102,
    104, 106, 164–165, 170–173
Vitamins, 51, 91

Warfarin, 101
Widowhood, 12, 15–18, 70, 71,
    139, 158–159, 162, 166, 217,
    243, 245, 256, 270